DOCTORS
in DENIAL

DOCTORS *in* DENIAL

WHY BIG PHARMA AND THE CANADIAN MEDICAL PROFESSION ARE TOO CLOSE FOR COMFORT

JOEL LEXCHIN, MD

Professor Emeritus, School of Health Policy and Management
York University
and
Emergency Physician
University Health Network
and
Associate Professor
Department of Family and Community Medicine
University of Toronto
Toronto, Ontario

FOREWORD BY DR. BRIAN GOLDMAN OF CBC RADIO'S *WHITE COAT, BLACK ART*

James Lorimer & Company Ltd., Publishers
Toronto

James Lorimer & Company Ltd., Publishers acknowledges the support of the Ontario Arts Council (OAC), an agency of the Government of Ontario, which in 2015-16 funded 1,676 individual artists and 1,125 organizations in 209 communities across Ontario for a total of $50.5 million. We acknowledge the support of the Canada Council for the Arts, which last year invested $153 million to bring the arts to Canadians throughout the country. This project has been made possible in part by the Government of Canada and with the support of the Ontario Media Development Corporation.

Cover design: Tyler Cleroux
Cover image: iStock

Library and Archives Canada Cataloguing in Publication

Lexchin, Joel, 1948-, author
        Doctors in denial : how the Canadian medical profession has been captured by big pharma / Dr. Joel Lexchin.

Includes bibliographical references and index.
Issued in print and electronic formats.
ISBN 978-1-4594-1244-6 (softcover).--ISBN 978-1-4594-1245-3 (EPUB)

        1. Physicians--Professional ethics--Canada. 2. Pharmaceutical industry--Corrupt practices--Canada. 3. Medical ethics--Canada. 4. Drugs--Canada--Marketing. 5. Physician and patient--Canada. 6. Conflict of interests--Canada. I. Title.

R725.5.L49 2017   174.2'6   C2017-900787-4
                                                             C2017-900788-2

James Lorimer & Company Ltd., Publishers
117 Peter Street, Suite 304
Toronto, ON, Canada
M5V 0M3
www.lorimer.ca

Printed and bound in Canada.

CONTENTS

TABLES

FIGURES

BOXES

ABBREVIATIONS

ARR = absolute risk reduction
BMJ = *British Medical Journal*
CFP = *Canadian Family Physician*
CJEM = *Canadian Journal of Emergency Medicine*
CMAJ = *Canadian Medical Association Journal*
NEJM = *New England Journal of Medicine*
NNT = number needed to treat
NSAID = nonsteroidal anti-inflammatory drug
R&D = research and development
RRR = relative risk reduction
SSRI = selective serotonin reuptake inhibitor
UBC = University of British Columbia
UHN = University Health Network

FOREWORD

A few months before the publication of this rather important book on the past and present relationship between physicians and the pharmaceutical industry in Canada, Joel Lexchin asked if I'd like to write the foreword.

Lexchin has been a colleague of mine in emergency medicine for more than thirty years. While I have pursued a less than serious second career as a medical journalist and broadcaster, Lexchin has worked on weightier issues that range from the factors that influence the prescribing habits of physicians, to the promotion and marketing of pharmaceutical drugs.

The subtitle of this new book made me freeze.

That's because of the considerable time I spent giving lectures and educational workshops to physicians and other health professionals that were sponsored by pharmaceutical companies — mainly Purdue Pharma Canada, the Canadian maker of OxyContin.

My career as a paid speaker began in the 1980s after I wrote a series of articles in the *Canadian Medical Association Journal (CMAJ)* on drug seekers. As part of my research, I interviewed police officers on the drug diversion beat and doctors who had lost their licences for caving in to bogus patients. They taught me little about drug diversion. If you really want to understand the patient as the boss, you have to talk to the experts — the drug seekers themselves. Police officers put me in touch with some of the smartest and most successful prescription drug con artists working in the Toronto area at the time.

They described the techniques they used to scam physicians into prescribing opioid pain relievers, benzodiazepines, barbiturates and stimulants that they sold on the street for large profits.

I turned those articles into a lecture that I gave hundreds of times to allied health professionals. Audiences found the material educational and amusing. At one point, a pharmaceutical company asked if I'd give the same speech to a group of doctors invited to dinner. Frankly, I couldn't see how my speech would do anything other than discourage physicians from prescribing controlled substances. So I said yes, thinking that there was no ethical issue whatsoever.

In the mid-1990s, my reputation as a speaker came to the attention of Purdue Pharma Canada. It had already launched MS Contin, the first long-acting opioid approved for patients with cancer pain, and later for chronic noncancer pain. The company was about to launch a suite of long-acting opioids, including OxyContin.

By then, on my own, I had begun treating patients with chronic pain. For the most part, I prescribed modest doses, and the patients benefited. There were patients for whom the treatment did more harm than good, and I'd like to think I monitored them closely for addiction and other harms, and tapered the opioid as soon as possible.

I became part of a small group of physicians recruited by Purdue Pharma Canada to develop and teach a curriculum on safe and responsible prescribing of opioid drugs to patients with chronic pain. The topics included patient selection, initiating and titrating opioid therapy, screening for addiction and monitoring red flags. I also contributed material on how to recognize drug-seeking behaviour and how to minimize the risk of diversion.

In an article entitled, "I was part of Big Pharma's influence," published in March 2012 in the *Globe and Mail*, I wrote that "I wanted to help teach doctors who were getting very little training in pain management and to help patients who were in pain. I never underplayed the risk of addiction, always urging colleagues to carefully assess patients and to make certain other remedies had been tried first."

Having been an expert in the abuse and diversion of opioid pain relievers, I was swayed by flimsy scientific evidence showing that opioid analgesics could benefit patients with chronic pain without causing addiction. For example, a case series published by Russell Portenoy, a pain specialist at Memorial Sloan Kettering Cancer Center in New York, showing what was then considered long-term use of opioid analgesics staggered the establishment with its counterintuitive message.

Later, a study conducted by Dwight Moulin, a neurologist at the University of Western Ontario, was arguably even more compelling because it was a randomized controlled clinical trial.

Today's critics of opioid therapy rightly say studies like these provided weak evidence in support of opioid therapy. Drug company money and marketing — coupled with recommendations from people like me — helped fuel a massive increase in the number of users of OxyContin (and other narcotics).

I was always aware of the potential for OxyContin to be misused. In 1998, the *CMAJ* published a study by Dr. Amin Sajan[1] that documented anecdotal reports of the street prices for diverted drugs. In an article commissioned by the *CMAJ* that accompanied the study, I wrote, "Now that controlled-release oxycodone has been licensed in Canada, we can expect that it and other controlled-release opioid analgesics will also find their way onto the black market."[2]

We know all too well what happened subsequently. OxyContin was not just another narcotic. The drug created a rising tide of abuse that floated all boats. It raised dramatically the rates of prescription drug abuse in North America along with overdoses causing hospitalization and death. More than that, the story of OxyContin was a stark reminder that doctors like me could literally kill patients with kindness — when such kindness came with a prescription.

In 2010, Purdue Pharma introduced a reformulated version of OxyContin in the United States. The purpose of the reformulation was to make it difficult for abusers to crush the tablets. In 2011, the *New York Times* reported that the pills had been found to resist freezing, baking, microwaving and attempts to dissolve them in solvents like acetone. In Canada, Purdue Pharma voluntarily removed OxyContin from pharmacy shelves in 2012 and replaced it with a tamper-resistant version called OxyNeo. The company and others have continued to reap huge profits from sales of opioid analgesics.

As an assessor with the College of Physicians and Surgeons of Ontario and as an expert witness for the defence, I saw up close prescribing practices that were frankly dangerous. I came to realize that some primary-care physicians were not taking the correct message from people like me to prescribe responsibly. I saw many examples of physicians prescribing large doses of opioid drugs with little rationale and even less documentation. In some cases, they kept on prescribing despite many indications that the patient was diverting drugs.

As I wrote in the *Globe and Mail*, "In recent years, I've seen doctors overprescribe opioids to patients without screening or monitoring them for addiction. I've seen doctors prescribe powerful narcotics in assembly-line fashion at walk-in clinics."

Because of my first-hand experience of what happened with OxyContin, I stopped giving educational lectures sponsored by Purdue Pharma or any other drug company. I believe pharmaceutical companies should not be in the business of educating physicians about their products. We thought we were providing a balanced educational message. It is obvious that the benefits of opioid therapy were exaggerated, and the risk underplayed. Unfortunately, in the case of OxyContin, the damage has been done.

Joel Lexchin's book explores the relationship between individual Canadian doctors, Canadian medical journals, academic health science centres, regulatory and professional bodies and medical associations and societies and the pharmaceutical industry from the early 1950s up to the present time.

Much has been reported regarding the influence of pharmaceutical companies on pain doctors in the US. A joint investigation by the *Journal Sentinel* and *MedPage Today* uncovered "a network of pain organizations, doctors and researchers that pushed for expanded use of the drugs while taking in millions of dollars from the companies that made them." For instance, the newspaper found that a University of Wisconsin–based organization in Madison "had been a national force in helping liberalize the way opioids are prescribed and viewed. While pushing a pharmaceutical industry agenda that critics say was not supported by rigorous science, the UW Pain & Policy Studies Group took in $2.5 million over a decade from opioid companies."

The newspaper also uncovered evidence that national organizations like the American Pain Society and the American Academy of Pain Medicine issued statements endorsing the use of opioids to treat chronic pain and claiming the risk of addiction was negligible — while receiving "substantial funding from drug companies."

Portenoy was a prominent advocate for the use of long-term opioid therapy while acting as a paid consultant to pharmaceutical companies.

Lexchin's chapter on key opinion leaders resonates with me because I was a key opinion leader myself. What the book demonstrates in detail is that there are key opinion leaders for every new pharmaceutical drug in the therapeutic arsenal. Despite calls for more regulations, physicians continue to be recruited by pharmaceutical companies to provide a patina of academic respectability to their efforts to promote products regardless of their value as better or even necessary drugs.

My experience as host of *White Coat, Black Art* — a show on CBC Radio One about the culture of modern medicine — has taught me that many physicians continue to believe they are immune to being influenced by pharmaceutical companies and other givers of gifts. It never ceases to amaze me that physicians feel that way about themselves.

In his chapter on guidelines for preventing conflict of interest, Lexchin is right to wonder whether provincial colleges are up to the task of enforcement. My sense is that the culture of the medical establishment in Canada continues to be relatively unconcerned about whether or not the new rules are being followed.

While there is much deserved attention on doctors and speaking engagements, I am glad that Lexchin has also devoted considerable space in the book to discussing the research dollars funnelled to Canadian doctors, health-care organizations and universities in Canada. These are important ways in which pharmaceutical companies exert major influence in this country — in some cases on a much grander scale than speaker fees.

His chapter on the attempts by pharmaceutical companies to influence medical students is frankly disturbing. More often than not, it's students who raise concerns regarding the involvement of drug companies in education, and mentors and administrators who have regarded that involvement as benign. As discussed by Lexchin, students in the US appear more ready to challenge that view than students in Canada.

Opioid addiction and deaths caused by opioid analgesics have reached crisis levels in Canada. The evidence continues to mount that increased prescribing was the cause. In BC, Kate Smolina and colleagues found that between 2005 and 2013, opioid consumption increased by 31 per cent, driven by longer duration of opioid therapy and by an increase in the use of stronger opioids.[3] The dramatic climb in the death rate soon followed.

Unfortunately, OxyContin is the index example against which other potential harms will be measured now and in the years to come. But it's not the only example. The book is filled with many others. Overall, Lexchin presents overwhelming evidence that prescribing practices almost invariably get worse whenever drug companies exert undue influence.

Can we do more? The answer is an emphatic yes. Lexchin's final chapter gazes at the example from the United States, where the culture of public reporting of speaker fees is now well established. That trend seems to have taken a pass in Canada, at least for now. One wonders how many key opinion leaders in this country would continue in that role were their speaking fees to be disclosed.

This book is an important summation of the past and present of an all-too-comfortable relationship, and what's at stake if we sit by and idly let it continue.

DR. BRIAN GOLDMAN
DECEMBER 27, 2016

NOTES

1   Sajan A, Corneil T, Grzybowski S. The street value of prescription drugs. CMAJ. 1998;159:139–142.

2   Goldman B. The news on the street: prescription drugs on the black market. CMAJ. 1998;159:149–150.

3   Smolina K, Gladstone E, Morgan SG. Determinants of trends in prescription opioid use in British Columbia, Canada, 2005–2013. Pharmacoepidemiology and Drug Safety. 2016;25:553–559.

INTRODUCTION
DOCTORS IN DENIAL: WELCOME TO THE COMFORT ZONE

I graduated from the University of Toronto medical school in 1977, finished a family practice residency in 1979 and for the past thirty-seven years have worked with hundreds of doctors in various emergency departments. Almost all of those doctors are highly ethical and caring people who want to do what is best for their patients. At the same time, most of the doctors that I know have very ambivalent attitudes about their relationship with the pharmaceutical industry. About eight years ago the emergency department where I work had a debate about whether to continue to allow drug companies to sponsor our monthly continuing medical education evening events. We chose the topic and the speaker, but a pharmaceutical company would pay the cost of the dinner, always in a good restaurant, and the speaker's fee. Meals at some of the restaurants could cost upwards of $150 per person and there were typically twenty-five to thirty people at these dinner events. When the votes were counted they were about evenly split between continuing on in the same manner and going to a self-financing model where we would pay for the cost of our own meals. Since there was no consensus, we continued to accept industry money for our meetings.

What happened in my emergency department mirrors the attitudes of Canadian doctors in general. Some are deeply offended at the suggestion that their ethics are called into question by their interactions with the pharmaceutical industry. One example comes from a letter in the *Canadian Medical Association Journal* (*CMAJ*) from a cardiologist in London, Ontario: "Over the last several years I have seen increasing correspondence about the reportedly unethical relationships physicians have established with the pharmaceutical industry . . . Virtually all the correspondence that I have read reflects the underlying (sometimes not very subtle) hypothesis that physicians are mindless idiots who cannot think for themselves and are easily swayed by material incentives into prescribing certain brands of medication to their hapless, unsuspecting patients."[1] Some are truly grateful for their relationship with the industry. One recounts encounters she had with drug company sales representatives: "When I moved to a larger office, a Pfizer rep helped me shelf my charts. A Wyeth rep framed and put up my pictures and certificates on the office walls. There are so many other reps I need to thank — in small ways and big."[2] Finally, a few are worried about the relationship and find it ethically problematic. In response to the previous quote, a family doctor replied that "I make a conscious effort not to use 'pens, note pads and paper clips' with any pharmaceutical branding out of concern they could influence my decision-making or be noticed by a patient. I also made the decision during my residency training not to attend any 'drug dinner' and am proud to say I have so far kept this commitment."[3]

Multiple studies have shown that doctors have doubts about the ability of their colleagues to remain unaffected by gifts from drug companies, attending sponsored dinners or other interactions with company representatives, but believe that they themselves are immune from being influenced. In an American study, 61 per cent of first- and second-year internal medicine residents stated that they were uninfluenced by industry promotions and contacts, but only 16 per cent believed other physicians were similarly unaffected.[4] Dr. David Collins from Vancouver is one Canadian example of this perception of invulnerability. He is aware that doctors can be influenced when accepting mugs with logos, free pizza and the occasional junket that includes a meal. (Mugs with logos and free junkets are generally no longer allowed under the Code of Ethical Practices from the Canadian pharmaceutical industry association, the organization that represents all of the major pharmaceutical companies operating in Canada.) But he's still confident he relies on the best evidence to make drug choices for his patients.[5] The more exposed physicians-in-training in Toronto were, i.e., the more money and promotional items they received, the more likely they were to believe that talking to company reps did not affect how they prescribed medications.[6] That same sense of invulnerability extended to doctors at some of the highest levels of authority in the profession. Dr. Roy le Riche, the registrar of the Alberta College of Physicians and Surgeons, the licensing body for doctors in that province, told a reporter in the late 1980s that "I don't believe for a minute that physicians are being bribed for the price of a meal. I have been taken out to dinner on a number of occasions and I most certainly do not succumb to the $15 or $20 cost of dinner."[7]

There are a number of explanations for what is happening, starting with cognitive dissonance, whereby the discomfort between what doctors do and what they believe has to be resolved.[8] Based on an analysis of transcripts from focus groups, Chimonas and colleagues describe the ways in which doctors resolve the dissonance: "They avoided thinking about the conflict of interest, they disagreed that industry relationships affected physician behavior, they denied responsibility for the problem, they enumerated techniques for remaining impartial, and they reasoned that meetings with detailers were educational and benefited patients."[9] Some doctors justify taking the gifts that companies offer in the belief that they are "putting something over" on the company. That happened to me back in my early years of practice. I received by mail a questionnaire from a company about drug company advertising, with an offer of a nice set of carpentry tools for answering the questions. My reasoning was that it was all right to accept the gift because the answers I was going to give would be extremely negative about advertising. On another occasion I answered a survey because I wanted the Cross pen that came as a reward and used the same logic of "sticking it to the industry."

When doctors thought about the sacrifices that they had made during their training and in their work, and rationalized taking gifts from industry on the basis of these sacrifices, their willingness to take a gift almost tripled, such that 60 per cent of the entire group ended up finding gifts acceptable.[10] Here is how one British Columbia doctor thinks about her sacrifices: "When I arrive home at the end of a busy day, and have committed to go out that evening to listen to a pharmaceutical industry–sponsored talk given by a practising specialist and eat a pharmaceutical industry–sponsored meal, most times my preference would be to stay at home. I nevertheless attend the gathering and listen to the speaker and the questions and discussions of my colleagues."[11]

Finally, there is the largely mistaken belief that doctors are being bribed by drug companies. In nearly all cases that is not what is happening at a conscious level. Instead, doctors are being affected at a subconscious level through the gift relationship. Dr. Robert Cialdini, a professor of psychology at Arizona State University, relates one example of how the gift relationship was successfully exploited by the Hare Krishna Society, an Eastern religious sect. "A robed Krishna would walk up to a person in an airport and give them a gift, such as a flower . . . Often, people attempted to return the gift, but the Krishnas declined to take them back, requesting a donation instead. People who didn't want the flowers often gave money anyway."[12] Another way to think about the gift relationship is with Christmas or other seasonal greeting cards. If you receive a card from someone who you didn't bother to send one to this year, chances are that next year that person will be on your list. Relationships with drug companies work in a similar fashion. Gifts may be meals, free samples of medications to give out to patients, educational items or just the break from the office routine that doctors get when they talk to sales representatives. But each of these gifts instills the feeling within doctors that they need to reciprocate.

What happens at the level of the individual doctor extends to how organizations behave with respect to their benefactors, although sometimes on a more overt level. In 2010, Barrick Gold founder Peter Munk gave $35 million to the University of Toronto to expand the Munk School of Global Affairs. Dr. David Naylor, who at that time was the president of the university, provided an assurance that this donation would not compromise academic freedom, as all donors had to sign an agreement not to interfere with research and teaching policy. However, under the terms of the donation, the university was required to present a report on activities every year to a board appointed by Munk. "The purpose of the report is 'to discuss the programs, activities and initiatives of the School in greater detail.'"[13] The Canadian Association of University Teachers documents a further eleven collaborations between universities and governments and corporations where the independence of the universities seems to have been subverted by the collaboration.[14]

The same phenomenon occurs in medical organizations. In the mid-1980s, the College of Family Physicians of Canada agreed to cooperate with Health Industries Research in a marketing survey designed for use by the pharmaceutical industry. In return for filling out the survey doctors would get one continuing medical education credit.[15] Dr. Donald Rice, the executive director of the college, defended the decision to be associated with the project on the basis that family doctors who participated in this survey would have an opportunity to indicate whether or not they wished to receive drug information from drug companies and would be able to provide information to the college on their prescribing habits that would be helpful in designing continuing medical education programs. The education credit was in lieu of a $2 payment, which Dr. Rice felt would have been insulting to doctors.[16] (Subsequently, the college decided not to participate in any further such surveys.)

The Canadian Dermatology Association announces on its website that it "has a number of sponsorship opportunities [for industry] including the annual conference, disease awareness campaigns, and special events."[17] In February 2013, its president penned an essay that, while containing some mild criticism of the pharmaceutical industry, was mostly positive about industry-doctor relationships on the basis that "[m]any of the activities that some perceive to be morally fuzzy, such as free lunches, drug samples and educational sessions, are actually common, governed by the [pharmaceutical industry association's] code of ethics and ultimately benefit the patient. While some view interactions between physicians and the pharmaceutical industry as an unsavory, clandestine type of relationship, they may be failing to see both the necessity and benefits related to it."[18] The Society of Obstetricians and Gynaecologists of Canada in the early 1990s was in serious financial distress and was ultimately bailed out by a number of drug companies through their sponsorship of a number of society meetings.[19] It later went on to defend a four-page advertisement from Berlex for its newly launched oral contraceptive pill that was, according to one doctor, thinly veiled as an educational document, complete with a stamp of approval from the society.[20] According to the organization's associate executive vice-president, this method of disseminating the results of a conference's highlight was preferable to healthcare professionals receiving information directly from industry itself.[21]

Just as medical societies can be seen as being biased by their association with the pharmaceutical industry, so can medical journals. In the early 1960s, the *CMAJ* was

editorializing against generic products[22] and in favour
of drug company advertising in medical journals on the
grounds that "the pharmaceutical manufacturer has been
and should continue to be a close and trusted ally of the
physician" and that advertising was necessary to inform
doctors about therapeutically beneficial new products.[23] In
the early 1980s, David Woods, the director of publications
for the Canadian Medical Association, was often penning
articles in the *CMAJ* highly favourable to drug companies.
When the *CMAJ* received a letter critical of his opinions,[24]
rather than directly rebutting it, he left that task to Gordon
Postlewaite, the director of communications for the industry
association.[25] In the mid-1980s, the same Mr. Woods was
effectively advocating for drug companies as he toured various
plants in Europe and the United States, singing their praises
in multi-page articles in the *CMAJ*.[26-29] As just one example,
in his article on Roche he concluded that "the industry
as a whole has a good story to tell and, indeed, individual
employees tell it with pride and enthusiasm."[26]

Whenever money is involved, the issue of conflict
of interest is not far behind. A conflict of interest exists
whenever individuals or organizations are placed in a
situation where there is a risk that judgments or actions
regarding a primary interest will be unduly influenced by a
secondary interest.[30] For individual doctors and the various
organizations that they belong to and that represent them,
those primary interests are promoting and protecting the
integrity of research, the welfare of patients and the quality of
medical education. Financial interests are the secondary
ones that people are most concerned about. A conflict does
not mean that secondary interests will prevail but it creates
the perception that they might. Next, there is the argument

that even if financial conflict of interest is a problem at the individual level, other forms of conflict of interest are equally bad and need to be dealt with. In December 2011, the United States Food and Drug Administration (FDA) refused to let Dr. Sidney Wolfe of Public Citizen's Health Research Group take his position as a consumer representative on the FDA's Drug Safety Advisory Committee when it was considering whether to pull the oral contraceptive Yasmin off the market. Since Wolfe's group had already advocated removing the drug, he was accused of "intellectual conflict of interest."[31] However, financial conflict of interest is fundamentally different from other types of conflict. As Dr. Jerome Kassirer, former editor of the *New England Journal of Medicine*, recognized, "there is a substantial difference between financial conflicts and others; namely financial conflicts are optional. When faced with the choice to agree to a financial relationship with a company or not to, one has a choice: either take it or leave it. In contrast . . . one cannot divest oneself of one's biases or prejudgments because they are so integral; one cannot easily disclose them because they are so internal."[32] At the organizational level, drug companies have far greater resources available to them than any other group and the influence from those resources is always in a single direction, benefitting the products that the companies are marketing. Financial conflict of interest is a recurring theme throughout this book.

This book is partly a history, so in a number of places I will be talking about practices of many decades ago. Sometimes, the goal is to illustrate the continuity between what happened then and what is happening now, and at other times the aim is to show how relationships have evolved and changed. As this is a book about the medical profession and industry, I will not be discussing the relationships that drug companies have with other healthcare professionals or with patient groups. Similarly, how doctors and government interact will largely be left out of this narrative, except insofar as I am describing the medical profession's response to various government initiatives and pieces of legislation in order to show the similarities and differences with the way that industry responded, or in Chapter 10 when I discuss actions that government should take.

Over the years, the organization representing the major pharmaceutical players has undergone various name changes, morphing from Canadian Pharmaceutical Manufacturers Association to Pharmaceutical Manufacturers Association of Canada to Rx&D (Canada's Research-Based Pharmaceutical Companies) to its present name, Innovative Medicines Canada. For the sake of clarity, I will refer to this organization as the pharmaceutical industry association throughout.

In early 2016, one of my colleagues made a presentation to a group of internists in Toronto about problems with the industry-medicine relationship and was confronted with criticisms on two grounds. The first was that he was relating incidents that had happened in the past and that the situation was now different. The second was that he was using American examples and he should not extrapolate from what happened there to make statements about what was going on in this country. As this is partly a historical analysis, much of what I have to say comes from events in the past, but to the extent possible I will also be incorporating material from the present so that readers can judge for themselves whether, or to what extent, things have changed over time. There are a number of books about the relationship between the American medical profession and the pharmaceutical industry,[33-37] but Canada is largely left out of these narratives. While I do not believe that there are any fundamental differences between what happens in the United States and here with respect to how industry and medicine interact, I use Canadian material whenever possible. As a result, there may be some issues, such as the movement of personnel between organized medicine and industry, that are only briefly touched upon.

The purpose of this book is to explore the relationship between individual Canadian doctors, Canadian medical journals, academic health science centres, regulatory and professional bodies and medical associations and societies and the pharmaceutical industry starting in the early 1950s up to the present time. Chapter 1 describes the historical basis for these relationships and discusses what effect they had on the positions that Canadian medicine took on controversial issues such as intellectual property rights, direct-to-consumer advertising and the way that Health Canada regulates pharmaceuticals. Chapters 2 to 8 look at how the ongoing industry-medicine relationship has played out in terms of the clinical practice guidelines that are produced to help doctors prescribe more appropriately and in the design and conduct of their continuing medical education, the behaviour of medical schools and academic medical centres, the promotion of drugs, the guidelines issued by various organizations about how doctors should relate to industry and the behaviours of individual doctors.

Finally, and most importantly, we need to be concerned about what happens between industry and medicine because of the effects (positive or negative) on how patients are treated and because the medical profession has a responsibility to society. That responsibility extends to ensuring that pharmaceutical policies are developed in the public interest, that the research behind medications is scientifically sound, that drug approvals are based on an objective analysis of the benefits and harms of medicines and not on their economic value to companies, that medical students and doctors-in-training (residents) are not exposed to commercially oriented messages, that the information that doctors and the public get about the medications that they prescribe and use is accurate and objective and that medications are used in a cost-effective way and only used when they are medically justifiable.

Medicines are a resource that need to be developed and used in a way that benefits the entire society. In this vein, Chapter 9 will look at whether the relationships that I have described have negative effects on the issues that I have just mentioned. The book closes with a series of recommendations about how to make sure that the medical profession is protecting patients and society and that doctors no longer remain in denial about the effects of their relationship with the pharmaceutical industry on their patients.

CHAPTER 1
MEDICINE AND INDUSTRY: A MARRIAGE OF CONVENIENCE OR A MARRIAGE MADE IN HEAVEN?

There is a natural affinity between doctors and the companies that make drugs. Pharmaceutical products are one of the mainstays of modern medicine and without them doctors would be far less able to help people. The drug makers, on the other hand, would not be able to earn revenue from the products that they produce without the collaboration of doctors who prescribe them. This symbiotic relationship was probably not of major importance in the first half of the twentieth century, largely because many of the medications were compounded by pharmacists instead of being produced in company factories. Furthermore, until 1941 a prescription was not necessary in order to purchase some medications.[1] After World War II, with the advent of the antibiotic era and other drug discoveries, such as steroids, compounding was dying out and the importance of the large pharmaceutical companies in supplying medicines dramatically increased. Although little evidence documents how this change affected the relationship between doctors and industry in Canada, it is quite likely the change made the relationship more important, just as has been shown in the United States.[2]

Evidence does exist to show the increasing collaboration between doctors employed by pharmaceutical companies and organized medicine. Whereas prior to World War II only three or four companies employed medical directors on a full-time basis,[3] by the late 1950s enough such doctors existed in Canada that they formed a Medical Section of the pharmaceutical industry association and the Consultant Secretary of the Canadian Medical Association congratulated the pharmaceutical industry for its foresight in organizing such a section.[4] As an affiliated society of the Canadian Medical Association, the Medical Section sent a representative to its General Council. (In later years, moving to industry became an attractive option for a number of doctors.[5,6])

In the US in the interwar years, scientific medicine reformers began to impose higher standards on the testing and promotion of pharmaceuticals. At the same time, as industry improved its methods of operation, a strong bond developed between medical scientists and the drug companies. This mutual accommodation, as Rasmussen terms it, meant that medical science ended up incorporating commercial values. As the research head of Smith, Kline described it, "now clinical and commercial values are almost identical."[7] It is possible that the same thing happened in Canada but once again we are faced with the lack of any documentary evidence one way or the other. The low level of pharmaceutical research done in Canada, even at the end of the 1950s, argues against a strong alliance between medically trained researchers and industry. According to the report from the Director of Investigation and Research, *Combines Investigation Act*, the total amount spent by twenty-two pharmaceutical companies in Canada in 1959 on research and development was $2 million, compared to $12 to $16 million by a single American company in the US.[8] One possible reason for this situation was that the two remaining Canadian-owned companies were too small to fund much research and the foreign-controlled companies, mostly American and a few British,[8] preferred to do their research in their countries of origin.

Economics seems to be a likely reason for the Canadian Medical Association wanting to align itself with the pharmaceutical industry, specifically the contribution from advertising in the *Canadian Medical Association Journal* (*CMAJ*) to the organization's overall financial health. All advertising, not only that from drug companies, contributed $317,000 (55 per cent) in 1957 to the total association revenue of $579,239, and the *CMAJ* made a profit of $30,000. "Dr. Kelly, general secretary of the [Canadian Medical Association], concluded at the time that 'we are not quite in the position of being dependent upon advertising revenue for our existence, but its absence would make Journal publication very expensive and would result in considerably increased membership fees' . . . Net profit in 1965 exceeded $100,000 for the first time since the journal began publication in 1911."[9]

Finally, contributing to the growing alliance were the actions of some companies such as Horner, one of the last

Canadian-owned pharmaceutical firms, that curried favour with doctors by sponsoring the Physicians' Art Salon at the annual Canadian Medical Association convention and then converting the winning paintings and photographs into a desk calendar that was distributed annually to all physicians in Canada.[10]

A COMMON ENEMY — THE CANADIAN MEDICAL ASSOCIATION AND MEDICARE

On their own, the combination of the factors just described was probably not enough to create the tight bond that developed between organized medicine and industry. What brought the two groups together and cemented an alliance was the presence of a common ideological enemy in the form of the federal government. Dr. Alan Davidson, a Toronto psychiatrist, reached the same conclusion in his brief to a House of Commons committee in the mid-1960s. "Organized medicine and the individual doctor seem to identify with the industry in a common fear of government control. Doctors are extremely uncomfortable about the prospect of Medicare and appear to sense that Industry is fighting a similar battle."[10]

The medical association's position on the question of a government-run national medical insurance plan had undergone a dramatic change between the early 1940s and 1960. The association approved the "adoption of the principle of health insurance" in 1943 and favoured a plan that would "secure the development and provision of the highest standard of health services, preventive and curative."[11] A year later, it revised the policy to make it clear that any plan should run on a collective nature and be compulsory for people who could not afford healthcare on their own and that such a plan should be administered by an independent, non-political commission. However, by 1960 that position had morphed considerably. While the association still recognized a limited role for government, the organization asserted that "a universal comprehensive medical care insurance programme financed through government-imposed taxes" was neither necessary nor desirable and a collective approach was no longer favoured.[11]

Ideologically the Canadian Medical Association was committed to protecting its members against the threat of government-sponsored medical insurance. This opposition was rooted in values that the medical profession felt were central to the way that it operated. First among those values was to avoid "control by third parties, particularly public medical care insurance commissions or agencies, over the conditions of work of the physician."[11] The extent to which that value drove the actions of organized medicine can be seen in its near hysterical reaction to the introduction of government-run medical insurance in Saskatchewan in the summer of 1962. Publicity kits were sent by organized medicine to almost all doctors in the province. As Badgley and Wolfe put it, one "entitled Compulsory Medical Care Needed (?), began with this reminder: 'The concept of universal medical coverage is not new and the approach by government to seek support is just the same as it was when first enunciated by Karl Marx in his Communistic Theories of the last century . . .'"[12] The president of the medical association sent a letter to the premier of the province urging him not to go ahead with Medicare and advocated for "the voluntary insurance principle with government assistance in areas of need" and at the association's annual meeting in

1962 the executive was unanimous in its opposition to the action being taken by the government of Saskatchewan.[12] Then, with the appointment of the Royal Commission on Health Services (usually referred to as the Hall Commission after its head, Justice Emmett Hall) in 1961, the association was faced with the prospect of Medicare on a national basis. In its brief to the Hall Commission, the association made its unequivocal opposition to universal medical insurance clear, stating bluntly "[w]e do not subscribe to the introduction of universal, compulsory, tax-supported comprehensive medical services insurance under Government auspices and we feel that public funds should not be applied to the self-supporting in the area of medical insurance."[13]

A COMMON ENEMY — THE PHARMACEUTICAL INDUSTRY AND PATENTS

While the medical profession was trying to stave off national Medicare, the pharmaceutical industry was feeling economically threatened over the issue of patents. Drug companies viewed, and still view, patents as vital to their business model as they allow companies to sell a particular drug without any competition until the patent expires. In the early 1960s, patents were valid for seventeen years. Between 1961 and 1964, three separate reports took a hard look at drug prices and all three concluded that drug prices in Canada were among the highest in the world and pointed the finger at patents as one of the main reasons for that finding.[8,14,15] (A fourth report also highly critical of the then-current patent system would follow in 1967. That report will be discussed in the next chapter.[16]) The first of these three, from the Director of Investigation and Research, *Combines Investigation Act*, stated "[t]he control exercised over the manufacture, distribution and sale of certain drugs through patents has virtually eliminated price competition."[8] The Restrictive Trade Practices Commission report agreed with that conclusion and recommended the abolition of patents for pharmaceuticals.[15] This recommendation was anathema to the industry and was bitterly opposed.[9]

The Hall Commission was willing to consider other measures for dealing with drug prices, such as compulsory licensing to import drugs, and it recommended a delay of five years in the abolition of patents to see if compulsory licensing was successful in lowering prices.[14] (A compulsory licence is granted by the government and allows other companies to either manufacture or import products that are still under patent even if the company controlling the patent is opposed to the licence. In return, the company receiving the licence pays the patentee a royalty. Canada had implemented compulsory licensing to manufacture drugs in 1923 but this provision was rarely used because the small size of the Canadian market made it uneconomical for most products.[17]) In opposition to these recommendations the pharmaceutical industry association mounted a large-scale lobbying campaign directed at politicians and enlisted the assistance of a wide variety of ideologically aligned groups, including the Canadian Manufacturers Association, the Chamber of Commerce and the Canadian Medical Association.[9] (The alliance between the industry and the Canadian Medical Association in opposing the extension of compulsory licensing will be extensively analyzed in Chapter 2.)

MUTUAL SUPPORT

Although the Canadian Medical Association declined to submit a brief to the Restrictive Trade Practices Commission,[18] once the report was released, the association's Department of Economics was at best tepid about the recommendation to abolish patents. It was of the view that this was a "very debatable subject" and that "doctors must be concerned about any adverse effects of the proposed recommendation and must resist any tendency to minimize medical and pharmaceutical research in Canada."[19]

By 1965, the former president of the medical association, Dr. William Wigle, had moved on to become the first full-time president of the industry association. By virtue of his previous position, he had a permanent seat on the medical association's General Council thus establishing what, in 1974, Lang called "an interlocking directorship between the decision-making bodies of both associations." Lang continued, "In this manner, [industry association] policy and opinions are injected directly into the policy-making processes of the [medical association] — as is the reverse. In addition, the two Associations have established a liaison committee that meets whenever submissions are to be made to royal commissions or government committees concerning interests that affect either or both of them. This liaison committee in turn reports to the appropriate [medical association] committee, recommending lines of action to be adopted as official [medical association] policy."[9]

Therefore, it should come as no surprise that a medical association delegation that presented a brief to a parliamentary committee in 1966 said that, although drug prices might be high, drug companies were not to blame. Instead, the delegation claimed that drug companies could be persuaded to voluntarily lower prices, it defended the need for an economically healthy drug industry and opposed the establishment of a Crown corporation to manufacture drugs because that would remove the "private enterprise initiative."[20]

One manifestation of the ideological agreement between the medical association and the pharmaceutical industry is found in their respective briefs to the Hall Commission. In its brief, the medical association's only recommendation about drug prices was the removal of the federal sales tax of 11 per cent. It did not mention the effects of patents on price.[13] In turn, the industry association's brief to Hall did not mention universal government-run medical insurance. The industry association asserted that the current system was working well and should not be abandoned. "Instead, the solution should be directed to the areas of indigency, rather than towards a Caligula-like method of reorganization which would also affect the majority of the people."[21]

Shortly following the release of the Hall Commission report, the president of the medical association attended the fiftieth anniversary meeting of the industry association, where he rejected the idea of government control of medicine, and the president of the industry association said that the Hall Commission did not understand that the industry and pharmaceutical companies were "disturbed" by the report's sections on drugs. In the industry's view, Hall would sacrifice the entire Canadian industry through massive imports of generic drugs.[22] A few months later, in January 1965, the chairman and general secretary of the medical association considered the Hall Commission's recommendations about prescription drugs at a meeting of the Liaison Committee with the industry association. Although the medical association's Committee on Pharmacy was in favour of reducing drug prices, it did not want that objective achieved through "discriminatory" changes to the *Patent Act* that "would prejudice the survival, initiative and research programs of Canadian pharmaceutical companies." (This statement seems to indicate that the Committee on Pharmacy was ignorant of the fact that by the early 1960s there were only two Canadian-owned companies of any size.[8]) Instead, it favoured voluntary price reductions.[23]

MEDICAL JOURNALS AND THE ALLIANCE

As the voice of organized medicine in Canada, the *CMAJ* articulated the alliance to the organization's membership. In the early to mid-1960s, editorials on various issues often echoed the positions of the pharmaceutical industry. A 1961 editorial supported advertising in medical journals;[24] one in 1963 warned against using generics, as "the best guarantee of quality in drug products is still the manufacturer's reputation as represented by his name or his trademark."[25] The following year saw an editorial favouring patent protection as one of the "cornerstones of free enterprise."[26] The *CMAJ* also printed articles from industry officials who warned of the dangers of the Alberta legislation that allowed generic substitution[27] and insinuated that the quality of some generic products could not be trusted.[28] The repeated statements about the safety of generic products were clearly just fear-mongering. In the mid-1960s, the Drugs Directorate in the Department of National Health and Welfare undertook a laboratory examination of a mixture of brand-name, generic and imported drugs and found no difference in quality among the groups.[29]

Other journals were just as effusive about the industry as the *CMAJ*. The November 1960 issue of *Canadian Doctor*, a journal solely supported by advertising revenue, carried an article by the general manager of the pharmaceutical industry association that, in the words of the journal, was designed to give Canadian physicians "a factual review of medical research" in the country, touting the growing amounts of money spent in Canada on pharmaceutical research.[30] The following year *Applied Therapeutics*, another journal financed by advertising and sent free to doctors, ran a series of articles about the cost of prescribing in various countries. The article dealing with Canada was authored by the consulting economist to the industry association, who concluded that the competitive nature of the pharmaceutical industry was socially desirable and the resultant growth, improvement of products and the general level of prices had been favourable to the public; furthermore, this healthy competition would be improved by the elimination of compulsory licensing.[31] Intriguingly, this article appeared at the same time as the three reports, referred to earlier, that had all consistently noted high drug prices caused by the suppression of competition due to patents. A few months later, the same journal editorialized that criticism of the cost of drugs and the promotion practices of companies was coming from those who had a "high index of irritability," and that their statements, which strike "very deep indeed into the structure of our Canadian community," were calling for state control of the industry.[32]

The generally laudatory tone of the material in the *CMAJ* and other journals was only infrequently countered by more critical pieces on promotion[33] and generic prescribing.[34] Even the Canadian Medical Association Committee on Pharmacy would occasionally raise objections to promotional practices such as direct mail advertising.[35] Other Canadian journals, such as the *Nova Scotia Medical Bulletin*, seemed slightly more inclined to voice opposition to industry activities,[36–38] but this journal had only a small, limited readership compared to the national reach of the *CMAJ*, *Canadian Doctor* and *Applied Therapeutics*.

CONCLUSION

In the end, the affinity between medicine and industry — found in a combination of the favours that companies doled out to the medical profession, the doctors who worked in industry, the income from journal advertising, the nearly unconditional support for industry from medical journals and, most importantly, the ideological opposition of both groups to an activist government — forged a bond between medicine and industry. The lone voices that were questioning the alliance were largely ignored.[10] The next chapter looks at how that alliance played out when it came to government initiatives that both threatened and supported industry objectives.

CHAPTER 2
GOVERNMENT, INDUSTRY AND THE MEDICAL PROFESSION: MÉNAGE À TROIS

The alliance between the medical profession and the pharmaceutical industry played an important part in how government initiatives rolled out from the early 1960s to the middle of the second decade of the twenty-first century. In some cases the alliance was opposed to what the government proposed, and in many cases it was a cheerleader pushing the government on, but, until roughly the turn of the century, it held firm. The alliance was largely engaged in legislation around intellectual property rights, but other issues were also present, such as direct-to-consumer advertising and reforming the drug regulatory process. This chapter looks at the five-decade history of the alliance.

COMPULSORY LICENSING
The battle over compulsory licensing that ran throughout the

mid to late 1960s is the first example of the alliance between the medical profession and the pharmaceutical industry in action. The beginning of this saga started in 1962 with the decision of the Conservative government to establish a special parliamentary committee, the Special Committee of the House of Commons on Drug Costs and Prices, ultimately known as the Harley Committee after its chair, to undertake a "full-scale investigation into Canada's drug history" including "a thorough study of our current law and practices concerning the introduction, marketing and use of drugs."[1] When the committee's attention turned from safety to drug prices, it was the fourth inquiry on this topic in Canada in the 1960s, coming after the three discussed in the last chapter.

THE HARLEY COMMITTEE, BILL C-102 — COMPULSORY LICENSING TO IMPORT BEGINS

In *The Politics of Drugs*, Ronald Lang describes in detail the development of the Canadian Medical Association's position presented to the Harley Committee.[1] The pharmaceutical industry association asked the medical association's Committee on Pharmacy in 1966 to reiterate its support for the industry association's "Principles Governing the Provision of Drugs to Canadians." The Committee generally agreed with the principles, but had trouble with one item that stated that "the respect of industrial property rights as represented by patents and trade marks is the essential foundation for progress in research and therapeutics." The reason for the Committee's reluctance was that it had no proof that this was "the essential foundation," but it still thought that "protection of the innovator of a new drug was important as a continuing stimulus to the development and introduction of new drugs."[2] However, it appears that the medical association was able to resolve its doubts by the time it presented its brief to the Harley Committee. One of eight recommendations was "No removal of patent or tariff protection for Canadian companies which could prejudice their economic survival, because of the need for a healthy pharmaceutical industry in Canada able to invest in research and development."[3] This conclusion seems inevitable, since the medical association utilized information about drug costs supplied by the industry association in the course of preparing its brief.[3] Not surprisingly, the medical association's brief also cautioned against the use of foreign imported generic drugs on the grounds that their safety could not be guaranteed.

When the Harley Committee reported in 1967, it concluded, as had the three reports before it, that Canadians were paying too much for drugs and recommended that the government amend the *Patent Act* to allow for compulsory licensing to import drugs.[4] The brief article in the *Canadian Medical Association Journal* (*CMAJ*) about the report was critical of it for assuming that generic drugs were equally as effective and safe as brand-name ones.[5] The Liberal government of the day eventually accepted the Harley Committee's recommendation about compulsory licensing and introduced the necessary legislation. The first iteration of the legislation, Bill C-190, drew an editorial in the *CMAJ* that questioned whether imported generics would actually be lower in price than brand-name drugs and once again raised the spectre of the safety of these drugs.[6] The medical association echoed the editorial, saying that the bill "could open the door to drugs whose safety and effectiveness are below the standards expected and deserved by the Canadian public. Although we favour the availability of drugs at a lower cost, we are not convinced that the implementation of Bill C-190 will accomplish this end, and we fear that the more important factors of safety and effectiveness may be compromised."[7] (The results of a 1965 analysis of generic, brand and imported drugs described in Chapter 1 shows that these concerns had no basis in fact.) A later letter from the executive secretary of the medical association to the government played on the fear that the legislation could impair drug research. In part it read, "Under present circumstances we rely on the products of reputable Canadian manufacturers and it would in our view be retrograde to impair the ability of such manufacturers to improve the quality of medication which is now available or may become available through pharmaceutical research."[8] Bill C-190 died when an election was called but was subsequently reintroduced as Bill C-102 after the Liberals were re-elected. Once the bill was tabled in the House of Commons, the medical association president sent a wire to the ministers of Consumer and Corporate Affairs and the National Health and Welfare again raising the question of safety and asking the federal government to guarantee the safety and effectiveness of drugs imported as a result of C-102.

After a protracted and bitter parliamentary battle, C-102 eventually passed, ushering in compulsory licensing to import generic drugs.[1] The new legislation seemed to trigger a wave of protest from prominent figures in Canadian medicine defending the pharmaceutical industry. Opening a scientific symposium in 1970, Dr. Jacques Genest, director of the Clinical Research Institute of Montreal and professor of medicine at the University of Montreal, thanked the directors of Merck Frosst Laboratories of Canada for making the symposium possible. He went on to laud "the courage of the Directors of Merck Frosst in investing . . . an important sum in pharmaceutical research in Canada, despite so unfavourable and so disturbing a climate of current legislation [Bill C-102], and the attitude of ignorance and distrust, if not antagonism, which is found among certain people who want socialization of the pharmaceutical industry and state control of drug manufacturing and marketing."[9] In his eyes, "the new law greatly diminishe[d] every advantage which a pharmaceutical company should have to establish research laboratories in Canada."[9] The following year, Dr. D.L. Kippen, the president of the Canadian Medical Association, at a meeting of the pharmaceutical industry association in Bermuda, said, "We see a deliberate threat to your industry by government 'acting on behalf of society,' enacting legislation which threatens your autonomy and reduces your profit potential."[10] Six years later, Dr. E.W. Barootes, a deputy-president of the medical association, again at a pharmaceutical industry association meeting, this time in Puerto Rico, concluded that the pharmaceutical industry was gradually being nationalized by an exclusive franchise system, by manipulation and by price controls.[11] In 1983, Dr. William Goodman, an associate professor in the Department of Medicine at the University of Toronto and a vice-president of the Association of Independent Physicians, a right-wing group that advocated opting out of Medicare by doctors, said that "civil conscription of . . . drug companies has already occurred" in Canada.[12]

THE EASTMAN COMMISSION — AFFIRMATION OF COMPULSORY LICENSING

The editorial pages of the *CMAJ* continued to decry the effects of Bill C-102. David Woods, the director of publications at the Canadian Medical Association, lamented that the change in the *Patent Act* "effectively eliminated ownership rights to newly discovered pharmaceuticals" and that "[i]ncentives to explore, invent and produce are being eroded because of a bureaucratic mistrust of private enterprise and a suspicion of the profit motive."[13] Despite these sentiments from physicians and the *CMAJ* and the continuing opposition from the industry association, sometimes through court challenges, compulsory licensing to import functioned well in encouraging generic competition and reducing drug expenditures in Canada.[14,15] However, the lobbying by the industry association was beginning to have an effect by the early 1980s. Much of the lobbying was concentrated on the federal Quebec Liberal caucus. The Liberal party formed the national government and almost half of their seats in parliament came from the province of Quebec, so continued support in that province was key to the Liberals' staying in power. Over half of the multinational pharmaceutical subsidiaries were located in and around Montreal and the industry association promised more investment in Quebec in return for an end to compulsory licensing. In 1983, André Ouellet was the minister of the Department of Consumer and Corporate Affairs, the department responsible for the *Patent Act* and compulsory licensing, and the deputy head and whip of the Quebec Liberal caucus. That year his department published a red paper that concluded with three proposals for substantially modifying compulsory licensing. That move was applauded by the medical association's Woods as "evidence of a belated realization that drug-company bashing has gone too far."[16]

With a federal election in the offing, the entire question of compulsory licensing was temporarily defused by turning the issue over to an inquiry headed by University of Toronto economist Harry Eastman. A superficial reading of the medical association's brief to the Eastman Commission makes it sound neutral in tone, with such statements as, "The Canadian Medical Association fully supports the objective of providing prescription drugs to patients at the lowest possible cost that is consistent with wise health-care delivery."[17] But, as in 1966, the medical association's position was philosophically in tune with that of the industry association. For example, the following passages appeared in the medical association's brief: "By focusing largely on the manufacture of drugs, government initiatives have seemingly lost sight of the fact that the reduction of expenditures on prescription drugs is not a goal in itself, but is merely one small component of the larger objective of providing the highest quality of health care at the lowest possible cost."[17] "The advantage of the patent system as a mechanism for inducing research and development is that . . . anyone willing to absorb the risks and costs of product development may test his concepts and products within the milieu of the marketplace. The patent system induces competition, but competition in the market for new ideas, products and processes."[17] Compare what was in the medical association's brief to statements in the one from the industry association: "Far too often in the past, the question of pharmaceutical patents and the public interest has been narrowly defined as an economic tool intended in the short term to lower drug prices to the consumer to the lowest possible level. Unfortunately, not enough attention has been paid to the longer term and a broader definition of where the public interest lies."[18] "All the available evidence strongly supports the conclusion that the patent system makes possible a significant portion of the research outlays by innovative drug companies worldwide. The literature contains voluminous statements asserting that this is so by those discharging decision-making responsibilities in the industry."[18]

In addition, the medical association's submission questioned the quality of generic products, suggested that compulsory licensing might cause a downturn in research and development in the near future, and posed the possibility of increasing the royalty rate for compulsory licences. All of these positions reflected industry association's policy. This interpretation of the bias in the medical association's brief is backed up by an anonymous civil servant who commented that although the brief supported the industry association's position, "it was full of mistakes, it didn't address costs or the savings from an aging population . . . it was oblivious to all that."[19] Similarly, the Fédération des médecins omnipraticiens du Québec also sided with the industry when they testified at the Eastman Commission hearings (Pierre Biron, personal communication, August 20, 2016).

When Eastman reported in 1985, he recommended retaining compulsory licensing to import but with modifications — a four-year period of exclusivity for the original manufacturer and an increase in the royalty rate paid to the patent holder.[20] These recommendations were not good enough for the medical association and its director of publications, who said that the entire report should be taken with a grain of salt.[21]

The Eastman Report should have ended the debate about compulsory licensing, but it didn't. By the time the report came out, the election had taken place and had been won by the Progressive Conservatives led by Brian Mulroney. During the election campaign Mulroney made statements very favourable to the multinationals' position against compulsory licensing.[22] After the election the Conservatives dominated the seats from Quebec and the indusry association made the same promises to them as it had made to the Quebec Liberals — increased spending on research and development in return for changes to the *Patent Act*. The most important change in favour of the multinationals was the fact that in 1985 the Conservatives became committed to a free-trade deal with the United States. This decision opened up the federal government to intense pressure from the American government in addition to the ongoing lobbying from its Quebec caucus and the pharmaceutical industry. In return for free trade with the Americans, the Conservatives produced Bill C-22, which proposed to give the industry a minimum of seven years of protection from compulsory licensing. In turn, industry pledged to increase spending on research and development (R&D) to 10 per cent of sales by 1996.[23,24]

Dr. Robert Gourdeau, the editor of the *Annals of the Royal College of Physicians and Surgeons of Canada*, was gratified that the new Conservative government was ready to roll back compulsory licensing. In his opinion, this was a policy that had stifled drug research in Canada and created an exodus of some pharmaceutical firms to more hospitable shores, and now the government was willing to "give back to the pharmaceutical industry the leverage it needs to prosper in Canada and to involve Canadians in drug research again."[25]

BILL C-22 — THE BEGINNING OF THE END FOR COMPULSORY LICENSING

The Canadian Medical Association General Council voted to support Bill C-22 at its meeting in the fall of 1987.[26] The association's brief to the parliamentary committee studying

C-22 did not leave any room for doubt as to the organization's stance when it came to compulsory licensing. "The Association has considerable sympathy for appropriate patent protection of intellectual property. We believe Canada should respect the spirit of international patent conventions for drugs as we expect other countries to honour patent protection for drugs or publishing copyright held by Canadians."[27] Although the medical association did not foresee a major increase in the amount of basic research being done, it was more hopeful about an expansion in clinical research with the resulting effect that clinical pharmacologists would be more knowledgeable about new drugs and would be better able to act as consultants to the medical profession, ultimately improving patient care. The industry association expressed its appreciation for the new legislation and the fact that companies' intellectual property would once again be protected as well as promising the creation of additional investments in medical research of $1.4 billion leading to three thousand direct and another three thousand indirect jobs.[24]

The promise of more research dollars and jobs drew in support from major figures and organizations in the Canadian medical research community. Dr. Stuart MacLeod, dean of health sciences at Hamilton's McMaster University, was bitter that the benefits of research undertaken by drug companies did not get counted in the costs of patent protection and wondered why this form of intellectual property was singled out for such harsh treatment.[28] The Medical Research Council of Canada, the major government funder for medical research in the country, was of the opinion that "the direction which the patent legislation will take if and when the new Act is passed cannot but be favorable to the expansion of medical research in Canada."[29] Dr. Stuart Smith, the chairman of the Science Council of Canada, told the House of Commons Legislative Committee that his organization commended the government for better protecting intellectual property and that although its members felt that Bill C-22 would not bring about a dramatic change in Canada's pharmaceutical industry "some research is better than none."[30] Dr. T. Spero, a clinical pharmacologist at the University of Toronto and a member of the Coalition of Scientists, testified before the same committee that "if industry does not decide to invest in research in Canada, those matching funds [to complement what the Medical Research Council provides] will not be forthcoming"[31] and that "early access to new drugs, which we would have if we had research in Canada, would bring new drugs with fewer side effects very quickly into the health care system."[31] (In fact, only about one in ten new drugs offer any significant therapeutic benefit[32] and little is known about the safety of newly marketed drugs.[33]) Dr. Michel Chrétien, the scientific director of the Clinical Research Institute of Montreal, "approve[d] of amending the Patent Act to give new impetus to pharmaceutical research and to make it internationally competitive."[34]

When the legislation was temporarily stalled in the Senate, David Woods, who had now moved on to become editor-in-chief of the *CMAJ*, attributed this delay to the "antibusiness attitude" during the "silly season" in Canadian politics.[35]

BILL C-91 — THE DEATH OF COMPULSORY LICENSING

On June 23, 1992, citing its obligations under the terms of the draft *Trade-Related Aspects of Intellectual Property Rights Agreement*, one of the treaties enforced by the newly created

Figure 2.1: Dr. Michael Sole praising the value of pharmaceutical industry-sponsored research

World Trade Organization, the federal Conservative government under Brian Mulroney introduced Bill C-91, which eliminated all forms of compulsory licensing, retroactive to December 20, 1991. Even before this announcement, the pharmaceutical industry association had been laying the foundation for further restrictions on compulsory licensing by running ads featuring Dr. Michael Sole, the Director of Cardiovascular Research at the University of Toronto, with the quote, "Most people simply don't realize what a significant contribution the pharmaceutical industry makes to medical research. I certainly do."[36] (Figure 2.1.)

In its brief to the Senate Committee on Banking, Trade and Commerce, industry played the research card again and pointed out that since the passage of Bill C-22 it had already invested $600 million in research and planned to spend a total of $2 billion by 1996.[37] This promise of research dollars is probably what drove individual scientists such as John Edward, an emeritus professor of chemistry at McGill University, and a coalition of the Association of Canadian Medical Colleges and the six-thousand-member Canadian Federation of Biological Societies to voice their strong support for the bill.[38,39] The lure of more research funding also seems to have convinced the Canadian Medical Association to support the legislation. The association's brief to the House of Commons Legislative Committee begins by acknowledging that "Bill C-91 seeks to afford the pharmaceutical industry the same patent protection already enjoyed by other sectors, thereby encouraging more research in Canada and enhancing the availability of quality drugs to Canadians,"[40] but this time it took a more nuanced position and attached conditions to its support. The medical association wanted the industry to commit to increasing the amount of money it invested in research with $300 million being dedicated over a five-year period through an arm's-length peer review mechanism and fines levied on companies for noncompliance that would be earmarked for pharmaceutical-related health research. The medical association also argued that profit margins should be taken into account when setting prices in Canada for new patented drugs.[40,41]

C-91 REVIEW: COMPULSORY LICENSING REMAINS DEAD

Bill C-91 had a four-year review built into it and so in 1997 the pharmaceutical industry association presented its case to the House of Commons Industry Committee that no changes should be made, and emphasized its commitment to research and the fact that it was spending over 12 per cent of sales on research and development, even more than it had pledged to commit. Judy Erola, the president of the industry association and former federal Liberal minister of Consumer and Corporate Affairs, proudly proclaimed that "as long as C-91 remains in place, we are committed to maintaining an R&D to sales ratio of no less than 10 per cent. Between 1996 and the year 2000, this will mean $2.5 to $3.0 billion in R&D investment."[42] This time the medical association did not get directly involved, but the industry association was supported by an array of organizations representing the medical research field including Dr. Barry McLennan, the chair of the Coalition for Biomedical and Health Research; Dr. Michel Bergeron, president of the Canadian Society for Clinical Investigation; Professor Mark Bisby, the head of the Department of Physiology at Queen's University; and Dr. Arnie Aberman, the dean of the Faculty of Medicine at the University of Toronto. Although some of the presentations were more enthusiastic than others, a representative flavour of what was said can be gleaned from the following quotes: "Above all, Bill C-91 has to protect inventions created here, because only inventions that are well protected can lead to major investment that will allow the pharmaceutical industry that's already present to develop further, as well as the creation of new Canadian firms in the areas of biotechnology and pharmaceuticals" (Dr. Bergeron), and "The Council of Deans [of the Faculties of Medicine] supports the principle of protection of intellectual property of those institutions and individuals involved in drug discovery. Such intellectual property deserves protection for the same fundamental reasons that we give protection to the intellectual property of songwriters, authors, software engineers, and inventors" (Dr. Aberman).[43]

Despite Erola's pledge, starting in 1998, spending on research and development as a percent of sales started to decline, fell below 10 per cent in 2001, and is now 4.7 per cent, well below its 1988 level.[44] How much Bill C-22, finally passed by the Canadian parliament in December 1987, and Bill C-91, passed in early 1993, actually contributed to pharmaceutical research in Canada is a matter of contention. Forty key medical figures engaged in pharmaceutical research in Canada were surveyed in 1990 and asked about how they viewed the additional research money then available. They were generally pleased about the increase in funds, but also expressed a number of misgivings about drug industry funding: 90 per cent foresaw a likely conflict of interest, 80 per cent deemed pharmaceutical clinical research as "me too" research, while 75 per cent saw it as "might as well" research and 40 per cent were worried about a potential delay in the publication of unfavourable results.[45] Anecdotally, other researchers believed that Bills C-22 and C-91 were essential for a positive change in the Canadian R&D environment.[46] As with the amount spent on research, scientific employment in the pharmaceutical industry initially increased, but has been on the decline since 2007.[47]

DIRECT-TO-CONSUMER — ADVERTISING OR INFORMATION?

As direct-to-consumer advertising began to be used more often to market products in New Zealand[48] and the US,[49] other industrialized countries, including Canada, experienced pressure to change laws prohibiting the practice. An example can be seen in the 1996 brief that Merck presented to the first national consultation on the introduction of direct-to-consumer advertising. Witness the opening paragraph in the Executive Summary of Merck's brief: "There are a variety of compelling legal, ethical, and financial reasons to permit direct-to-consumer advertising in Canada. Legally, the Industry has a right to commercial freedom of speech. It has also the legal and moral obligation to provide cautionary information to learned intermediaries and, according to its discretion, to patients. However, for patients to exercise their right to informed consent, they must understand their condition, its consequences, and the benefits and risks of treatment."[50] The pharmaceutical industry association echoed the sentiments in the Merck brief with the complaint that, since the 1995 Supreme Court's decision overturning the law regulating the advertising of tobacco, pharmaceuticals were the only products that could not be legally advertised to consumers in Canada. The industry association went on to claim that Canadians were better informed about breakfast cereals than about medications. Its solution to this issue was for "socially responsible" advertising assessed against specific criteria "either in the form of a code of advertising acceptance for advertisements directed to consumers, or through an extension of the current Code of the PAAB [Pharmaceutical Advertising Advisory Board, the organization that regulates advertising to doctors — see Chapter 3]. The [industry association] also believes that only those advertisements that have been precleared by the [board] should be carried by the consumer media in Canada."[51] The rationale and recommendation offered by the medical association was almost identical to what the industry association was advocating. "Consumers have a right to know about prescription drugs and manufacturers probably have a right to inform consumers, in an unbiased manner, about their products as long as they do no harm in doing so . . . A Board, similar to the [Pharmaceutical Advertising Advisory Board] should be put in place to study all public informational material to ensure that it follows this code and approve it before it appears in public. All public media should accept only advertising approved by this board. All manufacturers should be required to submit all advertising and other informational materials to the Board for approval before distributing it to consumers by any means."[52]

By 2003, the industry association was still repeating its same messages about advertising prescription medicines being beneficial to Canadians by helping them recognize early symptoms and letting them know about treatment options and about how the organization supported a regulated approach to direct-to-consumer advertising.[53] However, the medical association by now was opposed to this measure and called on the federal government to maintain the ban on direct-to-consumer advertising.[54]

BILL C-17 (VANESSA'S LAW) — A FURTHER PARTING OF THE WAYS

Bill C-17, which was signed into law in November 2014, gives Health Canada the power to recall drugs from the market for safety reasons and gives the minister of Health, among other powers, the authority to "order a person to provide . . . information . . . to determine whether the product presents . . . a serious risk of injury to human health."[55] In addition, the bill contains provisions to enhance the transparency of clinical trial information by giving the minister the power to release such information where risk of injury is suspected or for the protection and promotion of health. The minister is also given the power to make regulations that require companies to make "prescribed information" transparent and the regulations, once written, could extend the definition of prescribed information to postmarket studies.[55] (The regulations to implement Vanessa's Law have not yet been written as of February 2017.)

The pharmaceutical industry association's position on how much power C-17 should give Health Canada to unilaterally recall drugs was not initially clear. In his opening remarks to a House of Commons committee studying the bill, Walter Robinson, the vice-president for government affairs at the industry association, said, "We also note that, prior to any specific powers now proposed in C-17, [industry association] members have and will continue to work closely with Health Canada to recall products, update or change labels and implement any other important safety-related actions either of our own accord or those deemed warranted by Health Canada."[56] A few months later, testifying before the Standing Senate Committee on Social Affairs, Science and Technology, Robinson's colleague was clear that any disclosure of information must be done in a way to protect "Confidential Business Information," which the industry association defines as "any information that has economic value to a business or its competitors and that is not usually publicly available."[57] The only exception acceptable to the industry association would be where there was an imminent and serious threat to human health. The association proposed amendments at the Senate hearings that would have considerably narrowed the reasons for disclosure, instead of allowing disclosure "if the Minister believes that the product may present a serious risk of injury to human health."[58] It also proposed changing a clause in the bill from "if the purpose of the disclosure is related to the promotion or protection of human health" to read, "if the purpose of the disclosure is necessary for the protection of human health."[57]

None of these concerns resonated with the medical association as it felt that "the term 'serious risk of injury to health' . . . may limit the authority of the minister to take action when the concern may be serious, but not necessarily permanently debilitating or life threatening" and that instead of saying that the minister "may" take certain actions the legislation should read that the minister "shall" take certain actions.[59] When Dr. Jamie Meuser from the College of Family Physicians of Canada appeared before the Standing Senate Committee on Social Affairs, Science and Technology, he recommended that positive and negative decisions about drug authorizations and clinical trial information should all be made publicly available.[60] (Health Canada does not release any information about drugs where approval has been denied and also upholds industry's characterization of safety and efficacy information as confidential business information and will not release that data without the consent of the companies.)

CHANGE AND THE CANADIAN MEDICAL ASSOCIATION

As in many cases where the orientation of organizations has changed, it is often difficult to identify a single precipitant. The move away from industry by the medical association was probably due to multiple factors. The older generation of leadership that was vehemently opposed to government-run health insurance was gone and was replaced by doctors who had grown up with Medicare. These leaders were not necessarily on friendly terms with government, as witnessed by the Ontario doctors' strike in the mid-1980s over extra billing (charging patients beyond what the government paid), but, for the most part, they had accepted the fact that Medicare was here to stay. This change in attitude may have weakened the ideological bond — government as the enemy — that was one of the reasons why the medical association and the pharmaceutical industry formed an alliance. The 1980s had also seen the emergence of a left-wing group of doctors in Ontario, the Medical Reform Group. While the organization's membership was relatively small, in the range of a couple of hundred, there are indications that it had the silent support of a wider group of doctors. The Canadian Medical Association's position on Bill C-91 also indicates that it had become more sensitive to the issue of drug prices and was no longer willing to back industry without a guarantee that patients would be protected against high prices. In line with a concern about prices, the use of generics was no longer a major issue for the medical association, as it had been in the 1950s through to the 1970s.

However, there are also questions regarding how sincere the medical association is about severing its relationship with industry. Chapter 6 deals with the 2003 position of the medical association president about changes in the industry's code of ethics and with the 2009 joint venture on continuing medical education that the association forged with Pfizer. A third event that raises concerns relates to a two-day conference in Ottawa in September 2016. Back in 2004, the federal and provincial governments signed a ten-year health accord designed to "fix" the perceived problems in the Canadian healthcare system. A couple of years after that accord began, the Conservatives were elected and adopted a hands-off approach to healthcare, leaving all major decisions to the provinces. As a result of that philosophy, as the accord approached its expiry date of the end of 2015, the Conservatives unilaterally decided not to negotiate its renewal. One of the planks of the successful Liberal campaign in 2015 was a renewal of the accord with a focus on issues such as home care, dealing with the aging Canadian population and high drug prices. In anticipation of the start of negotiations, the medical association and the think tank Canada 2020 co-organized a two-day conference in Ottawa, titled "A New Health Accord for All Canadians," featuring the association's president Dr. Avery Granger as one of the speakers. The pharmaceutical industry featured prominently in this conference with a representative from Amgen as the moderator for a panel about a new health accord. Sponsors of the conference included the Pharmaceutical Research and Manufacturers of America (the lobbying arm of Big Pharma in Washington), Johnson & Johnson and Amgen.[61]

CONCLUSION

The alliance between the pharmaceutical industry and the medical profession that was formed in the 1950s to respond to government initiatives held solid for almost fifty years and set the stage for cooperation over a period of many decades. The bond was clearly evident in statements by the leadership of the Canadian Medical Association and other leading Canadian doctors and researchers and from reports and briefs from the association when it came to issues involving intellectual property rights, direct-to-consumer advertising of prescription drugs and the value of pharmaceutical research and development. The result was that, up until the early 1990s, the medical association repeatedly supported the industry in its positions when it came to government legislation. Although the alliance is not as solid as it once was, it does not appear to be completely dead.

Over the five decades covered in this chapter, the industry was acting in its own self-interest to preserve its ability to generate the largest possible profit. The question is whether support for industry's positions by the medical profession was compatible with what should be its primary goal — protecting public health.

CHAPTER 3

MEDICAL JOURNALS — ADVERTISEMENTS, MONEY, REGULATION, REBELLION AND POSSIBLY RETRENCHMENT

For a long time, medical journals were the primary way that doctors had to communicate with each other and to learn about new research findings and new approaches to diseases and treatments. Even now, with the Internet, Facebook, Twitter and other means of delivering information, journals still retain a central importance. They are usually seen as sources of authoritative information. However, they also exist in a world where survival means earning revenue and, in the case of journals, in the past that revenue primarily came from the drug advertisements that they ran, and for some journals, from the sale of reprints of articles to drug companies that were then distributed to doctors for marketing purposes. The most prestigious medical journal in Canada, the *Canadian Medical Association Journal* (*CMAJ*), has vigorously defended itself against the charge that its editorial content is determined by the advertising it runs[1] and there is no evidence that I have found to contradict that assertion. This chapter tracks how the *CMAJ* and other Canadian journals have responded to criticisms about taking ads, looks at how advertising in journals is regulated and examines editorial positions that the journals have taken on various issues related to pharmaceutical policy.

There are two ways of looking at the usefulness of drug ads in medical journals. When Canadian doctors are asked about them, as they have occasionally been, the response is that they are not very valuable. In a 1966 survey about which commercial source of information they found most valuable, only 19 per cent of doctors ranked ads as their first choice, behind sales representatives and exhibits at medical meetings at 46 per cent and 20 per cent, respectively.[2] Thirty-four years later when doctors were again asked their opinions, 53 per cent had used ads for information, compared to 82 per cent, 66 per cent and 59 per cent for journal articles, sales representatives and continuing medical education, respectively, and journal ads ranked at the bottom of a list of ten sources in terms of credibility.[3] Ask the industry and the answer is quite different. Guy Beauchemin, executive vice-president of the pharmaceutical industry association, said, "If advertising doesn't influence doctors, then a hell of a lot of people are wasting a lot of money."[4] Beauchemin's comment backs up what an American study found. For products generating greater than $500 million in revenue per year between 1998 and 2000, for every $1 invested in journal advertising companies got a return of $12.20. Even for low-revenue-generating drugs (sales of $25 to $100 million) the return on investment was $7.20 for each $1 spent.[5] Journal promotion was still touted by marketers as the best way to access the hard-to-reach Canadian family physician as recently as 2005.[6] The economics of industry advertising may mean that ads are used by doctors much more than they care to admit.

A DEFENCE OF ADVERTISING: MONEY

Companies in Canada traditionally invested tens of millions of dollars in medical journal advertising. Figure 3.1 shows that from about 1990, spending had been above $50 million annually until 2005, peaking at just under $80 million in 2004. In 2000, companies bought 22,000 pages of advertising in Canadian medical journals and there were more than a thousand pages of advertising for one product alone.[7] More recently, advertising spending has shrunk considerably and by 2015 totalled only $13.3 million and the total number of advertising pages had plummeted by almost 90 per cent to 2,383.[8] These figures may paint a bleak picture, but at least up until 2012 advertising revenue for the *CMAJ* seems to have been relatively robust. Between 1990 and 2012, the *CMAJ* averaged about sixty pages of ads per issue although there was year-to-year variation, and in 2012 the journal reported total advertising revenue of over $2.5 million.[9] Since 2012, the situation has probably deteriorated as there was an average of just fourteen pages of pharmaceutical advertising per issue of the *CMAJ* in the first half of 2016.

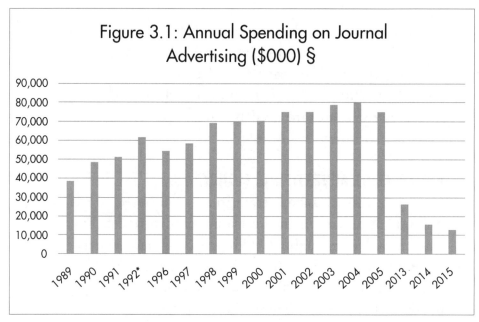

Figure 3.1: Annual Spending on Journal Advertising ($000) §

§Data from 1989–92, 1996–2005, 2013–15 are from three difference sources and the method of data collection may not be the same.
*First 8 months of year.
Source: Chiasson[10]; CAM Corp International[11]; imshealth I brogan[8,12]; ims I brogan[13]

As a result of the money that flowed in from advertising, Canadian medical journals have a long history of supporting the appearance of advertisements on their pages and editorial writers have defended journals' decision to run ads based on the need for the revenue that journal advertising generates. While an anonymous editorial writer said in 1970 that he would like to be able to assure advertisers that doctors get some measure of education from the ads, he also admitted that the most important source of revenue in medical publishing was advertising.[14] The saga of how the *CMAJ* changed the placement of ads illustrates just how important advertising revenue was to the journal. Whereas in 1965 the journal was in the black to the tune of $100,000, by 1969 it had lost $101,631, giving its owner, the Canadian Medical Association, an overall loss of $38,000. But by 1970, the *CMAJ* was budgeting for a loss of only $43,271 and expected it could be lower.[15]

The reason for this turnaround in the *CMAJ*'s fortunes can be directly traced to a change in advertising policy commencing with the October 4, 1969, issue. Before that time, ads had been grouped at either the front or the back of the *CMAJ*, separate from the scientific and medical content, the way that ads in many American medical journals, including the Canadian edition of the *New England Journal of Medicine*, are still placed. Beginning October 4, ads were scattered throughout the body of the journal, at some points interrupting articles. An editorial in the *CMAJ* defended the move, stating that "under the present circumstances, there *are* logical reasons why the advertisements cannot be placed at the front and back of the Journal in their entirety"[16] [emphasis in original]. The editorial never did supply the logical reasons, but it is safe to assume that they were economic. Seeding ads throughout the scientific content made the *CMAJ* unique in comparison to forty other medical journals.[17]

The *CMAJ* published nine letters on the issue of its change in advertising policy in mid-1970; seven of these were critical of the new policy, but the ads remained where they were.[18] A few weeks later, when two Montreal doctors wrote an additional letter about the change in the placement of ads,[19] the editorial response was that this change in where the ads appeared was necessary because of economics. "Advertisers in Canada are no longer content with the automatic scheduling of advertising in a well esteemed periodical. They are now demanding good exposure for their money. If the Journal is to be self-sustaining it must recognize this change in the advertisers' attitude."[16]

By 1974, according to the Canadian Medical Association president, Dr. Bette Stephenson, those ads were worth $1 million a year. In 1980, $1.5 million of the *CMAJ*'s total revenue of $2 million came from pharmaceutical advertising.[20] When asked about the ads, David Woods, director of publications for the association, said, "We still get letters from readers who wonder why the journal chooses to mix pure science with grubby commerce by carrying advertisements . . . Were we, as some purists have urged, to turn up our editorial noses at advertising we'd very quickly have them rubbed in red ink. Without ads this journal would cost each of its 35,000 readers about $40 a year."[21]

Periodically the *CMAJ* continued to raise the point about the need for advertising revenue. In 1984, Dr. Peter Morgan, the journal's scientific editor, said that "Even the journals with the highest circulations could not forgo their display advertising without threat to some of their editorial capacity."[22] In 1993, it was the turn of Dr. Bruce Squires, the *CMAJ*'s editor-in-chief, to repeat the point that except for possibly the *New England Journal of Medicine*, no journal could survive without advertising and certainly the *CMAJ* could not afford to publish its 1,600 pages semiannually without the money that ads brought in.[23] At one point, the *CMAJ* was so positive about the ads that were appearing in its pages that it was giving out an annual award for the best ad.[24]

The relationship with the pharmaceutical industry that other Canadian journals have may also be affected by the income from ads. One president of the College of Family Physicians of Canada bluntly admitted that her college's journal, *Canadian Family Physician* (*CFP*), depended on revenue from journal advertising.[25] As an emergency department doctor I read the *Canadian Journal of Emergency Medicine* (*CJEM*) and estimated that from 2005 to 2008 it took in between $65,071 and $129,666 annually from pharmaceutical advertising, compared to $49,677 to $80,079 from other types of advertising.[26] Eliminating drug ads from *CJEM* would have raised annual individual membership fees to the Canadian Association of Emergency Physicians by $47 to $113 or 13 per cent to 32 per cent depending on the year.[26] The response from the president of association, as a representative of the board of the organization that owned *CJEM*, to the possibility of removing the ads, was that "[The association's] current position is that relationships between [the association] and industry, including pharmaceutical companies, are acceptable. This applies by extension to *CJEM*, as [the association] is the parent organization of *CJEM*, and pharmaceutical advertising in *CJEM* is a component of these industry relationships."[27] (*CJEM* has subsequently become an online-only journal and so the question of advertising is now moot.)

DEFENCES FOR ADS — THEY ARE EDUCATIONAL, BLAME THE DOCTORS, LET THE ADVERTISERS RESPOND

Over the years, journals have employed a number of other arguments to justify their decision to continue to run ads. As far back as 1961, the *CMAJ* was editorializing in favour of ads on the basis of the "considerable educational influence" of "sound, reliable advertising."[28]

The editorial writer in a 1970 issue of *CMAJ* hoped to be able to assure advertisers that "Canadian doctors derive some measure of their education in a complex field from the announcements of advertisers."[14] Another *CMAJ* editor from the 1980s also claimed that ads had educational value. According to Dr. Peter Morgan, "The physician who reads nothing but the ads and the 'package inserts' in a medical journal would at least be getting an accurate update on frequently used drugs."[22]

Margaret McCaffery from the *CFP* offered a novel defence of journal advertising. She agreed that the function of ads was to remind doctors about the form and availability of drugs but, at the same time, made the point that ads were not a substitute for education in therapeutics. According to her, it was up to doctors to ensure that they read more than the ads, including other material in her journal, before they prescribed a drug.[29] When I responded to her editorial and pointed out problems with ads that the *CFP* had recently run,[30] her response was that I had missed the point of her editorial and she repeated her message about the need for doctors to seek other sources of information.[31] She was correct, of course, in saying that doctors should use objective sources of information, but what she was effectively saying was that it's acceptable to run advertisements that may be misleading since doctors are the ones who should be blamed for using only the ads. The "blame the doctor" defence was subsequently taken up by others. Dr. Tony Dixon, again in the *CFP*, also accepted that there will be biases in advertising but said that it's up to doctors to spot those biases and then sanction the drug companies by refusing to prescribe their products.[32] In effect what he was saying was that if we, as doctors, are not up to being able to analyze the ads then it's our problem and the journals that run the ads should not be blamed.

Essentially the same message — ads are deceptive but it's up to doctors to recognize that fact and look elsewhere for information, so don't blame journals for running the ads — was picked up by others. Dr. Squires from the *CMAJ* echoed what McCaffery and Dixon wrote when he said, "Although it seems to me that pharmaceutical firms would increase their credibility were they to give more useful information in their display ads, physicians must ultimately be responsible for ensuring that they are fully informed about any product they prescribe. Physicians who rely solely on an advertiser's claims for a product might be interested in a magnificent new bridge that I have for sale."[33] A variation of the message was extended to "onserts," quasi-reports that are included in the polyethylene bag that journals are often mailed in. A reader wrote to the *Canadian Family Physician* to complain about an onsert, "Meeting Report. Acid-related Gastrointestinal Disorders," that accompanied the January 1997 issue of the journal, saying that it was "distasteful, inaccurate, and obviously biased."[34] In defending the decision to include the onsert, the editor said that the journal does not publish, edit or promote onserts, they are merely a source of revenue. Since onserts are not prescreened by the Pharmaceutical Advertising Advisory Board as ads are, the editor said that the *CFP* had developed a series of criteria that it used in deciding whether to accept them and in the opinion of the editor this particular onsert met those criteria. Finally, according to the editor, it was up to readers to "examine onsert material and decide for themselves whether it is relevant to their practices."[35]

One further line of defence is not to say anything at all and let the advertiser do the defending. This was the tactic that the *CMAJ* chose to use[33] when two clinical pharmacists wrote an article criticizing the way that ketorolac (Toradol) was being depicted in advertisements. Ketorolac is a nonsteroidal anti-inflammatory medication (NSAID) useful in controlling pain and reducing inflammation, but essentially no different from any of the many other anti-inflammatories on the market, such as Advil (ibuprofen) or Naprosyn (naproxen). However, as they pointed out, that was not the picture that doctors were being given in the ads running in journals such as the *CMAJ*. Their point was that the ads selectively focused on comparing the analgesic properties of ketorolac with those of narcotics and tried to set ketorolac apart from other NSAIDS through statements that it was "unlike conventional NSAIDs." The implication was that it was pharmacologically unique. The problem with this portrayal is that all NSAIDs, including ketorolac, can cause serious adverse effects such as acute renal failure, gastro-intestinal tract ulceration and hypersensitivity reactions. A number of European countries either never approved ketorolac or else suspended sales of the drug because they viewed its benefit-to-harm ratio as unfavourable.[36] If ketorolac is seen as somehow different from other NSAIDs, then these problems might be overlooked, with disastrous consequences for patients.[37] The *CMAJ* editor turned over defending the product and its advertising to the vice-president and director of medical research of the company marketing ketorolac.[38]

REGULATION OF JOURNAL ADVERTISING: PHARMACEUTICAL ADVERTISING ADVISORY BOARD

In 1963, the *CMAJ* published the first Canadian statement on journal advertising, in a brochure entitled, "Advertising in Canadian Medical Association Publications." This statement was subsequently adopted by the pharmaceutical industry association and formed the basis for its policy about how drug companies should advertise in journals.[14] Amongst the provisions in the indsutry association's policy were that promotion should be in good taste, it should in no way be offensive, it should give doctors as complete a picture as possible about the product and it should reflect an attitude of caution about using drugs, particularly those that were relatively new. The code was supposed to be binding on all industry association members.[39] However, by the early 1970s it was clear that companies were largely ignoring the code. An ad from G.D. Searle pictured a man suffering from such "gut issues" as student demonstrations, hijacked airplanes and the rising cost of meat, with its drug as the solution for the man. One from Mead Johnson showed a man wearing water skis, standing on sand, in an ad for its laxative. The message to the doctor was that "it's hard going without water" and the promise was that its product would "get the water in to make movements easier." Ads featuring nude women were plentiful — Glaxo-Allenburys had one showing a full-length nude basking in the rainbow colours cast by its new product; Lederle showed a full-length nude in its ad for a skin cream (Figure 3.2); Schering advertised its skin cream with a series of tattoos, appropriately placed over nude bodies[40] (Figure 3.3). Other ads promoted hydroxyzine (Atarax) as the solution for the child who was a "troublemaker, bed-wetter, picky eater" or who had a "nervous stomach"[41] (Figure 3.4). If you wanted to find out why the male bus driver was suffering from estrogen deficiency you turned the page and saw that it was because the emotional, menopausal woman on his bus was out of control[42] (Figure 3.5). Scientific-looking charts were sometimes included with the ads but many of the studies that they cited were out of date, used out of context or were directly sponsored by the company making the product.[40]

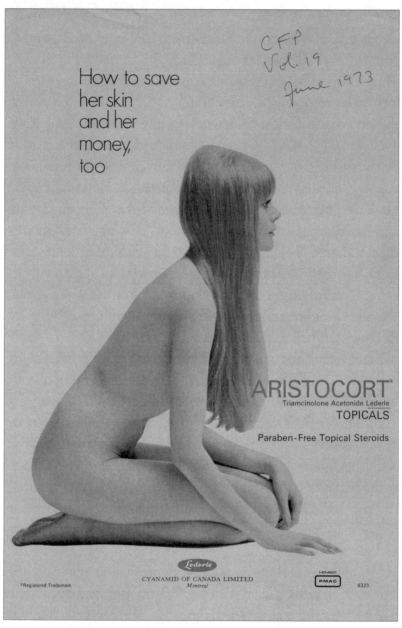

Figure 3.2: Lederle ad for steroid cream

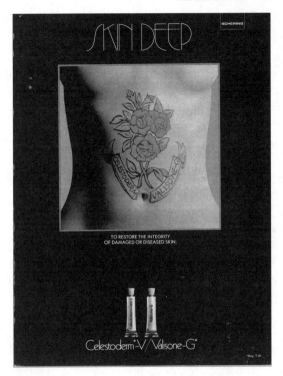

Figure 3.3: Schering
ad for steroid cream

Figure 3.4: Pfizer ad for
treatment of children who are
troublemakers, bed-wetters,
picky eaters or who have a
nervous stomach

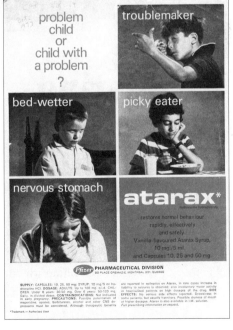

Figure 3.5: Ayerst ad explaining why the bus driver is suffering from estrogen deficiency

she is the reason why

Behind the long-suffering man is the suffering woman. She may be suffering from any one or more of a multitude of symptoms — irritability, depression, headache, loss of vitality, loss of libido, tension or emotional instability — apart from the more obvious signs of estrogen deficiency. And through no fault of her own, she makes life miserable for everyone she comes in contact with.

But it doesn't have to happen. Many of these disruptive processes may be minimized or prevented. PREMARIN®, the *natural* and *complete* estrogen complex, acts as a metabolic regulator and exerts a protective effect on many systems, organs, and tissues of the female body.

Moreover, PREMARIN has the intrinsic ability to impart a sense of well-being — of vital importance in this period of psychologic adjustment and emotional imbalance.

"If we consider the number of aging changes that take place in the body after estrogen deficiency begins, it would seem logical to treat all women . . . estrogens are as essential to good health as a well-balanced diet."[1]

1. Willson, Beecham, Carrington Obstetrics and Gynecology 2nd Edition, 1963

when symptoms point to estrogen deficiency, prescribe

premarin Ayerst

the original conjugated estrogen

Complete prescribing information and references on request
*T.M. Reg'd.
850/71/B PMAC

In the face of this type of medical journal advertising, a 1973 meeting of federal and provincial health ministers recommended that the federal government "review controls on the advertising of drugs with the aim of strengthening them where necessary."[43] In response, Marc Lalonde, then federal minister of Health and Welfare, issued an ultimatum to the industry to reform its practices or else face the prospect of government action. The pharmaceutical industry association, as might be expected, was very much in favour of self-regulation over direct control by government and initiated a sequence of events that resulted in the creation of the Pharmaceutical Advertising Advisory Board in 1975. The first chair of the board was an employee of the Upjohn company and the industry association's promotion code formed the basis for the one adopted by the board.[43] The board was given the responsibility for advertising/promotion systems, i.e., the media presentation of promotion in all forms — print, audio, visual, audio/visual and later electronic and computer means of communication. Advertisements in any of these forms have to be submitted to the board for preclearance to ensure compliance with the provisions of its code before they can be used.[44] The industry association's own code mandates compliance by its membership with the advisory board's code[45] and Canadian medical journals will not run ads that have not been first prescreened by the board. From the beginning, the Canadian Medical Association has had a representative on the board.

Support for the advisory board was forthcoming from the *CMAJ*. In 1980, David Woods enthused that the board "ensures among other things that advertising has a sound scientific basis, provides complete and accurate product information and doesn't make outlandish or extravagant claims."[21] A decade later Dr. Squires was "surprised and pleased to learn how effective this unique form of self-government is . . . In 15 short years [the board], with the cooperation of pharmaceutical manufacturers, has come a long way in restoring the confidence of government and the public in drug advertising and is a model for promoting truth in all advertising."[46] When I wrote about the deficiencies in the board's code in a challenge to Squires's championing the organization,[47] his response did not deal with any of my criticisms. Instead he indulged in personal criticisms of me, saying that I had an "overdeveloped penchant for self-righteously tweaking the noses of pharmaceutical firms" and "utopian standards."[48] He did admit that the board was not perfect but, on the other hand, he also felt that pharmaceutical advertising had come a long way under the board.

I was not the only one who was unhappy with the quality of journal advertising after the advisory board took over regulation. In 1980, Dr. Murray Katz took a look at advertisements and produced numerous examples of questionable ads. One for an antibiotic to treat urinary tract infections featured a seductive woman with a ring of entwining hearts on her figure; the caption on the ad was "The Power to Perform." An ad for an oral contraceptive read, "Expectations . . . Realized. The Class of 1980." The picture appeared to be a graduating class of young girls who looked no more than seventeen or eighteen, implying that all teenage girls are sexually active and should be on the Pill.[20] A 1991 survey of 111 different advertisements in eleven medical journals, two pharmaceutical journals and one nursing journal found that while benefits were discussed in 91 per cent of the ads, risks were mentioned only 53 per cent of the time and, of the ads that mentioned risk, 94 per cent referred to the product as free of certain risks or side effects. Moreover, risks and benefits were included on the main page of ads in only 39 per cent of cases. Prescribing information accompanied the ad only 18 per cent of the time; otherwise, it was at the end of the journal in small print, far away from the ad.[49]

When a special task force convened by the Canadian Public Health Association released a 1992 report on communicating about the risk, benefit and cost of pharmaceuticals, panel chairwoman Dr. Linda Strand, executive director of laboratory and disease-control services for the Saskatchewan Department of Health, said that Canadian medical journals should pay less attention to gloss and more to fact in the drug advertisements they carry. According to her, "We need stringent, clear guidelines for advertising regulations. Obviously, the way things are now, this kind of advertising is going to promote benefits without mentioning cost or the various adverse effects in large print."[50] Dr. David Naylor, later president of the University of Toronto, talked about a recent full-page ad that was dominated by a vivid colour photograph of the dim, menacing eyes of a black panther, barely visible against a dark jungle background. Over the picture, in large letters, were the words, "Blending Into The Environment Can Work Just As Well For a Vaginal Antifungal." The advertised product promised "faster symptomatic relief, higher microbiological cure rates (and) low relapse rates." Although the ad appeared on page 3, the fine print with the references to back up the claims for the drug appeared only on page 81 of the journal. Naylor said these sorts of ads had no place in respected journals and likely increased public spending on drugs.[50]

In previous years I've criticized the Pharmaceutical Advertising Advisory Board for its poor reporting about sanctions levied on companies whose ads have been found to violate the organization's code: the companies involved were not identified, the complainant was not identified except to divide up the numbers of complaints into those made by pharmaceutical companies that were competing with the one being complained against and others types of complainants, the nature of the violations was not described, the product involved was not named, when the violation took place was not disclosed and reasons for the Commissioner's decision were not given.[51] Along with a colleague, I examined twenty-two ads in issues of the *CMAJ* published in 1992 for their use of references to see if they were being used in accordance with the requirements in the board's code. The mean methodologic quality score, a measure of the methodological soundness of the reference, was 58 per cent and the mean relevance score, i.e., evaluating whether the reference was appropriately cited, was 76 per cent.[52] At that time, the wording of the code required that references reflect current medical *opinion* rather than current medical *evidence*. The code also did not explicitly require that references accurately reflect the statement(s) in the advertisement that the references were supposed to support.[53] Evidence and opinion are two different things — opinion is often subjective whereas evidence ideally is objective.

The lack of specificity in the 1997 code about how statistics should be presented in ads allowed companies to use the more liberal relative risk reduction (RRR) rather than the more conservative absolute risk reduction (ARR) or the more reader-friendly number needed to treat (NNT).[54] (See Box 3.1 for a definition of RRR, ARR and NNT.) Various authors have noted that when results are presented as RRR, doctors are much more willing to prescribe a drug than when an ARR or NNT is used. My study of twenty-two ads found none of them gave an ARR or NNT, although in half the cases it was possible to calculate an ARR or NNT.[55]

BOX 3.1: DEFINITION OF RELATIVE RISK REDUCTION (RRR), ABSOLUTE RISK REDUCTION (ARR) AND NUMBER NEEDED TO TREAT (NNT)

A relative risk reduction (RRR) is the percent reduction in the risk of targeted complications between two groups: e.g., a drop in mortality from 50 per cent to 25 per cent would be a RRR of 50 per cent (25/50 × 100). An absolute risk reduction (ARR) is the absolute percent difference in the risk of targeted complications between two groups: e.g., a drop in mortality from 50 per cent to 25 per cent would be an ARR of 25 per cent (50 - 25). The number needed to treat is the number of patients that have to be treated in order to prevent one complication of their disease: e.g., a drop in mortality from 50 per cent to 25 per cent would be a NNT of 4 (100 / ARR or 100 / 25).

According to the board's code, advertisements are acceptable as long as printed material from pharmaceutical companies is consistent with the contents of the government-approved Product Monograph. Therefore, if the Product Monograph lacks a statement indicating that the medication has not been shown to have an effect on a hard clinical endpoint such as life expectancy, then advertisements do not need to contain a statement saying that the effect of the drug on survival is unknown. When I complained about this problem to the board, the response was that this was an issue for Health Canada to deal with, i.e., Health Canada needed to modify the Product Monograph to contain this kind of information. Health Canada declined to make any changes[56] and as a result the board did not take any action and ads remain unchanged.

Some of the weaknesses that I previously identified in

the operations of the board have been corrected and some remain unchanged. Code violations are now reported in reasonable detail in "PAAB Views," found on the organization's website.[57] After publication of my analysis of the use of RRR, ARR and NNT, the board's code was changed to require that if results were reported as an RRR, "they must also include an indication of the absolute treatment effect. This can be presented as absolute risk reduction (ARR), number needed to treat (NNT) and/or the actual comparative clinical results or rates."[44] On the other hand, the current version of the code, revised in 2013, only requires that references "be consistent with current Canadian medical opinion and practice,"[44] not with current evidence.

The code continues to contain other significant weaknesses. It requires a "fair balance of risk to benefit" but there is no specific requirement that equal space in the ads be devoted to harms and benefits and there is no provision for the font used to describe benefits and harms to be equal in size. Although the font size for the print in an ad has a lower limit, the generic name of the drug is not required to be the same size as the brand name; additionally, the generic name does not have to be used each time that the brand name is given, despite evidence that use of the generic name leads to better prescribing.[58] Companies are allowed to make statements in journal ads about effects of drugs, even if the clinical significance of those effects is unknown, as long as the ad also includes that caveat. Finally, and maybe most significantly, the only sanctions explicitly listed for violating the code are "immediate withdrawal of offending advertising, to notices in annual reports or newsletters, to public letters of apology."[44] Withdrawing ads doesn't correct the misinformation that they contain; doctors may still tend to remember that misinformation and continue to prescribe based on the inaccurate or incomplete data in the ads.

The last positive statement from the *CMAJ* about the board seems to have been back in 1994[59] and since then the journal has been quiet about the organization. The question to ask is whether this silence is reasonable given the board's ongoing weaknesses and the way that the board reacts to its critics with threats of legal action and ad hominem attacks (See Box 3.2). In addition to the *CMAJ*'s lack of an editorial voice about the adequacy of the board, the Canadian Medical Association has remained publicly silent with any criticisms it may have and continues to sit on the board.

BOX 3.2: HOW THE PHARMACEUTICAL ADVERTISING ADVISORY BOARD REACTS TO ITS CRITICS

There are two vignettes that illustrate how the Pharmaceutical Advertising Advisory Board responds to its critics. Since I'm one of the few vocal people criticizing the board, this is largely a personal story.

The first episode started in the late fall of 2010 at a workshop in Toronto that was organized by me and Dr. Barbara Mintzes to discuss some interim results from a project that she was leading that was looking into how much safety information drug company sales representatives give to family doctors. One of the attendees at the workshop was Dr. Walter Rosser, the chair of the board. Dr. Rosser has also at one time or another been head of the department of family practice at almost all of the medical schools in Ontario.

Dr. Rosser took exception to a quote about lack of transparency from an interview study on drug regulation in Canada, France and the United States that was presented in a preliminary report. He apparently believed this quote was about the board, although to maintain confidentiality neither respondents' names nor national affiliations were presented. A second statement referred to the board's standards as weak. These statements were made at a seminar with ample time for open discussion and Dr. Rosser briefly aired his views. About a month and a half later, Dr. Mintzes and I received a letter from Dr. Rosser on the letterhead of the board. In that letter he once again complained about the way that the board was represented and requested that we send a letter of apology to all of the people who had attended the meeting, a letter that would be reviewed first by the board's lawyers.

Our reply to Dr. Rosser pointed out that primarily we were talking about the regulation of sales representatives, not of journal advertising, we were presenting preliminary results and that if we were successful in obtaining further funding we would be contacting the board to get its views. We heard nothing further from Dr. Rosser but shortly thereafter we were contacted by Ray Chepesiuk, the Commissioner of the board. Mr. Chepesiuk invited Dr. Mintzes and me to visit the offices of the board to meet and speak with the people who reviewed the ads.

At the time, Dr. Mintzes was working at the University of British Columbia and we replied that we would be glad to take up the offer of a meeting but since Dr. Mintzes was not planning to be in Toronto until the fall of 2011 any meeting would have to wait until then. Mr. Chepesiuk took our request to delay a meeting for about six months as a refusal to meet at all and expressed his disappointment. He ended his email with a request that Dr. Mintzes and I stop making "false and/or misleading" comments about the board in public.

The second event unfolded at the end of April 2016. I was
in the final editorial stages for my previous book, *Private Profits
versus Public Policy: The Pharmaceutical Industry and the Canadian
State*, and in that book I wanted to reproduce a 2004 email
exchange between Mr. Chepesiuk and me about the role of
the board. In the exchange, I described what I found to be the
very small and difficult to read font that the board allows for
harm information and references, and contrasted this with ads
for the same products in the United States, with larger, much
more readable print and more safety information. I wrote to
Mr. Chepesiuk to request permission to use his emails and
he declined because he felt that his opinions in 2004 did not
reflect the situation in 2016 with respect to the way that the
board functioned. He also expressed his belief that the board's
guidelines about journal advertising may be the best in the
world, although he did not provide any evidence to back that up.
In the course of formulating his reply to me, Mr. Chepesiuk also
sent on my email to the Executive Committee of the board. One
of the members of the executive congratulated him on his refusal
to allow me to use the emails, characterized me as "a loose
cannon" and advised him to avoid anything that I am involved
with. Mr. Chepesiuk replied to the Executive Committee
member that I invariably talked about issues that happened
decades ago and that I inhabit my own "perfect world."

There are two ways to interpret these vignettes. The first
is that I have an axe to grind against the Pharmaceutical
Advertising Advisory Board and that I engage in irrational
criticisms and that, in fact, recounting these events is just
another attempt to unfairly malign the organization. The
second interpretation is that when faced with criticisms of the
organization, board officials resort to veiled legal threats and ad
hominem attacks against its critics.

REBELLION AND POSSIBLY RETRENCHMENT

Despite the widespread criticisms that I have levied against Canadian medical journals in general and the *CMAJ* in particular, it is fair to say that more recently, at least the *CMAJ* has been willing to take on the pharmaceutical industry over some issues. The first, somewhat timid, evidence of independence came in 1992 when Dr. Bruce Squires, the *CMAJ* editor, said that although the *CMAJ* would consider publishing the reports of drug company–supported consensus conferences, the journal needed to be assured that the academic organizers of the conference had full control of the content and the authors had to declare all conflicts of interest.[23] The conflict created by publishing non–peer-reviewed supplements to the *CMAJ* continued to plague the journal into the mid-2000s without any adequate resolution. The acting editor-in-chief identified a number of ongoing problems: companies had the opportunity to knowingly and selectively sponsor a supplement that directly related to their product or product areas and, since sponsorship was necessary to cover publishing costs, the topic selection for supplements was limited to those areas that could attract industry funding. The editor could not offer any immediate solution to these issues but admitted that "a resolution must be found — the current relationship with industry is too cozy."[1]

In 1994, in replying to an author inquiring about why his article was rejected, the anonymous editor who responded said that it was the policy of *CMAJ* not to accept articles where the author had been paid to write them, although *CMAJ* would publish original research funded by companies provided that before the research was started it was understood that the sponsors had no control over the result of the study.[60] Shortly into the new millennium, the *CMAJ*, along with ten other leading medical journals that were part of the

International Committee of Medical Journal Editors, signed on to a statement about the publication of industry-funded research that tightened up the previous policy of the journal. Under this new policy, the *CMAJ* committed to routinely requiring authors to disclose details of their own and the sponsor's role in the study and requiring the "responsible author to sign a statement indicating that he or she accepts full responsibility for the conduct of the trial, had access to the data and controlled the decision to publish."[61] Moreover, the *CMAJ* agreed not to publish a study where the sponsor could withhold publication. When asked about the increased scrutiny, Dr. John Hoey, the *CMAJ* editor, said that given the large amount of money required to get a drug to market, there was pressure from drug companies on researchers to deliver positive results, although he was also quick to say that he didn't think that this was happening all too often.[62] The following year, the *CMAJ* was editorializing against conflict of interest, saying that conflicts should be disclosed by "physicians who receive money to enrol patients in phase IV trials [trials of drugs already on the market]; by participants in consensus conferences; by the writers of CPGs [clinical practice guidelines] and reviews. Prescriber beware: marketing departments are experts in disguise, and one of those disguises is science."[63]

In 2004, the *CMAJ* editorially questioned whether disclosure of conflict of interest was enough to allay fears about bias in the material being presented in articles. Although it did not go as far as to exclude authors with conflicts from publishing in the journal, it did impose restrictions on their level of conflict of interest. The policy announced that "Commentaries and narrative reviews or other similar articles, whether commissioned or spontaneously submitted, will not be accepted for consideration for publication if any author has any financial investments (such as equity, shares, derivatives, bonds, but excluding publicly traded mutual funds), receives royalties or similar payments, that in total over the past year have exceeded US$10 000 per company; or holds a patent (or is likely to or has applied for one or more) in a company that markets a product (or a competitor's product) mentioned in the article. Nor will we accept for publication papers by authors who are employed by such companies, who have a contractual relationship of any type with such companies, or who are named officers or board members of said companies."[64] A few years later, the *CMAJ* went on to question the commercialization of the knowledge base of medicine and to call for the elimination of "the influence of commercial interests whose values require a primary commitment to increasing value for shareholders, not patients" in the provision of information to doctors.[65] (Chapter 5 will return to the question of the commercial influence on knowledge that physicians receive.)

Although the *CMAJ* was increasingly willing to take an independent stance on many issues important to the pharmaceutical industry, there are two episodes that demonstrate how far its owner, the Canadian Medical Association, is willing to let it go in that direction and how far it will go on its own. The first episode was the 2006 abrupt dismissal of the *CMAJ*'s then editor Dr. John Hoey and the journal's senior deputy editor Anne Marie Todkill. On February 20, 2006, the president of Canadian Medical Association Media, the arm of the association in charge of publications, Graham Morris, announced the firing of Hoey and Todkill with the claim that "it was time for a fresher approach."[66] The immediate reason for the firings seems to have been related to two stories that the *CMAJ* planned to run, the first one about how readily pharmacists were dispensing Plan B (levonorgestrel), the so-called "morning-after pill," to women and a second one that was critical of the Health minister in the Conservative government.[67] The association was mostly silent about the entire affair, although six weeks after the firings its president, Dr. Ruth Collins-Nakai, wrote in a letter to association members that the two were sacked because of "irreconcilable differences" with Morris. Her letter did not go into details about what these differences might have been.[68]

The first of the two articles, that was never published, generated a complaint from the Canadian Pharmacists Association, alleging that the research leading to the article was unethical. Following the complaint and before they were fired, the *CMAJ* editors appointed an ad hoc committee headed by Dr. Jerome Kassirer, former editor of the *New England Journal of Medicine* and a member of the *CMAJ*'s Editorial Board, to report on the entire situation. Kassirer's committee released its draft report condemning the association on February 17, three days before the firing, and supported the way that material for the article was gathered. Collins-Nakai's letter hinted about clashes between the editors and what she calls "the responsibility of the publisher to protect the organization's [Canadian Medical Association's] legal, financial and liability interests." Concretely, what she may have been referring to can be inferred from Kassirer's report, which documented a history of interference in the editorial freedom at the *CMAJ*.[69] The report said that there had been tensions over the past few years regarding articles in the *CMAJ* "unflattering to the journal's advertisers" and that conflicts had arisen between the *CMAJ* and Canadian Medical Association Media because of controversial articles. Kassirer's report did not identify which group of advertisers had been subjected to unflattering articles but since the vast majority of the advertising in the journal comes from the pharmaceutical industry it seems clear that these were the advertisers in question.

The second incident involved a three-part series on conflict of interest that ran from late summer of 2015 to the early winter of 2016. Importantly, these articles were in the News section of the journal, which means that they were not peer-reviewed but only read by the editorial team. The first of the trio of articles featured extensive quotes from Dr. Jeffrey Drazen, editor of the *New England Journal of Medicine* (*NEJM*), who was concerned that an anti-industry sentiment was creeping into medicine. Highlighting what Drazen said is especially significant because the *NEJM* itself had just run a much criticized[70] set of articles, written by Dr. Lisa Rosenbaum, whose thesis was that too much concern about conflict of interest was counterproductive to medical research and that people who criticized conflict of interest were using the language of rape and child abuse.[71–73] The only other person who was mentioned by name in the *CMAJ* article was Dr. Thomas Stossel, someone who has a long history of promoting physician-industry interaction and downplaying concerns about conflict of interest.[74] Part 2 of the *CMAJ* series was revealingly titled, "The costs of vilifying pharma," and was based on the thesis that "There is concern in some corners that the quest to ferret out conflicts of interest in medical research has become over-zealous, that it has morphed into a religious-like crusade based more on morality than evidence of harm."[75] Once again the people who appeared most extensively were Drazen and Stossel, this time accompanied by Rosenbaum. The final part of the

CMAJ series starts with Rosenbaum defending her articles and Drazen saying that he ran them "because I wanted a conversation to start." According to Roger Collier, who wrote the series, the responses to Rosenbaum's articles were "often ireful." Stossel again makes an appearance but this time, and for the first time in the series, someone who is a critic of conflict of interest is included. Near the end of the article, Collier brings in Dr. Roy Poses who "said that advocates for more physician-industry 'collaboration' appear to have 'largely dismissed the evidence and logic underlining concerns about conflicts of interest in health care.'"[76]

At one point, it seemed as if the *Canadian Family Physician* (*CFP*), the other large-circulation general medical journal in Canada, was poised to challenge the pharmaceutical companies. In May 1999, it announced that henceforth it would start reprinting reviews from the independent French drug bulletin, *La revue Prescrire*, on a monthly basis. *Prescrire* was, and still is, solely supported by subscriptions and has a reputation for very critical and objective reviews of new drugs and new indications for existing drugs, reviews that often elicit negative responses from the companies that make the products. The announcement from the *CFP* made it clear that the editors at the journal were attracted by the rigorous quality of *Prescrire*'s reviews. Dr. Tony Reid, the editor, said, "Our editorial staff have reviewed a number of editions of *Prescrire International* [the English-language translation of *La revue Prescrire*] and believe it is particularly well suited to our readership because the reviews are conducted by good scientific methods, many of the reviewers are family physicians, and we liked the presentation of results in a format that is applicable to practice."[77] However, after two years (May 2001), an announcement, this time unsigned, appeared in the *CFP* saying that the journal was discontinuing reprinting *Prescrire* reviews, although, in fact, no reviews had actually appeared since October 2000. The stated reason for the decision was that "competition for publishing space [meant that the journal] could no longer sustain the large number of pages needed for the bilingual versions of *Prescrire*'s reviews."[78] One review did take up nineteen pages in the journal, but overall the fourteen *Prescrire* reprints occupied an average of 4.7 per cent of the pages in the issues in which they appeared. Moreover, in 2000 there were a total of 2,524 pages in the *CFP*, and the next year there was actually an increase of eighty pages, so the idea that there was competition for publishing space is difficult to justify. (The following year, 2002, long after the *CFP* had ceased to reprint material from *Prescrire*, the journal did shrink by 624 pages.) Finally, the companies making the products that were reviewed, or consultants working for them, were not happy with the reviews and on five separate occasions wrote to the *CFP* objecting to the reviews.[79–83] The lack of objective data about the claim that space for the reviews was lacking and the frequent complaints from companies raise the question about whether there were other factors that lead to the decision to drop the reviews. Aside from running *Prescrire* reviews, the only significant statement from the *CFP* that could be construed as mildly critical of industry that I'm aware of was in 2011 when its scientific editor said that the journal would be more demanding in its requirements for authors to declare their conflicts of interest.[84]

CONCLUSION

From the mid-1960s to the early 1990s, the *CMAJ* consistently and unreservedly supported the positions of industry. That support may have partly come because of its heavy reliance on advertising revenue, but it also seems to have been ideologically based, coming from an attitude that journal advertising had a legitimate role to play in helping companies market their products and a belief that physicians should recognize advertising for what it was and use other sources of information beyond what was in the ads. Since the early 1990s there has been a growing gap between the *CMAJ* and industry and the *CMAJ* is now willing to challenge drug companies on some issues. This gap preceded the decline in advertising revenue and may have resulted from an ideological shift in the leadership of the journal, although the firing of the *CMAJ* editor in the mid-2000s and the recent series of articles about conflict of interest raises questions about how large that gap is. Other journals such as the *CFP* continue to be even more timid about confronting industry interests.

The *CMAJ* and all other Canadian journals still do not publicly disclose the amount of revenue that they obtain from advertising or the sale of reprints of articles that they publish. As stated earlier, the *CMAJ* reported advertising revenue for 2012 at $2.53 million. (Although the bulk of that probably came from drug ads, the breakdown between revenue from drug and other types of ads was not given.) With a print circulation of just over 69,000 in 2012, it would have cost each reader about $35.50 annually if the *CMAJ* carried no advertising in that year.[9] Is that amount too much to ask of readers? Given the precipitous decline in journal advertising in recent years, then the cost to readers of replacing advertising income is even less, raising the question as to why the *CMAJ*, and other Canadian journals, continue to accept pharmaceutical advertising.

CHAPTER 4
ACADEMIC HEALTH SCIENCE CENTRES: RESEARCH, MONEY, CONTROVERSIES, CONFLICT OF INTEREST AND INDEPENDENCE

Academic health science centres are at the pinnacle of the healthcare system. These are the universities housing medical schools, the medical schools themselves and their affiliated teaching hospitals, places where cutting-edge medical research is done. (Medical schools and medical students are considered separately in Chapter 7.) All told, there are seventeen universities with medical schools, seventeen medical schools by themselves and about fifty teaching hospitals scattered across the country. Because these centres are at the heart of medical research, they are also on the receiving end of large amounts of research funding and grants from pharmaceutical companies. Are disinterested research and patients' interests being put above the economic interests of pharmaceutical companies? This chapter looks at the money that these centres get from the pharmaceutical industry for research and the conflicts that this money may create.

ACADEMIC HEALTH SCIENCE CENTRES, RESEARCHERS AND CONFLICT OF INTEREST

Government research funding is increasingly being restricted. On a per capita basis, funding for research from the American National Institutes of Health is thirty-two times larger than that of the Canadian Institutes of Health Research[1,2] although the population difference is only nine-fold. Drug companies have partly stepped into the breach and in 2014 they provided $107 million to fund research in Canadian universities and hospitals.[3] Table 4.1 shows the amount of corporate research funding for sixteen of the seventeen universities with medical schools, excluding the Northern Ontario School of Medicine.

Table 4.1: Universities with medical faculties: corporate research income 2010–2014*

University	Research income ($000)	Corporate income as a percent of total research income
McMaster University	588,745	35.1
Université de Montréal	382,267	14.4
University of Toronto	358,695	7.2
University of British Columbia	307,048	10.9
University of Calgary	189,943	12.6
Western University	163,128	13.9
Queen's University	158,051	18.2
University of Alberta	156,276	6.6
Dalhousie University	151,882	22.5
McGill University	145,769	6.1
University of Ottawa	117,675	8.3

Université Laval	102,293	6.6
University of Manitoba	55,802	7.1
University of Saskatchewan	55,650	6.1
Université de Sherbrooke	52,539	7.7
Memorial University of Newfoundland	49,588	10.6

*Not all of the funding necessarily comes from pharmaceutical companies.

Source: Research Infosource Inc.[4]

Companies want to conduct high-quality scientific research, but if the clinical trials that they fund turn out badly, it can affect their ability to get their products approved for marketing or the sales of products already on the market. Back in 1992, there didn't seem to be very many concerns about academic medical centres conducting pharmaceutical industry–funded research. According to Dr. Martin Hollenberg, dean of medicine at the University of British Columbia in the early 1990s, industry funding was viewed in the past as a threat to the autonomy of universities but "the view is much more positive now" and the relationship was seen as "a true partnership with very high standards."[5] The Faculty of Medicine at the University of Toronto released a set of guidelines for the ethical conduct of research in 1994. The guidelines said, "Clinical researchers must not permit their clinical practices to be swayed by such [industry] support and they must be free to think independently, to conduct research freely and to publish negative as well as positive results promptly. When such freedom is not assured, accepting financial support from interested commercial parties threatens the ethical standards of the faculty and its teaching hospitals."[6] Representatives from both the university and the pharmaceutical industry were quick to deny that there was any problem with their relationship. John Pye, director of public affairs with the pharmaceutical industry association, maintained that "We all want to produce things that benefit mankind . . . I think they [industry and academe] are complimentary. The relationship has come a long way; the two solitudes are moving together now."[6]

In the ensuing years, researchers, including me, have documented that clinical research funded by companies that Hollenberg and Pye were so positive about is significantly more likely to produce both positive results and positive conclusions compared to research funded by any other source.[7] This finding fuels concerns about conflict of interest between the researchers receiving the money and the companies giving it. Dr. Penny Ballem, then vice-president of British Columbia Women's Hospital and board chair of the Centre of Excellence in Women's Health at the University of British Columbia (UBC), put it quite bluntly in a 1996 interview with the *Vancouver Sun*: "I believe that drug company funding and the insidious way that it is basically overwhelming our biomedical research is a grave threat to our health care system."[8] Dr. Ken Renton, a pharmacology professor at Dalhousie University, was worried that "if a clinician has access to a product for research, it might influence his treatment of a particular patient . . . They'll use the compound and enter the patient in a trial . . . It's not that the route they go is wrong, it's that there were other choices that weren't considered."[9] What Ballem and Renton were particularly concerned about is that when pharmaceutical companies direct research funding, money that should be going to address the most pressing problems in healthcare is instead often being directed towards health problems that hold the greatest potential to generate profits for the companies.

Universities and hospitals were assumed to have developed and put in place conflict-of-interest rules to mitigate the effects of any conflicts, but back in 2001 these rules varied considerably across the country. In a series in the *Globe and Mail*, reporter Anne McIlroy described the hodgepodge of policies in different universities. At McGill University, scientists had to inform patients about their financial conflicts of interest, such as being a principal shareholder in a firm funding a trial, but not so at UBC. "'We don't include that. We look very carefully at the experiment, but I am not sure the corporate stuff makes a huge difference,' Richard Spratley, the associate vice-president of research at UBC, said."[10] Although McGill expected researchers to disclose potential conflicts annually, a senior university official conceded that often they forgot.[10] Queen's University, like UBC, did not require disclosure regarding owning shares in a company that was paying for a clinical trial. Dr. Renton said that researchers at his university felt pressure from their superiors to land industry contracts, because the academic institution takes upward of a 40 per cent cut to cover overhead. "We are told all the time by everyone from the department heads to the deans that we as individuals should be going after more contract-type research, no matter what it is. This is because universities are desperate for money."[10]

McMaster University in Hamilton is near or at the top of academic centres receiving research money from the pharmaceutical industry. Between 2002 and 2004, company funding to the university and its teaching hospitals virtually quadrupled from about $34 million to almost $129 million.[9]

As part of a 2005 series on the pharmaceutical industry, reporters with the *Hamilton Spectator* identified ninety-seven researchers at McMaster University who had received money from pharmaceutical companies and attempted to contact them to get their comments about their relationships. Only twenty-one replied at all out of the ninety-seven. Of those who did, some were quite defensive about taking money: "I've always found it insulting and offensive that it is assumed that if I read a study that is funded by a pharmaceutical company, it is immediately a bad study . . . If the methodology was appropriate then who funded it is not that critical"; some maintained that the money did not influence them: "I turn away three of four trials I get offered. I turn away different companies. When I give talks, I use my own slides, I use my own setup. It's very important that I be independent"; and one or two used the opportunity to comment about how little federal funding there is for medical research: "The essential remedy is more public funding for research. There are all sorts of issues about dealing with the pharmaceutical industry . . . The long-term goal would be to have more productive use of the money."[11]

Among the doctors at McMaster who had relationships with pharmaceutical companies were Dr. Richard Hunt and Dr. Barry Jones. Hunt was the lead researcher of a clinical study funded by Merck that compared Vioxx (rofecoxib) against ibuprofen or a placebo to see which product best protected patients from developing gastrointestinal bleeding when they took the drug for inflammation or pain. Besides Hunt, among the other eight authors on the paper were five people affiliated with Merck Research Laboratories. The study found that Vioxx was better at protecting the gastrointestinal tract from bleeding than a traditional anti-inflammatory painkiller. When Merck announced the approval of a new use for Vioxx in a press release in 2002, the first doctor quoted in the release was Hunt. The release didn't mention that Hunt was a consultant, investigator and speaker for Merck. When the *Hamilton Spectator* asked Hunt if his relationship with Merck had any influence on his findings, he responded that it was "A very important question . . . I don't believe so."

The *Spectator* continued, "In November 1996, Eli Lilly touted [olanzapine] Zyprexa in a press release as a breakthrough treatment for schizophrenia that had just been approved by Health Canada. The first doctor quoted in the press release was Dr. Jones, described as associate vice-president of research and development for Eli Lilly Canada and a clinical professor of psychiatry at McMaster." Although Jones had been with Lilly since 1995, he was allowed to maintain his affiliation with McMaster.[12] Dr. John Kelton, dean of McMaster's Faculty of Health Sciences, said, "the university has never tried to keep track of faculty members' relationships because 'We've got, we think, pretty careful checks and balances . . . It's a relationship that has to be managed carefully,'" and "McMaster has no plans to change the way things are done." He believed that "the basic integrity of scientists — and the fact that academic peers are closely watching one another — is a satisfactory control on potential conflict." Kelton was also firm that "The investigators, not the research sponsors, own the research data, and investigators may not be prohibited from publishing the results. Investigators work for the patients, not the study sponsors, and they are obligated to alert patients about any potential side-effects."[9]

A decade earlier, Dr. David McLean, vice-president of research at Vancouver Hospital and assistant dean of medicine at the University of British Columbia, also thought that ethical guidelines about the relationship between university and hospital researchers and industry were a good idea. But he too did not seem to be fully committed as he was not convinced that there was a big problem. He also worried that cumbersome and time-consuming rules for industry-financed research might drive research out of the province.[8] Likewise, Dr. Richard Reznick, the current dean of the Faculty of Health Sciences at Queen's University, recognizes the need for policies to govern the relationship between academia and industry but he clearly comes down on the side of needing to maintain industry-physician interactions. Without these, in his view, "[a]ll 'unrestricted' educational grants would disappear. Capital donations that support centers, buildings, and hospital wings would vanish. Collaborations that reward excellence in the form of industry funded academic chairs would be eliminated."[13] The title of his 2010 blog piece pretty well sums up his outlook: "The relationship between health professionals and the pharmaceutical and device industries is under attack."[13] In another blog, five years later, he commented that when he became dean, "the pendulum, with respect to industry-academic relationships had swung far to the left [i.e., was too restrictive], communications were not open, relationships were fractured." His response was to recruit the previous CEO of the Canadian subsidiary of GlaxoSmithKline to "proactively buil[d] relationships with senior executives of pharmaceutical and medical device companies."[14]

At other centres, debates about conflict of interest have generated controversy due to a perceived industry bias in the nature of the debate. The Departments of Psychiatry and

Family Medicine at McGill University staged a half-day conference in April 2013 entitled, "The Medical Profession and the
Pharmaceutical Industry — Ethical, Clinical, Scientific and
Financial Issues at the Interface."[15] The initial announcement
about the event did not mention that some of the funding
was coming from various pharmaceutical companies, something later admitted in a clarification issued by the psychiatry
department. The clarification also claimed that "The balance
between 'pro' and 'con' positions should be well addressed
by the various speakers. They were chosen because of their
expertise, different perspectives, and the variety of their
involvements in this area."[16] However, out of the five people
on the panel only one, Dr. Ashley Wazana, who published a
systematic analysis of the effects of physician-industry interactions on prescribing and professional behaviour in 2000,[17]
was truly independent of industry. The most controversial
person on the panel was Dr. Alan Schatzberg. While conducting research funded by the US National Institutes of Health
into a drug for the treatment of depression, Schatzberg simultaneously owned almost 2.5 million shares in the company
making the drug, worth about $6 million.[18] (Schatzberg and
Stanford University, where he was employed, said that this
conflict was disclosed to the institutes.) Out of the other three
panel members, Dr. Carl Salzman received grant support
from four pharmaceutical companies.[19] One of Dr. Roger
McIntyre's 2016 publications listed him as a consultant to
and receiving speaker fees from nine different companies and
one of his coauthors worked for the company whose drug was
being studied.[20] On one website, Dr. Denis deBlois was listed
as having over seven years of experience as a scientific consultant for the pharmaceutical industry in Canada and the US.[21]

FUNDING & ACADEMIC HEALTH SCIENCE CENTRES

It is not just individual researchers who are on the receiving end of money from pharmaceutical companies, it is the academic health science centres themselves that also are beneficiaries of the donations from companies. Table 4.2, based on the relationships that have come to light, summarizes those relationships and is most certainly only the tip of the iceberg. It shows a more than two-decade history of company grants to universities and hospitals across Canada. (In addition to the examples given in the table there was a $200,000 donation from Purdue Pharma to a pain clinic at Western University but the timing of that gift is not clear.[2])

Table 4.2: Endowments, research chairs and money

Year	Institution	Interaction	Reference
1989	University of Western Ontario (now Western University) and Victoria Hospital Research Foundation	Upjohn Company of Canada (now part of Pfizer Canada) donated a $1 million 5-year endowment to Victoria Hospital Research Foundation and a $2.4 million 2-year grant to University of Western Ontario to study central nervous system disorders	Helwig[23]
1993	Mount Sinai Hospital	Miles Canada (now part of Bayer Canada) donated $5 million over a 10-year period to cover the operating costs of the hospital's Cardiovascular Clinical Research Laboratory	Morrissey[24]
1993	Ontario Cancer Institute & Princess Margaret Hospital (now part of the University Health Network)	Amgen Canada Inc. contributed $100 million over 10 years for the establishment of the Amgen Institute to study human immunology	Johnston[25]
1993	Dalhousie University	Nordic Laboratories (now part of Sanofi-Aventis) donated $1.3 million to help fund the Cardiac Prevention Research Clinic	Moulton[26]
1999	University of Toronto	University of Toronto was negotiating with Apotex for a $20 million grant to help fund its proposed $90 million Centre for Cellular and Molecular Biology Research and possibly an additional $35 million grant	Foss[27]

1999	Humber River Regional Hospital	Apotex donated $5 million for hospital's emergency services	Foss[27]
2007	Queen's University	Sanofi-Aventis donated $400,000 over three years for the Centre for Obesity Research and Education	Tripp[28]
2009	University of Saskatchewan	Pfizer Canada, AstraZeneca and Merck Frosst Canada contributed $400,000 each along with $500,000 from the provincial government to establish the Chair in Patient Adherence to Drug Therapy	Stewart[29]
2013	McGill University, Université de Montréal, Université de Sherbrooke, Université Laval	Merck Canada donated $4 million to each university to support health research with a translational component conducted in areas of unmet medical need	Merck Canada awards $4 M to faculty of medicine[30]
2015	Faculty of Pharmaceutical Sciences, University of British Columbia	Amgen Canada Inc., AstraZeneca Canada Inc., Eli Lilly Canada Inc., GlaxoSmithKline Inc., Merck Canada Inc., Novartis Pharmaceuticals Canada Inc., Pfizer Canada Inc., Boehringer Ingelheim (Canada) Ltd., Hoffman-La Roche Ltd., LifeScan Canada Ltd., Lundbeck Canada Inc. provided $2.4 million to establish the Initiative for, and Professorship in Sustainable Health Care	Professorship in sustainable health care established at UBC[31]
2016	Faculty of Medicine at McGill University	Boehringer Ingelheim donated $3 million to establish the Albert Boehringer (1st) Chair in Pharmacoepidemiology	McGill University installs inaugural chair in pharmacoepidemiology[32]

These grants were usually met with enthusiasm from university and hospital officials grateful for the money. When Mount Sinai Hospital in Toronto received its gift from Miles Canada, the president of the hospital, Ted Freedman, said, "Through the generosity of Miles . . . the Mount Sinai Hospital . . . cardiovascular centre can play a major role in understanding, treating and even eliminating a disease which has caused too much hardship to too many people."[24] The University of Saskatchewan president, Peter MacKinnon, accepted that partnerships with drug companies were necessary for future research, saying, "It is well known across the country that so much of the research that is being done now and will be done in the future will be done pursuant to partnerships."[29] When McGill got its $4 million from Merck Canada in 2013, Dr. David Eidelman, vice-principal of Health Affairs and dean of the Faculty of Medicine, called the collaboration fundamental in advancing his university's biomedical research and said that the faculty was "tremendously proud to be partnering with Merck Research Laboratories."[30] Three years later, Eidelman was equally effusive in praising Boehringer Ingelheim for its donation that established the chair in Pharmacoepidemiology at McGill.[32]

While grants may have appeared altruistic on the surface, they had an underlying commercial motivation. Sanofi-Aventis gave its money to Queen's University for the new obesity centre at the same time that it was seeking Health Canada's approval for a new anti-obesity drug, rimonabant, but the company denied that there was any connection between seeking approval and providing the money. (The product was never approved in Canada and was pulled from the market in Europe because of safety issues.[33]) Dr. Robert Ross, the Queen's University researcher who headed the obesity centre, said the money was coming to the university through an unrestricted educational grant and that "We have no accountability [to the company] . . . We make no reports. We have no advice to give them or them us . . . They do not sit on our council. They no not advise us on any issue."[28] Despite Ross's denials two issues remain — the first is the appearance of a conflict of interest and the second is whether a centre funded by a pharmaceutical company would be willing to offer an unflattering opinion about a drug made by its funder. Dr. Ross was a speaker for, on the advisory board of and received consulting fees from Sanofi-Aventis. He was also one of the coauthors of a Sanofi-Aventis–funded study investigating rimonabant that concluded that in abdominally obese patients with elevated cholesterol, the drug significantly improved multiple risk markers for cardiac disease.[34]

Sometimes officials seemed to understand that there might be potential downsides to taking the money but accepted them as a necessary trade-off. When Princess Margaret Hospital got its $100 million over ten years, Amgen gained the exclusive right to the hospital's pending patents that dealt with developments and discoveries in the new Amgen Institute research area, including ownership of two strains of mice with partial immune systems. The president of the hospital said it weighed the options and chose to go for the positive developments it would get now rather than wait for something that might happen years later.[28] In some cases, the grants seemed to come with a quid pro quo. Dr. John Ruedy, dean of medicine at Dalhousie University, wrote a letter to the federal government in support of Bill C-91, the piece of legislation that eliminated compulsory licensing of pharmaceuticals, at the same time as the Faculty of Health Professions received a $1.3 million donation from Nordic Laboratories.[26] (See Chapter 2 for details about Bill C-91.) Robert Prichard, president of the University of Toronto, wrote to the government in 1999 in support of the position of the generic companies, and Apotex in particular, asking the government for a thirty-day extension to a review of drug-patent-protection regulations. An official from Humber River Regional Hospital also did the same. Apotex had given money to the hospital and was negotiating with the University of Toronto for a substantial grant.[27]

On at least one occasion hospitals have allowed companies to directly advertise their products on the hospital grounds. In a backlit box on the first floor of the Montreal General Hospital there was a picture of two people who appeared to be healthcare professionals with an ad for Lipitor (atorvastatin) and the message (in French) that these professionals endorsed the use of Lipitor.[35] (The ad was quickly removed after the hospital received a few letters of protest. (Pierre Biron, personal communication, August 20, 2016.)) In the mid-1990s, the Vancouver Hospital and Health Sciences Centre was permitting company sales representatives to attend or host hospital continuing education events (rounds). Almost one in every five visits by sales representatives were to attend rounds and in nearly half of these cases drugs were promoted to individual doctors. Rounds appeared to be a "good method of making contact with an individual practitioner for the purpose of follow-up, one-to-one detailing. Almost one in every ten visits to the hospital was devoted" to hosting a "drug lunch."[36] In the early 2000s, I was involved with a process to change how the University Health Network (UHN) in Toronto dealt with sales reps. One clause in the proposed new policy banned the use of drug samples for personal use (i.e., self-treatment or treatment of family members) by UHN staff. When the policy reached the Medical Advisory Committee of the hospital, the body that makes decisions about clinical issues, that clause was removed.[37] The rationale for this change was not recorded in the minutes of the meeting. (As of May 2014, the UHN policy was changed and now the use of samples by UHN staff or family members is not allowed.[38])

A recent public controversy at an academic health science centre involved the ophthalmology department at Western

University. That dispute lead to the appointment of lawyer Elizabeth Hewitt in the fall of 2013, in an attempt to resolve allegations that a pharmaceutical company exerted "undue influence."[39] When Hewitt reported in late winter of the following year, the nature of the allegations from Dr. William Hodge, who had been chair of the ophthalmology department, were finally revealed. Hodge alleged, among other things, that Novartis created a conflict of interest when it provided "kitbags," that included vitamins and drugs, to be given directly to patients, in exchange for the patients making a $5 donation to the St. Joseph's fundraising arm; that Novartis proposed buying TVs for the waiting room of the institute's "retina pod," where macular degeneration is treated, along with educational videos that included material sponsored by the company and others, an offer rejected by Hodge; and that Novartis paid for another educational video, featuring three doctors who treat macular degeneration, that discussed the condition and its treatments. Ms. Hewitt's report rejected all three allegations: the bags benefited no doctor directly, raised money for charity and did not constitute a conflict; the video for the patients could have been implemented simply by controlling its contents; and the physicians got no personal gain from the educational video and the video did not promote one particular drug.[40]

CONTROVERSIES AND GHOSTWRITING

Ghostwriting is the practice whereby pharmaceutical companies, or companies paid directly by them, engage medical writers to write up the results of clinical studies or to write commentaries, letters to the editor or other material for publication. The companies then find well-known doctors or researchers, typically at academic health science centres, who are willing to sign on as authors of the pieces. Sometimes these doctors review the manuscript and make changes and sometimes they just accept what has been done. There are no estimates as to how often this happens in Canada but the practice has been investigated in the United States and other countries and is all too common.[41,42] Ghostwriting first came to public light in a Canadian context in 2003 on *Marketplace*, a CBC television show. The show tracked down a ghostwriter who they called Blair Snitch, who was interviewed wearing a hood. Snitch was making over $100,000 per year. He said that he was "given an outline about what to talk about, what studies to cite. They want us to be talking about the stuff that makes the drug look good . . . There's no discussion of certain adverse events. That's just not brought up . . . As long as I do my job well, it's not up to me to decide how the drug is positioned. I'm just following the information I'm being given."[43] On the same show, Dr. John Hoey, then editor of the *CMAJ*, said that his journal did not have the resources to check whether the person claiming to be the author actually was. Dr. Paul Hébert, a subsequent editor of the *CMAJ*, estimated in 2009 that he turned down five to ten ghostwritten articles per year.[44]

In 1997, SmithKline Beecham, now part of GlaxoSmith Kline, found its antidepressant Paxil (paroxetine) under attack from competitor Eli Lilly, makers of Prozac (fluoxetine), because Paxil's short half-life, the time taken to clear the body, allegedly led to Paxil having more side effects than Prozac. SmithKline hired the public relations agency Ruder Finn to help prepare medical journal publications to counter this attack. One letter to the editor of the *Journal of Clinical Psychiatry* appeared under the name of Dr. Bruce G. Pollock, a psychiatrist at the University of Toronto. The letter did not acknowledge that SmithKline Beecham or Ruder Finn had any role in writing it, nor that Pollock had any financial relationship to the drug company.[45]

Julia Belluz chronicles probably the best known example of ghostwriting in Canada, involving psychologist Dr. Barbara Sherwin of McGill University. In response to class-action lawsuits in the United States from women who claimed that they had been harmed by being prescribed hormone replacement therapy, Wyeth, now part of Pfizer, hired the New Jersey-based medical communications company DesignWrite to produce articles defending hormone replacement therapy that would appear in medical journals. One of those articles under the authorship of Sherwin appeared in the April 2000 edition of the *Journal of the American Geriatrics Society*. Sherwin's involvement was revealed when documents from the class-action suit were made public. She issued a statement, which she says was written by McGill's public relations department, saying that "I made an error in agreeing to have my name attached to that article without having it made clear that others contributed to it. It is an error I regret and which had never occurred before or since." McGill carried out an eight-month investigation that was never made public. The investigation cleared Sherwin but reprimanded her for not acknowledging the "editorial assistance" she received.[44]

As of mid-2015, a Canadian class-action lawsuit was pending against Janssen, makers of the antipsychotic drug Risperidal (risperidone), alleging that the company ghostwrote articles about the drug — "utilizing hired medical writers, who are not researchers or scientists, to write articles and then submitting them to selected opinion or 'thought' leaders to attach their names to them as authors without making any meaningful contribution to the article, to lend false credence to these articles." Should the case proceed, Janssen said it "plans to vigorously defend itself."[46]

As might be expected, ghost authorship occurs more often in industry funded, compared to non-industry funded research. A 2006 survey of 844 Canadian investigators found that more than two-thirds reported that ghost authorship was present in all of their industry-sponsored trials experience compared to less than one-third for non-industry trials.[47] Moreover, the intent behind ghost authorship is different in non-industry trials compared to industry ones. In the former, medical writers are employed mainly for efficiency to produce a manuscript more quickly but the researchers are the ones who own and analyze the data. In the latter, it is the companies who own the data and are crafting the message that the ghostwriter delivers.

CONTROVERSIES — NANCY OLIVIERI AND DAVID HEALY

The story of Dr. Nancy Olivieri is all too well known. Olivieri, the director of the Hemoglobinopathy Research Program at Toronto's Hospital for Sick Children and with an appointment in the Faculty of Medicine at the University of Toronto, was doing research in the mid-1990s on L1, a product to be used in the treatment of iron-overload in patients with thalassemia, a blood disorder that requires frequent transfusions. But she had also signed a confidentiality clause with Apotex, the Canadian company with rights to the drug. The clause gave Apotex the right to control communication of trial data for one year after termination of the trial. When Olivieri became concerned about the safety of L1, she contacted Apotex and explained to the company that she needed to inform the patients in the trial of these new safety concerns. Apotex disputed the interpretation of her safety data, refused her request and threatened to take legal action against her if she made her concerns public. Neither the University of Toronto nor the Hospital for Sick Children provided effective support for Olivieri and her rights, or for the principles of research and clinical ethics, or for academic freedom, during the first two and a half years of the controversy.[48] This lack of support came despite the 1994 statement from the university about the ethical conduct of research that explicitly said that researchers "must be free to think independently [and] to conduct research freely."[6] At the time the Olivieri controversy broke, the University of Toronto was negotiating with Apotex for a large grant to help pay for the cost of a new building.[49] When the controversy was at its peak, Michael Strofolino, president of the Hospital for Sick Children, said: "Our goal is to be the best hospital in the world, to be number 1. How do we do it? Do we close down commercialism? Do you think the federal government is going to give us the money? Do you think we're going to get scientists to come up to Canada in an environment like that?"[48] It seems that Strofolino was willing to tolerate conflict of interest in the interest of getting industry money.

A few years after the case of Olivieri became public, another controversy erupted at the University of Toronto, this time involving Dr. David Healy. In the late 1990s, Healy, a psychiatrist, was Director of the North Wales Department of Psychological Medicine. As Trudo Lemmens, who teaches law at the University of Toronto, describes it, in 2000, Healy was offered the position of the Director of the Mood and Anxiety Disorders Program at the Centre for Addiction and Mental Health, a psychiatric hospital affiliated with the University of Toronto.

Prior to starting his job, in November of 2000, "he gave a public lecture at a special conference organized by the Department of Psychiatry at the [Centre for Addiction and Mental Health] in which he reiterated his controversial but well-known view that pharmaceutical companies should have investigated further the link between suicide risk and selective serotonin reuptake inhibitors (SSRI), and that they had failed to do so."[50] The SSRIs are a group of antidepressants, of which Prozac, made by Eli Lilly, was the best known and best-selling. A week after this talk, Healy received an email from Dr. David Goldbloom, the physician-in-chief at the centre, telling him that the job offer was withdrawn on the grounds that Healy's talk had shown that his "approach [was not] compatible" with the rest of the department.[51] Although twenty-seven leading neuropsychopharmacologists, including two Nobel prize winners, signed a letter of protest at Healy's firing, the hospital did not reverse its decision.[52]

Various people have raised the question about whether Healy's firing was an example of conflict of interest caused by the relationship between the Centre for Addiction and Mental Health and Eli Lilly. Shortly before the affair with the centre, Healy, along with three philosophers, had written articles in the *Hastings Center Report*, one of the leading bioethics journals, that contained criticisms about the way that Prozac was being used.[53] Eli Lilly was one of the major funders of the Hastings Center and after Healy's article appeared, Lilly withdrew its funding.[52] The Hastings Center had Healy's article peer-reviewed a second time, but found nothing amiss with it and did not apologize to Lilly.[52] At the time Healy was fired by the Centre for Addiction and Mental Health, Lilly was the "lead" donor to the centre according to its website, contributing more than $1 million to its $10 million capital-fundraising campaign.[54] Even Healy doesn't believe that Lilly directly intervened in this dispute,[52] but the question of whether this represents self-censorship by the centre remains unanswered. The Centre for Addiction and Mental Health "steadfastly denies that it has allowed fundraising concerns to interfere with academic freedom. 'If you are asking me if his comments influenced our decision, let me be clear that there were a number of factors involved. We regret that our actions have been misinterpreted as an attack against academic freedom and as a conflict of interest,'" said Dr. Paul Garfinkel, CEO of the centre.[54] Dr. David Naylor, then dean of the Faculty of Medicine at the university, also believed that this was not a question of academic freedom but a "lack of fit" with other staff at the centre.[55]

AFTER OLIVEIRI AND HEALY AT THE UNIVERSITY OF TORONTO

Following the controversies about Olivieri and Healy, the University of Toronto Faculty of Medicine, its dean and all eight university-affiliated teaching hospitals began a process to ensure the independence and integrity of industry-sponsored research. To that end, they developed a set of principles to govern clinical research contracts with third parties. Working groups were established to harmonize five areas of research policy and practices including clinical study agreements, ethical conduct of research and intellectual property. Four principles were adopted to guide negotiations of research contracts. "First, agreements should not allow research sponsors to suppress or otherwise censor research results . . . [Second,] investigators should generally be able to submit work for publication within 6 months of sharing the findings with a sponsor . . . Third, researchers must retain the right to disclose immediately any safety concerns that arise during the study."[56] Finally, there was a provision for dispute resolution. An analysis of the first seven months of experience with the new process found that "a co-operative and solid foundation ha[d] been laid for continued ethical enhancement of contract clinical research in the Toronto academic health science complex . . . Non-compliance in recent months appear[ed] to be exceedingly uncommon."[56] According to Naylor, in 2002, the various institutions were in the process of refining the agreement.

Although there is no doubt about the importance of the initiatives that Naylor described, what was absent from the agreement is also important; especially missing was anything about the quality of the research ethics boards that approve all research involving humans in hospitals and other institutions and the financial relationships between the researchers and the companies funding the research. In 2000, Health Canada acknowledged that not all research ethics boards have the expertise and funding to ensure that drug trials can be conducted according to generally accepted principles of good clinical practice.[57] Naylor's article did not go into the status of the ethics boards at the teaching hospitals affiliated with the University of Toronto. Did they have the time and the expertise to adequately review the proposals that came before them? Did board membership include people from outside the hospital community, particularly representatives of patient organizations? Did the board monitor ongoing research activity? What happened when there was a conflict of interest between a member of a board and a company funding a research project? Has there been any independent audit of activities of the research ethics boards?

The March 26, 2001, edition of *Med.E.Mail*, the weekly email bulletin from the dean of the Faculty of Medicine at the University of Toronto, stated that the university and the hospitals agreed to adopt policies and procedures to address real and potential conflicts of interest in the conduct of research at their institutions. Investigators would be required to disclose funding sources for the research, their direct or indirect financial interests in the outcomes of the research and any past or ongoing direct financial relationships they had with the sponsor of the research.[58] These guidelines were vague and broad and therefore were unlikely to solicit a detailed response. Have the university and the hospitals gone beyond this limited declaration to develop explicit criteria on this topic? Without detailed information on the policies of the hospitals and university and without ongoing monitoring we do not know whether or not there are instances of conflict of interest, how often they occur and how serious they are. Finally, there was the issue of the relationship between institutions and private companies sponsoring research activities. What was the policy, if any, of the university and its affiliated teaching hospitals regarding public disclosure of any conditions attached to donations of money or other resources by such companies?

A task force chaired by Dr. David Goldbloom, from the Department of Psychiatry at the University of Toronto, published a statement in 2003 about interactions with the pharmaceutical industry. There were recommendations in five areas: education of residents, research in the teaching hospitals and the department, clinical care, conflict of interest and society.[59] Some of these recommendations were promising, such as a ban on sponsorship of speakers, a ban on allowing speakers' topics to be selected by industry and a ban on all gifts from industry directly to individual faculty and residents regardless of their financial value; the promotion of faculty and resident discussion on the issues raised in the task force report at each teaching hospital; and the dissemination of the report to promote faculty development. Others were more half measures: research presented at the hospital or departmental level needed to include a disclosure of conflicts of interest but there were no details about the level of disclosure required; all physicians holding University of Toronto appointments were required to annually disclose to their psychiatrist-in-chief and university program/division head potential sources of conflict of interest related to industry (honoraria, consultancies, advisory boards). But what would happen to these disclosures? There was no mention about whether they would be made generally public or publicized even within the department.

Four years later, there was a policy from the Governing Council of the University of Toronto on conflict of interest and conflict of commitment.[60] The main thrust of the document was in the opening couple of paragraphs that said, "The University of Toronto is dedicated to supporting and fostering research, teaching and learning . . . in accordance with the highest standards of academic integrity . . . These standards include freedom from conflicts of interest and conflicts of commitment as well as transparency in all processes and relationships." This was an aspirational document and didn't have any details about how these goals were to be achieved.

CANADIAN ACADEMIC HEALTH SCIENCE CENTRES AND POLICIES ON CONFLICT OF INTEREST

In 2006, I was part of a team led by Dr. Paula Rochon that undertook a project funded by the Canadian Institutes of

Health Research to look at researcher and institutional conflict of interest in academic health science centres. For the former, we surveyed 844 Canadian researchers and for the latter we looked at seventy-two academic health science centres consisting of sixteen universities with medical schools, the sixteen medical schools themselves and forty-two of the forty-seven teaching hospitals in the country. Full adherence to preferred clinical trial practices by researchers was spotty at best. It was highest for the institutional review of signed contracts and budgets (82 per cent and 75 per cent of researchers, respectively), where the practices were required and enforced by an external agent and under these conditions the practices were equally likely to occur in industry- and nonindustry-funded trials. Lower rates of full adherence were reported for the other two practices in the clinical trial preparation stage (avoidance of confidentiality clauses, 12 per cent; trial registration after 2005, 39 per cent). Lower rates of full adherence were reported for seven practices in the trial conduct (35 per cent to 43 per cent) and dissemination (53 per cent to 64 per cent) stages, particularly in industry-funded trials. Two hundred and sixty-nine investigators personally experienced (n = 85) or witnessed (n = 236) a financial conflict; over 70 per cent of these situations related to industry trials.[47]

When it came to institutions, we examined thirty-eight distinct policies in the various academic health science centres looking for the mention of sixteen core policies around institutional financial conflict of interest, such as those dealing with royalties from the sale of the investigational product being researched, institutional officials having a direct responsibility for research in humans who held a significant financial interest in a commercial research product, the existence of an institutional conflict-of-interest committee and procedures for conducting institutional-level audits for conflict of interest. We found that over half of the Canadian centres lacked institutional financial conflict-of-interest policies at the time of our survey. "On average, individual policies contained 20 per cent of the 16 core "standard" items: no individual policy contained more than 65 per cent of the core [financial conflict of interest] items. Even when the content of up to three policies per site was combined, less than half of the core items were addressed. Less than a quarter of policies addressed royalties, equity interest, or ownership interests. Where policies existed, they were not comprehensive and were frequently difficult to access."[61] Finally, out of the total of sixty-one different items that we asked about, only one, the definition of faculty and staff, was addressed by all centres that responded. Thirteen items were present in fewer than 25 per cent of centres. Fewer than one-quarter of hospitals required researchers to disclose financial conflicts to research participants. The role of research ethics boards in hospitals was marginal. At the time of the survey in 2006, no single policy in any Canadian centre informed researchers about the broad range of investigator financial conflict-of-interest issues, and some areas, such as strategies for managing financial conflicts and publication rights, were not addressed at all.[62]

Since 2006, some academic health science centres have gone on to also develop or revise their policies about their relationship with industry. An example is the one from the University of British Columbia from February 2010.[63] This policy covered a variety of topics including research, education, educational resources, gifts, samples and detailing. Like most policies it contains a mixture of strong points, e.g.,

"No faculty member should enter into an agreement with industry without the power to publish study results" and weak ones, e.g., "Travel and accommodation arrangements, social events, and venues for industry-sponsored educational activities should be the same as if there were no industry sponsorship."

CONCLUSION

Academic health science centres' primary mission should involve serving the public interest through the research that they do, but they need money to be able to fulfill their mission. At present they are heavily dependent on industry for funding of research programs and research chairs. When the money is coming from industry it brings both benefits and risks, and the most obvious risk is conflict of interest. Conflicts of interest are real. Even if the secondary interests do not prevail, there is still the perception that they may have, and academic centres need to guard against that perception in order to maintain the trust of doctors, patients and society in general in the research that is done in them. Concretely, what that means is not merely having policies about the disclosure of conflict of interest, but avoiding conflicts entirely, something that academic health science centres have not yet been willing to do.

CHAPTER 5
KEY OPINION LEADERS, CLINICAL PRACTICE GUIDELINES AND MEDICAL SOCIETIES: GETTING THE MESSAGE OUT

Many influential Canadian researchers and Canadian medical societies are linked to pharmaceutical companies. The former because of money that they receive from companies for doing clinical research and for speaking on behalf of companies, and the latter because the companies help fund their general activities as well as the continuing medical education that they offer. Just as conflict of interest is a concern when academic health science centres take money from industry, it is also present when researchers and medical societies do the same. Some researchers are direct spokespeople for companies and/ or sit on committees that develop clinical practice guidelines. These conflicted relationships help to send out messages to doctors about the benefits of collaborating with industry. Medical societies talk to their membership about a wide range of issues including government policy, relations with industry and clinical practice. Does conflict of interest play a role in what researchers and societies say?

KEY OPINION LEADERS

Over the past four decades, companies have evolved from controlling the development of new drugs to also controlling the knowledge about those drugs, ensuring that theirs is the primary message that reaches doctors.[1] However, companies know that messages coming directly from them are likely to be viewed very skeptically. As a result, companies' use of "key opinion leaders" as an "independent" source of information has significantly expanded since the mid to late 1990s.[2] The Pharmaceutical Inquiry of Ontario (Lowy Report) looked into the acquisition, distribution, prescribing, dispensing and use of prescription drugs in Ontario in the late 1980s. It commented that "Pharmaceutical manufacturers are well aware of the impact that specialists and respected consultants have on the prescribing habits of community physicians."[3] Key opinion leaders are typically well known and highly respected leaders in their field who are especially effective at transmitting messages to their peers. Reid and Herder found that "1 or more of the top 5 publishing cardiologists at each of 12 out of 13 Canadian medical schools had disclosed receipt of 'lecture fees' or a 'speaker's honorarium,' had been 'paid to speak for,' and/or had participated on a speakers' bureau on one or more occasions" for pharmaceutical companies.[4]

KEY OPINION LEADERS AS TRUE BELIEVERS

Pharmaceutical companies hire key opinion leaders to consult for them, to give lectures and to run continuing medication education sessions.[5] In some cases, key opinion leaders talk about the industry generally rather than a single company or product. For instance, in the early 1990s, when the question of industry investment in medical research was at the centre of the debate about whether compulsory licensing should be abolished, three prominent Canadian researchers, Drs. Michael Sole, Fernand Labrie and Calvin Stiller, were appearing in TV commercials or medical journal advertisements to tout the benefits of industry sponsorship of research. Table 5.1 provides a very partial list of some key opinion leaders and their activities. (See also Figure 2.1.) (In the United States, a 2007 survey found that 16 per cent of physicians received payments for serving as a speaker or being part of a speakers' bureau.[6] If that figure can be translated into Canada it would mean that over twelve thousand have given talks on behalf of drug companies.)

Table 5.1: Physicians and their relationship to the pharmaceutical industry and individual companies

Year	Physician	Company	Message	Reference
1990	Michael Sole	Industry in general	Contribution the pharmaceutical industry makes to medical research	Advertisement[7]
1991	Fernand Labrie	Industry in general	Pharmaceutical manufacturers are among the leading contributors to medical research	Dr. Labrie will now speak for PMAC[8]
1992	Calvin Stiller	Industry in general	Advances in Canadian medicine and the role that pharmaceutical companies play in this effort	Dr. Cal Stiller: now a TV star[9]
1992	Robert Nelson	Glaxo	Imitrex for migraine	Regush[10]
1993	Carter Thorne, William Bensen	Searle	Arthrotec for arthritis less likely to cause stomach problems	McLean[11]
Mid-1990s	Brian Goldman	Purdue	OxyContin for pain	Goldman,[12] Blackwell[13]
1997 +	Gideon Koren	Duchesnay	Diclectin for nausea during pregnancy	Blackwell,[14] Mendleson[15]
2000+	Roman Jovey	Purdue Pharma	OxyContin for pain	Ubelacker[16]
2002	Paul O'Byrne	AstraZeneca	Symbicort for asthma	Morrison[17]
2005	Peter Selby	Pfizer	Unnamed smoking cessation medication	Weeks[18]
2014	Andre Lalonde	Eli Lilly	Cymbalta for back pain	Bruser[19]
c2014	Louis Liu	Actavis	Constella for irritable bowel and constipation	Bruser[19]

Other key opinion leaders directly talked about specific drugs on behalf of their makers. Sometimes promotion of particular products took place in academic health science centres, for instance when Dr. Paul O'Byrne appeared with Kevin Smith, the president of St. Joseph's Healthcare in Hamilton, to talk about a new combination asthma product.[17] Other times, doctors such as Carter Thorne and William Bensen attended press conferences. In their case it was the one that announced the release of Arthrotec, a combination of a pain killer/anti-inflammatory and a drug to protect the stomach from the side effects of anti-inflammatories.[11] Dr. Vivien Brown, an assistant professor of family and community medicine at the University of Toronto, was hired by Novo Nordisk, a company that has sponsored some of her research, to accompany Cathy Jones, star of CBC's *This Hour has 22 Minutes*, when Jones did media interviews on behalf of a Novo Nordisk vaginal hormone pill used to treat vaginal atrophy.[20]

Key opinion leaders are almost uniformly resolute that they are promoting the product because they believe in its effectiveness and that they are independent and able to say what they believe. Dr. Peter Selby said his relationship with Pfizer didn't influence his research. "Rather, he stands behind the products because they provide options for people who want to quit [smoking], including those who may not otherwise have access to counsellors or other quitting methods."[18] Similarly, Dr. André Lalonde, when speaking to a reporter from the *Toronto Star*, said that he did "the same presentation whether the event host is a drug company or doctor college. '(The company knows) that I am free and independent and I speak my mind, not theirs . . . I do not sell anything.'"[19] Rheumatologist Dr. Walter Maksymowych also expressed disbelief that he could be swayed by taking speaker's fees from drug companies. "If I was out there and gave a talk to some of my colleagues and was very effusive in my praise of a particular therapeutic that was clearly unjustified, I would lose my credibility."[21]

Dr. Roman Jovey, on the speakers' bureau for Purdue Pharma, maker of OxyContin (extended-release oxycodone), had no qualms about leaving behind textbooks for medical students to pick up that he coauthored and that were paid for by Purdue. "It was a gift from Purdue. I'm not at all embarrassed or ashamed. I think it's a darn good book . . . If we all want to be politically correct and have the appearance of being politically correct, then I guess I get it, that nothing that has any kind of pharma logo or name or ownership should be given out to medical students . . . But the losers are the medical students because I think it's a high-quality book, it's very readable and they're deprived of it this year because of this controversy. And I guess they will be in the future." (See Chapter 7 for more about Jovey.) Others were not as positive about the book. Dr. Irfan Dhalla, a staff physician at St. Michael's Hospital in Toronto, said, "There are definitely things [in the book] that are not consistent with the evidence." Dhalla went on to say that the book pays little attention to issues of addiction and deaths from overdose.[16] The introduction of long-acting OxyContin onto the public drug formulary in Ontario was associated with a major spike in the number of oxycodone-related deaths.[22]

The relationship between Purdue and doctors goes beyond the actions of just one physician. As of 2011, Purdue had a marketing budget of $14 million in Canada for its pain relieving medications and much of that money may have been spent paying $2,000 per talk to the one hundred doctors it reimbursed annually for giving talks.[13] In the spring of

2016 when Dr. Jane Philpott, the federal minister of Health, indicated that her government was planning on changing the rules about tamper-proof OxyContin, she received a letter from forty chronic pain and addiction specialists asking her not to proceed. Nearly 60 per cent of the signatories had declared financial ties on various websites to Purdue as consultants, speakers or researchers.[23]

Are doctors like Selby and Jovey "selling out" when they take money and speak on behalf of companies? The evidence would suggest that this is not the case. Doctors are not being bribed. The most likely scenario is that companies predominantly recruit people who already have genuinely held opinions favourable to the drugs they are speaking about. In taking the position that they will not be affected by conflict of interest, key opinion leaders are echoing the stance taken by doctors in general when questioned about their relationships with industry. These belief patterns are consistent with cognitive dissonance theory, discussed in the Introduction, whereby the discomfort between what doctors do and what they believe has to be resolved.[24] However, even when doctors do find themselves uncomfortable with the message that they are asked to deliver, they sometimes indulge in self-censorship to avoid the risk of losing funding for research and attendance at conferences. That was the reason given by one Canadian researcher for removing negative material from a talk about a drug, even though he was not asked to do so by the drug company involved.[25]

A RECENT CONTROVERSY: GIDEON KOREN, MOTHERISK AND THE HOSPITAL FOR SICK CHILDREN

The most recent controversy regarding key opinion leaders involves Dr. Gideon Koren, who used to run the Motherisk

Program for the Hospital for Sick Children in Toronto. Koren was a long-time supporter of the drug Diclectin (doxylamine and pyridoxine) used for morning sickness, made by Duchesnay, a Quebec-based company. He coauthored a key study in 1997 that established the safety of Diclectin when used in early pregnancy.[26] (A recent reanalysis of the data used in that study found that the safety data for Diclectin was based on many fewer women than the original study claimed and that its use was not associated with a decreased risk of malformations as reported in the study by Koren.[27])

Koren was a paid consultant to Duchesnay and also spoke on behalf of the company.[15] However, according to a review done by the hospital, Koren's relationship to the company was not always transparent. Motherisk provided information on Diclectin in a variety of formats without consistently declaring Duchesnay's role as a funder of Motherisk. Koren usually disclosed his relationship with Duchesnay in publications related to Diclectin, but in a number of them Koren acknowledged funding through the "Research Leadership for Better Pharmacotherapy during Pregnancy and Lactation," a fund created by him, but he neglected to mention that most of the money for this fund came from Duchesnay.

Koren coauthored a booklet on morning sickness featured on the website of Motherisk. Duchesnay was involved in underwriting the cost of the electronic version of the booklet, but its role was not acknowledged.[15,28] Maclean's reported that between 1994 and 2002 Koren received $240,000 from Duchesnay, but the article did not say what the money was for and Motherisk itself received just under $4.3 million in research funding from the company between

2000 and 2013.[29] For its part, Duchesnay has denied any wrongdoing, saying "it is common practice for drug companies to support independent groups and work with medical experts. 'Duchesnay offers unrestricted grants to numerous programs . . . Canadian researchers are highly respected and accomplished individuals who dedicate their lives to evidence-based medicine. Casting a doubt that their opinions are bought or influenced is at best disrespectful.'"[15] Although such grants are "unrestricted" it would be naïve to think that they come without reciprocal obligations on behalf of the recipient. It would be very unlikely that a researcher who received a grant from a company would publish an article or give a talk that was unflattering to the products that the company makes.

OCCASIONAL SKEPTICS

Some doctors, such as Dr. Brian Goldman, host of CBC Radio's *White Coat, Black Art*, start out as true believers but later recant and stop doing talks for pharmaceutical companies. Goldman is an emergency physician at Mt. Sinai Hospital in Toronto and in the course of his work became interested in pain management. As he tells it in his Foreword to this book and his own book *Night Shift*, "In the early 1990s, I began to be paid by a pharmaceutical company to lecture health professionals at hospital rounds or at continuing medical education events, such as conferences and dinner meetings. As well, I appeared in a number of educational videos on pain management and prescription drug abuse that were supported by educational grants from drug companies. If I travelled to another city to give the talk, it was on the company's dime. I was put up in five-star hotels and taken to nice restaurants. When I travelled across the continent, I was invariably given a ticket in business class. To my knowledge, the companies that sponsored my talks had no direct input into the opinions I expressed."[12] "As I gave these talks, I convinced myself that I was able to educate thousands of health professionals and law enforcement officers. I also got the sense that the entire world of organized medicine was blasé about growing links between Big Pharma and continuing medical education . . . One conference organizer told me that without sponsorship from pharmaceutical companies, the cost of conference tuition would double, driving tens if not hundreds of physicians away."[12] Eventually, Goldman stopped his activities on behalf of drug companies and, as he told a reporter from the *National Post*, any physician who undertakes that type of work is "likely to be influenced by" payment from pharmaceutical companies.[13] Goldman believes that it is not "possible for educational courses paid for by drug companies to be free of corporate bias" and has called on legislators, drug companies and doctors in Canada to require the reporting of company payments to doctors.[30]

KEY OPINION LEADERS AND REGULATION — MOSTLY NONEXISTENT

When the pharmaceutical industry association revised its Code of Conduct in January 2008, it included for the first time a section on the training of company speakers. According to the organization's president, Russell Williams, the revisions came about because pharmaceutical companies previously had no standards for speaker training. (Williams retired from his position in June 2016.) Williams said, "The idea is to get a small group of selected health-care professionals, whether they are specialists or other doctors, who will be trained with the sole purpose of telling them about products and new indications. So they would be key leaders to be able to talk about the requirements of Health Canada, et cetera," to other practitioners.[31] However, the revisions to the code made little mention of the quality or completeness of the information that speakers delivered. The new clauses mainly dealt with paying for travel and related expenses to meetings where the training would take place and how many people could attend a training session at a time.[32]

The Code of Ethics from the Canadian Medical Association explicitly prohibits peer selling: "Peer selling occurs when a pharmaceutical or medical device manufacturer or service provider engages a physician to conduct a seminar or similar event that focuses on its own products and is designed to enhance the sale of those products. This also applies to third party contracting on behalf of industry. This form of participation would reasonably be seen as being in contravention of the [association's] Code of Ethics, which prohibits endorsement of a specific product."[33] (See Chapter 6 for more on the Canadian Medical Association's code.) Reid and Herder convincingly argue, and I agree, that being on a speakers' bureau is equivalent to peer selling and should be prohibited by the medical association's code.[4] The Canadian Medical Association is a voluntary organization and can exercise only moral suasion in trying to get physicians to follow its code, but many regulatory colleges across Canada, i.e., the bodies that license doctors, have adopted the code and they do have enforcement powers including barring doctors from practising. In addition, both the Royal College of Physicians and Surgeons of Canada and the College of Family Physicians of Canada, the accreditation bodies for specialists and family physicians, respectively, have endorsed the medical association's code. However, there is no record of any of these organizations having disciplined physicians who accepted payment for endorsing a drug company's products.[4]

CLINICAL PRACTICE GUIDELINES

With the exponential increase in medical information, doctors are finding it harder to sort out the wheat from the chaff and deciding how to manage their patients. Many doctors are increasingly turning to clinical practice guidelines to help them in preventing illness and diagnosing and treating it once it occurs.[34] Clinical practice guidelines are print and/or electronic documents that, when they are rigorously done, involve "defining the primary clinical question the guidelines will address, surveying stakeholders (physicians, patients, policy makers) to identify priority areas, conducting an extensive systematic review of the scientific literature on the chosen topic . . . rating and synthesizing the evidence, convening a panel of experts to discuss the evidence and make clinical recommendations, submitting the recommendations for review to independent experts, and finally, publishing the guidelines and creating knowledge translation tools to push the information out to clinicians."[35]

CLINICAL PRACTICE GUIDELINES: FUNDING AND CONFLICT OF INTEREST

The creation of clinical practice guidelines often generates heated controversy about conflict of interest, both because industry funds many of the guidelines and because of the relationship between those sitting on the guideline committees and pharmaceutical companies. For example, the Canadian Thoracic Society's 2012 update of its guidelines on asthma management received "unrestricted grants [from] . . . AstraZeneca Canada, Boehringer Ingelheim Canada,

GlaxoSmithKline Inc., Pfizer and Talecris." According to a statement in the guidelines, funders did not play "a role in the collection, review, analysis or interpretation of the scientific literature or in any decisions regarding the recommendations or key messages presented in this document."[36] On the other hand, speaking of the 2010 version of these guidelines, Dr. Niteesh Choudhry, who has previously investigated the conflicts of interest of guideline authors, said "Collectively, the physicians on the [Canadian Thoracic Society] Asthma Committee have on at least one occasion acted as consultants for, received research funds from, and received speaker's fees from these pharmaceutical companies."[37]

The Canadian Diabetes Association's website states that the "Association maintains editorial independence and operational separation from our corporate sponsors,"[38] but it's not readily apparent who sponsored its 2013 Clinical Practice Guidelines for the Prevention and Management of Diabetes in Canada. There were ninety-three people involved in producing the 2008 version of the association's guidelines and 78 per cent had conflicts of interest. A decade earlier the association also had problems with its guidelines. At that time, it said that the process for developing the guidelines was rigorous and systematic and the eleven pharmaceutical companies that sponsored the creation of the guidelines were acknowledged.[39] But one of the controversial features of those guidelines was the recommendation in favour of using a new type of insulin. The Common Drug Review, the organization that evaluates new products for listing on provincial drug formularies, had recommended that this new insulin should not get public funding.[40] In its guidelines, the Canadian Diabetes Association did not disclose whether the members of their expert panel had financial links of any kind with the manufacturer of this particular version of insulin, nor did it respond to inquiries from the *Canadian Medical Association Journal* about this question.[41]

All twenty-three panel members of the Canadian Cardiovascular Society involved in its 2009 guidelines had conflicts, defined as direct compensation of guideline authors by drug companies in form of grants, speakers' fees, honorariums, consultant/adviser/employee compensation and stock ownership two years before and including the year of guideline release.[42] While funding and financial conflicts of interest do not automatically produce biases, Choudhry notes, "We wonder whether academicians and physicians underestimate the impact of relationships on their actions because the nature of their professions is the pursuit of objective unbiased information . . . Unfortunately, bias may occur both consciously and subconsciously, and therefore, its influence may go unrecognized."[43]

In 2010, Dr. Charles Kerr, president of the Canadian Cardiovascular Society, defended the society, saying that its guideline development is funded through the society's budget and it accepts no money from industry for this process and that approval of the chair and panel members of guideline committees and of the guidelines themselves is a multi-stage process. He said that the society was trying to minimize the number of guideline panelists with conflicts of interest, but "it's one of those difficult things because the most advanced people and involved people in the field do work with industry, just because industry seeks them out because they're the brightest and the best in the country."[44] This sentiment was echoed by the next president of the society, Dr. Blair O'Neill, who said that the society's process had been updated to address the issue of conflict of interest. Each of the society's panels had two chairs, none of whom, as healthzone.ca reported, had "done research funded by industry. And of the remainder of the panel, 50 per cent plus one of the members can have no such ties. But, O'Neill added, it's impossible for all of them not to have such ties because the level of expertise would be diluted. He explained that there is a limited pool of experts in Canada to begin with and the best ones inevitably have their research funded by industry because the government funding just isn't there. 'The experts in the field . . . have done research funded by industry because government granting agencies' purse strings have become ever tighter,' O'Neill said."[45]

One of the coauthors of a Canadian Cardiovascular Society guideline on the use of cholesterol-lowering medications did not take kindly to his guideline being criticized by Dr. Michel de Lorgeril, a cardiologist and investigator with the National Centre for Scientific Research in France. De Lorgeril reanalyzed one of the key studies that the guideline used. According to him, "The results of the trial do not support the use of statin treatment for primary prevention of cardiovascular diseases and raise troubling questions concerning the role of commercial sponsors."[46] Dr. Jacques Genest from McGill University took the position that de Lorgeril had an "extremist" position on cholesterol that didn't have much place in science and said, "I would not trust him to treat any of my patients or my own family."[44]

Out of the forty-nine people on the National Opioid Use Guideline Group, a collaboration of thirteen medical groups, that produced a 2010 policy guideline on the use of opioids for treating pain due to causes other than cancer, twelve disclosed that they had received $5,000 or more in speaking or consulting fees annually from Purdue or Purdue and other companies.[13]

Perhaps the medical society most resistant to disclosure and most defensive about its position is the Society of Obstetricians and Gynaecologists of Canada. The society's 2010 contraception guidelines, which focused on Bayer's oral contraceptives Yaz and Yasmin (drospirenone and ethinyl estradiol), were an almost identical copy of a consensus statement from a Bayer workshop. "The [Society of Obstetricians and Gynaecologists of Canada] guidelines, and the statement from Bayer's workshop — both written by Dr. Robert Reid, professor of obstetrics and gynecology at Queen's University, Kingston, Ontario — are identical, aside from the cover page and a few stray paragraphs ... Dr. Reid insist[ed] the company had no influence on the [guidelines]. Dr. Reid's conflict of interest as a company consultant [wa]s also not disclosed, and neither [wa]s the fact that the [society] receives funding from Bayer" although this was revealed on the society's website.[47] Dr. André Lalonde, the society's executive vice-president, explained that the society's guideline process follows very stringent principles directing how the society's clinical practice guidelines are prepared, vetted and approved. "However, the issue of conflict declarations reaches a level of absurdity when a document is reviewed and vetted by some 30 or more individuals as is the case with our [clinical practice guidelines] ... To some, the mere indication that a physician has been a consultant to industry is enough to lead to suspicion and conspiracy theories . . . it is our view that it is responsible for pharmaceutical companies to consult with these [subject matter] experts to undertake an objective review and analysis so that consumers can be assured of the safety and efficacy of pharmaceutical products. The issue of declaring conflict of interest in the minds of some seems to have superseded the assessment of the scientific validity of the document under scrutiny."[48] As to whether Dr. Reid personally had a conflict, Lalonde said that "While some members assume expert roles with pharmaceutical firms, it is understood that when they take part in the guideline development process, they do so as a subject matter expert, not as a spokesperson for a particular company or firm . . . I fail to see how one could perceive Dr. Reid as having 'conflicting interests.'"[49]

The Society of Obstetricians and Gynaecologists of Canada was joined in its position about conflict of interest disclosure by the Canadian Paediatric Society, an organization that also did not routinely disclose conflicts of interest of its guideline members. The society's executive director said that the "board of directors assesses individual contributors and the development process in general to determine if there was a conflict. 'If they felt it should be disclosed publicly in a guideline, it would be. But so far [May 2011] it hasn't come up.'"[49]

Even when guidelines are developed by public agencies that is no guarantee that panelists will not have conflicts. Three out of fifteen members on the government-sponsored Canadian Task Force on Preventive Care that produced a guideline on diabetes had a conflict,[42] whereas the panels that produced two other diabetes guidelines, both under the auspices of the non-profit Canadian Agency for Drugs and Technology in Health, had six out of twelve and seven out of twelve members, respectively, with conflict of interest.[50]

Conflict of interest among members of guideline committees appears to be pervasive in Canada. With Adrienne Shnier, one of my former PhD students, as the lead investigator, we evaluated conflict of interest in 350 authors from twenty-eight guidelines that were listed in the Canadian Medical Association Infobase (www.cma.ca/En/Pages/clinical-practice-guidelines.aspx) and that were published or most recently reviewed between January 2012 and November 2013, inclusive. In 75 per cent of guidelines at least one author, and in 21 per cent of guidelines all authors, disclosed conflicts of interest with drug companies. In 54 per cent of guidelines at least one author, and in 29 per cent of guidelines over half of the authors, disclosed conflicts of interest with manufacturers of drugs that they recommended. Since we did not cross-check disclosures in the guidelines with other sources our numbers are likely underestimates. Twenty of forty-eight authors on multiple guidelines reported different financial conflicts in their disclosures. Eight guidelines identified affiliated medical organizations with financial relationships with manufacturers of drugs recommended in those guidelines.[51]

CLINICAL PRACTICE GUIDELINES: A BETTER APPROACH

There is another side of the debate. While content experts bring a certain level of expertise to the evaluation of medical literature, Dr. Andreas Laupacis, executive director of the Li Ka Shing Knowledge Institute at St. Michael's Hospital in Toronto, argues that the most important criterion for guideline developers is not clinical expertise, but the ability to review the available literature competently and objectively.[52] On the question of whether financial conflicts should be disclosed, Dr. James Wright, managing director and chairman of the Therapeutics Initiative, based at the University of British Columbia, which publishes evidence-based reviews of drug therapies, said that people developing guidelines should not be in a position of conflict, declared or otherwise. "There are people who are independent . . . and that's who they should be getting to do it."[44] Dr. Alan Detsky, a professor in the health policy, management and evaluation department at the University of Toronto, succinctly summarized the counter argument as to why drug companies should not be funding clinical practice guidelines. He said that just as company-sponsored clinical trials are biased, it would be naïve to think that clinical guidelines that recommend drugs made by the companies sponsoring the guidelines are any less likely to be free of bias.[35]

INDUSTRY ATTEMPTS TO SUPPRESS A CLINICAL PRACTICE GUIDELINE

There is one twist to the issue about corporate involvement with clinical practice guidelines that has not yet been explored. That's the case where proposed guidelines might have negative effects on sales of a company's product. This was the situation that Dr. Anne Holbrook of McMaster University encountered. In 1997 she was asked by the government of Ontario to chair a panel of experts to formulate a guideline about the use of gastrointestinal medications. The panel's draft report concluded that AstraZeneca's drug, Losec (omeprazole), a drug used for disorders such as ulcers and reflux ("heartburn"), was no better than two less expensive products in the same drug class. The draft was sent to multiple parties, including AstraZeneca, for review and comments. Instead of engaging in a scientific debate about the recommendations, the company engaged a law firm that sent Holbrook a letter claiming that if her report was released, she would be contravening the *Food and Drugs Act* and "In the event that you proceed notwithstanding this warning you should assume that our client will take appropriate steps including the commencement of appropriate legal proceedings in order to protect its interests and to obtain compliance with the law."[53] AstraZeneca quickly apologized to Holbrook and claimed that the letter had been misdirected to her and should have instead been sent to the Ontario government.[54] In a later letter to the *British Medical Journal*, Sheila Frame, AstraZeneca's vice-president of corporate affairs, claimed that her company "has never prevented nor had the intention of preventing, any doctor or researcher from publishing or communicating the results of their studies. AstraZeneca has a passionate interest and a long history of supporting independent, peer-reviewed research that leads to the development of truly beneficial products for Canadians and patients around the world."[55]

MEDICAL SOCIETIES

The medical societies from the various branches of medicine are supposed to represent the interests of their membership, and ultimately the interests of patients, but many of them also are the recipients of money from pharmaceutical companies. The website of the Royal College of Physicians and Surgeons of Canada lists fifty-eight different Canadian medical specialty societies and in addition there is the Royal College itself and the College of Family Physicians of Canada.[56] Twenty-three of these state on their websites that they receive industry money for general activities and forty-nine receive industry funding specifically for continuing medical education programs.[57] The Introduction to this book has already highlighted some instances where societies have backed industry — the College of Family

Table 5.2: Medical societies supporting industry/company positions and receipt of money

Medical society	Year	Receives pharmaceutical money for general activities*	Receives pharmaceutical money for continuing medical education activities*	Supportive position	Reference
Canadian Cardiovascular Society	1997	Yes	Yes	Supported industry position against reference-based pricing	A position paper on drug-pricing strategies for prescription pharmaceutical in Canada[59]; Reference-based pricing of prescription drugs[60]
Canadian Dermatology Association	2013	Yes	Yes	Supported doctor-industry interactions in general	Industry[61]
Canadian Hematology Society	2011	Yes†	No	Value of cooperation between industry and doctors	Nevill[62]
Canadian Society of Transplantation	2012	Yes	Yes	Advised caution in the use of generic immunosuppressive drugs in solid organ transplantation	Harrison[63]
College of Family Physicians of Canada	1984	No	No§	Endorsed marketing survey of doctors designed to be used by industry	Rice[64]
Society of Obstetricians and Gynaecologists	Early 2000s; 2004; 2005; 2009	No	Yes	Accepted sponsorship from Duchesnay, makers of Diclectin, including for tennis tournaments at continuing medical education events; Criticized Canadian Cancer Society for its position that women should avoid hormone replacement therapy except when severe postmenopausal symptoms have not responded to other measures; Defended advertisement announcing launch of new oral contraceptive; Defended not including COI of the authors in new guidelines on the use of hormone replacement therapy	Mendleson[15]; Smith[65]; Senikas[66]; Eggertson[67]

* As stated on website as of January 2016.
† Statement of funding found in newsletter.
§ Accredits continuing medical education events that have industry support through unrestricted educational grants.

Physicians backing a marketing survey designed to be used by drug companies, the president of the Canadian Dermatology Association supporting doctor-industry relations in general and the Society of Obstetricians and Gynaecologists of Canada defending a four-page advertisement from Berlex announcing the launch of a new oral contraceptive. Chapter 2 presented instances where various medical research associations backed stronger intellectual property rights for drug companies. Here, I give a number of further examples of the interactions of societies and drug companies, although this list is likely to be far from complete as it only documents relationships that have been in the media. (See Table 5.2.)

In the face of annual cost increases of 16 per cent for the provincial Pharmacare plan, the British Columbia government brought in its Reference Drug Program in 1995.[58] Under this system, also used in many European countries and New Zealand, a reimbursement price is set for a therapeutic category where all of the available drugs are considered to be equally safe and effective. Patients are required to either accept the reference product or pay any difference between the cost of the product prescribed and the reference price, unless there is a valid medical reason for the costlier drug.

Four months before the policy came into effect, the pharmaceutical industry association initiated a series of ads in major BC newspapers in an attempt to discredit the policy, proclaiming "The Provincial Government wants to change your medication" and "RBP [Reference-Based Pricing] has begun. Where will it end?"[58] The industry association charged that the reference product was usually an older therapy, which was inferior to newer products that offered better efficacy and/or side effect profiles for many patients. The industry association maintained that reference-based pricing would likely lead to overall health costs rising, offsetting any drug savings.[68] However, aside from some anecdotal evidence, the association never produced any concrete data to back up its claims. The Canadian Cardiovascular Society publicly backed the industry association's position with both a position statement and an editorial[59] in its *Canadian Journal of Cardiology*. Two later independent publications that looked at the cardiovascular drugs that were included in the reference-based pricing program did not find any negative effects on patients' health.[69,70]

In the early 2000s, the Society of Obstetricians and Gynaecologists of Canada accepted sponsorship for research and educational events from Duchesnay, the makers of Diclectin, discussed above. Sponsorship included the support of tennis tournaments held during continuing medical education conferences in sunny destinations such as Costa Rica and Cuba.[15]

On two other occasions, the society sought to expand the indications for the use of hormone replacement therapy for postmenopausal women; once by criticizing the Canadian Cancer Society for issuing a recommendation that hormone replacement therapy should be used for severe postmenopausal symptoms only when other measures were not successful,[65] and a second time when it defended the fact that its new set of recommendations about the use of the therapy did not include any statement about conflict of interest from the authors.[49] In the former instance, Dr. Vyta Senikas, associate executive vice-president of the society, said that the Women's

Health Initiative study that found a negative benefit-to-harm ratio for the long-term use of hormone replacement therapy had "unfortunate limitations" that made it hard to apply directly to the way the therapy is used.[65] According to her, the average age of women in the Women's Health Initiative trial was sixty-three and these are not the women who should be getting hormone replacement therapy in the first place. (Of the 8,506 women who were randomized to take hormone replacement therapy, 2,839 (33 per cent) were between fifty and fifty-nine.[71]) In the latter case, we have already seen that Dr. André Lalonde defended the lack of disclosure of conflict of interest of guideline panel members. The Society of Obstetricians and Gynaecologists of Canada has defended its relationships with its various sponsors as "'unbiased' and stressed that all of these relationships 'are bound by strict policies to mitigate conflict of interest and adhere to all (Canadian Medical Association) guidelines.'"[15]

In the Spring 2011 newsletter from the Canadian Hematology Society, its president wrote about the relationship between physicians involved in the treatment of hematological diseases and pharmaceutical companies. In his view, there was "a tremendous willingness on the part of drug companies to engage and work with physicians to complete pivotal clinical trials and develop evidence-based guidelines for the use of new drug therapies . . . and that these companies appear committed to this support over the long run."[62]

The Canadian Society of Transplantation considered that the evidence supporting the equivalence of generic formulations of immunosuppressant medications in solid organ transplant recipients was lacking and established an interprofessional working group to look at the available data and come up with a set of recommendations. The bottom line as far as the working group was concerned was that "until more robust clinical data are available and adequate regulatory safeguards are instituted, caution in the use of generic immunosuppressive drugs in solid organ transplantation is warranted."[63]

One board member of the Canadian Dermatology Association challenged his organization to be the first in the country to mandate disclosure of drug costs in lectures, posters and commercial marketing-display booths at association conferences. While others agreed with his stance, Dr. Harvey Lui, professor and head of the Department of Dermatology and Skin Science at the University of British Columbia, said price disclosure was not likely to become policy for the association or other physician organizations in the near future. "We're not ready for the debate yet, but it should happen."[72]

OCCASIONALLY CLINICAL PRACTICE GUIDELINES DON'T SUPPORT INDUSTRY

Not all medical societies that accept industry money end up supporting industry positions. A number of years ago I was a member of a panel with representatives from the Canadian Neurosurgical Society and the Canadian Spine Society that looked at the evidence about whether steroids should be given to people suffering spinal cord injuries. The Canadian Neurosurgical Society acknowledged receiving industry money both for general operations of the society and for continuing medical education events; however, the conclusion of the panel was that there was insufficient evidence to support using steroids.[73]

CONCLUSION

There is a tight nexus among key opinion leaders, the people who sit on clinical practice guideline committees and the societies that most of the key opinion leaders and committee members belong to. The point is not the personal integrity of key opinion leaders, but that the information they are given and trained to deliver has been shaped by the companies whose primary goal is to increase sales of their drugs. The data that key opinion leaders and committee members present and evaluate may be scientifically valid, but data needs to be interpreted and biases may have entered into that process. Interactions with pharmaceutical companies can lead to subconsciously acquired biases. Other views about the data are not being heard to anywhere near the same extent, because no other stakeholder in the pharmaceutical world has resources to match those of the drug companies. Doctors who end up on clinical practice guideline panels are usually there because of their clinical expertise and oftentimes that expertise has been acquired by virtue of conducting industry-funded clinical trials. When it comes to the medical societies themselves, they are products of their membership and if the influential members of the organizations are biased, consciously or subconsciously, it stands to reason that those biases will also be seen in the actions of the societies. Even if conflict of interest plays no role in the positions that various societies take, there is still the appearance that conflict of interest may have influenced what they said and appearances can be damaging to the trust that the general public places in medical societies.

CHAPTER 6

GUIDELINES ON RELATIONSHIPS BETWEEN INDUSTRY AND THE MEDICAL PROFESSION: A GUIDE TO SALVATION?

As we have seen in earlier chapters, for a long time there were only lone individuals voicing concern about the relationship between doctors and the pharmaceutical industry. Usually, people either took a benign approach or assumed that this relationship was mostly positive. However, by the 1980s the thinking had started to change and various medical organizations were becoming concerned enough to look at developing guidelines about what should be considered ethical. This chapter looks at how that process played out, mainly in five organizations — the Canadian Medical Association, the voluntary organization that represents the vast majority of the country's seventy thousand doctors; the College of Physicians and Surgeons of Ontario, the body that licenses doctors in Ontario and sets out standards of care; the Royal College of Physicians and Surgeons of

Canada, the organization that accredits specialists and over-sees guidelines for continuing medical education for them; the College of Family Physicians of Canada, the organiza-tion that is the equivalent of the Royal College for family physicians/general practitioners; and the Conseil québécois de développement professionnel continu des médecins (prior to 2005, the Conseil de l'éducation médicale continue du Québec), the Quebec coordinating body consulted by its member organizations that accredit continuing medical education in that province. How did these organizations develop their guidelines, how were they accepted, are they being enforced and have they had an impact on the way that doctors and industry interact?

THE CANADIAN MEDICAL ASSOCIATION

The Canadian Medical Association was responding to complaints about industry-sponsored continuing medical education events in the early 1980s with a promise that guidelines were being developed that would ensure that these events were not compromised by the provision of financial support from pharmaceutical companies.[1] Its Council on Medical Education was apparently drafting guidelines in 1981 on accepting contributions to medical education from the pharmaceutical industry.[2]

The first formal set of guidelines on continuing medical education were not actually issued by the association until 1986,[3] and in 1990 it released a discussion document that outlined a proposal for guidelines covering a broader set of interactions between doctors and industry.[4] According to one person who was closely involved with developing the guidelines, the association held hearings and consultations across the country for two years including meeting with patient advocacy groups and industry representatives to discuss the contents. When the guidelines were presented to the association's annual meeting in August 1991 they were unanimously passed. "[Canadian Medical Association] officials hailed the rules as more far-reaching and specific than any similar code in the world. 'Bags, pizzas and personal gifts — they're out,' said Eike-Henner Kluge, director of the [association's] department of ethics and legal affairs." Dr. Robert Woollard, chair of the committee that drew up the guidelines, said, "We were in danger of drifting into a variety of unacceptable practices which might have meant a danger to the profession . . . These guidelines provide all physicians in Canada with a very clear expression of what their peers think should be the relationship between physicians and pharmaceutical companies."[5] Some doctors objected to the guidelines,[6] but overall the reception seems to have been positive. Judy Erola, president of the pharmaceutical industry association and former federal Liberal minister of Consumer and Corporate Affairs, said that the industry supported the medical association's guidelines. "They reinforce our own code of marketing practices," she said. "We're preaching from the same bible."[5]

The guidelines themselves were a mixed package.[7] Doctors were advised to only get involved in industry-sponsored research activities if they were ethically defensible, socially responsible and scientifically valid; continuing medical education organizers and their delegates could not be in a position of conflict of interest by virtue of any affiliation with the company or companies that funded education activities; and doctors should not accept payment to attend continuing medical education events. On the other hand, the guidelines were quiet about interactions between doctors and sales representatives (reps) from companies and did not require doctors to tell patients about any money that they were receiving for participating in postmarketing studies. (A postmarketing study is one that looks at a product after it has been approved for sale.) However, the most significant weakness in the guidelines was that the medical association had no way to enforce compliance with them since it is a voluntary organization. As Woollard said, "We only have moral suasion."[5] Moreover, the association did little to disseminate and implement its guidelines. Here is Woollard again: "The greatest disappointment of the [Canadian Medical Association] process has been the lack of effective implementation at the level at which physicians work and interact with the pharmaceutical and health care supply industries."[8]

Having only moral suasion and lacking a dissemination plan meant that less than a year after the guidelines were passed, there were reports of them being violated. Burroughs Wellcome Inc., makers of the anti-AIDS drug AZT, paid to fly doctors from all over the country to Toronto to hear a panel of experts discuss HIV/AIDS treatment. But doctors only heard one side of the story — the need to start treatment early. The opposing view, that treatment should be delayed, was not presented. Dr. Francois Lebel, medical director for Burroughs Wellcome, said some parts of the association's guidelines were just plain unrealistic, thereby contradicting what Erola had said earlier. "If someone doesn't pay for physicians' travel expenses, only big-city doctors will be able to stay current on medical knowledge," he said. Dr. John Gill, a well-known HIV researcher from Calgary, had no idea he had violated the new conflict-of-interest guidelines until told so by a reporter.[9] In the early spring of 1993, sixty doctors and their spouses enjoyed

$110-a-night rooms, nouvelle cuisine and free drinks at the Chantecler Hotel in southwestern Quebec where they had been taken courtesy of Searle Canada to hear about one of the company's products. In the morning they listened to a few lectures and in the afternoon there was alpine skiing.[10]

By the fall of 1992, the Canadian Medical Association started the process of revising the guidelines by sending out notices to 150 groups and individuals including medical associations, health organizations, industry groups and deans and directors of continuing medical education at medical schools. The revisions were going to focus on three areas. First, the guidelines would be more direct in asking doctors to be aware of their individual moral responsibility "to inform their consciences in making decisions about whether relationships with industry are appropriate or inappropriate, on a day-to-day basis." Second, the guidelines were going to be more stringent about product identification in conjunction with drug-company-funded continuing medical education, in order to deter what Dr. John Williams, director of the association's Department of Ethics and Legal Affairs, called "The long-standing practice of companies putting on events which are really designed to promote specific drugs held with a speaker who will speak about that drug and nothing else." Finally, the guidelines would include principles and practices that applied to medical students, residents and interns. Williams also said that there had been reluctance from both doctors and drug companies to fully cooperate with the first set of guidelines although, based on anecdotal reports, he thought that compliance was getting better.[11]

The new 1994 guidelines did expand on how drugs should be referred to during continuing medical education sessions, saying that "If specific products or services are mentioned, there should be a balanced presentation of the prevailing body of scientific information on the product or service and of reasonable, alternative treatment options. If unapproved uses of a product or service are discussed, presenters must inform the audience of this fact."[12] However, they dropped the stipulation that "Samples should be distributed solely for the purpose of allowing physicians to evaluate the clinical performance of the medicaments . . . Any departure from this use must be justifiable in terms of otherwise applicable principles of ethical medical practice."[7] The guidelines continued to say nothing about interactions with sales reps and there was virtually no change to recommendations regarding medical students, interns and residents. The guidelines were updated again in 2001[13] and 2007.[14] By the time of the last revision, they contained statements about disclosing conflicts when submitting articles to medical journals, disclosing the source of funding of industry-sponsored research (but still nothing about whether physicians were being paid or not by the companies sponsoring the research), disclosing the source of funding of continuing medical education material, a warning to doctors that if they were asked to sit on company advisory or consultation boards that they "should be mindful of the potential for this relationship to influence their clinical decision making" and a caution not to accept personal gifts or any significant monetary or other value. ("Significant" was not defined.) The guidelines also allowed the use of trade names in continuing medical education events, but they needed to be accompanied by generic names.

Dr. Woollard, who had moved on to be chair of the Canadian Association for Continuing Health Education, an alliance of officials from medical schools and industry, observed that the medical profession has "an obligation to tell our colleagues how it is appropriate to act." He further believed that there was "an ethical responsibility to define what's appropriate, to assess whether or not we and our colleagues are living up to that, and to have consequences if we're not, and to facilitate best behaviour insofar as we can."[15] (As of 2010, the position of the Canadian Association for Continuing Health Education's membership was that the medical profession and industry working together for continuing medical education was the best arrangement "as long as there are some rules of clarity on the terms [of] the engagement."[16]) As the Canadian Medical Association guidelines evolved they became more restrictive than those from the industry, as even the pharmaceutical industry association's president, Russell Williams, admitted.[17] (Williams retired from his position in June 2016.) However, it's questionable whether most medical association members even knew about the guidelines or if they did, were convinced that they were necessary. In addition, since they could not be enforced, they were largely ineffective.

Two events cast doubt on the medical association's commitment to its guidelines. In March 2003, Dr. Dana Hanson, the association's president, penned an open letter to the organization's membership under the heading, "Message from the President." The purpose of the letter was to congratulate the pharmaceutical industry association for revising its code to eliminate the exemption that allowed companies to pay for specialists to attend conferences in Canada even if they were not speaking. Hanson said that this change brought the industry association's code into compliance on this issue with the code from the medical association.[18] Accompanying that letter in the same issue of *CMAJ* was an "Announcement" of this recent change to the industry association's Code of Marketing Practice, co-signed by the presidents of the industry association, the College of Family Physicians of Canada, the Royal College of Physicians and Surgeons of Canada and the Canadian Medical Association.[19] However, while the industry association had taken a step forward it had also moved backwards, a move glossed over in Hanson's message. In 2002, the industry association had added a provision to its code that allowed companies to fund any physician to attend a conference outside of Canada under certain conditions.[20] As summarized by Dr. Michael Yeo in a commentary in the *CMAJ*, before these two changes the industry association had allowed companies to fund specialists to attend conferences in Canada; now it was allowing companies to fund any doctor to attend conferences outside of Canada.[21] Hanson's reply that the medical association "look[ed] forward to further discussions to bring the [industry association's] code fully in line with the [Canadian Medical Association's] guidelines"[22] was not reassuring to either Yeo[23] or to Dr. Keith Ogle, deputy chair of the Department of Academic Family Medicine in Saskatoon. The latter noted that the overall effect of the two changes to the industry association's code may leave it less compliant with the medical association's than it was before. In his words, "The moral basis of [Canadian Medical Association] policy on physicians and the pharmaceutical industry has always been clear: conflicts of interest can harm our patients. If we continue to accept gifts, we remain beholden to the giver."[24]

The other event that calls into question the medical association's commitment to its guidelines occurred in 2009 when it announced a partnership with Pfizer for a new online continuing medical education program for physicians across Canada. The press release that accompanied the announcement said that "collaboration between the [Canadian Medical Association] and Pfizer is based on a shared belief that evidence-based continuing medical education, including online learning, improves the quality of health care in Canada by enhancing physician clinical decision-making, resulting in improved patient outcomes."[25] The program was going to be overseen by an Administrative Board consisting of two staff members from the medical association, two staff members from Pfizer Canada and two members independent from the two organizations. An independent Content Committee, composed of one staff member from the medical association and two outside members, was responsible for selecting specific topics for individual modules and overseeing the development of content for the modules. Pfizer was going to contribute $780,000 to the initiative, but according to Dr. Sam Shortt, the director of knowledge transfer at the medical association, the company would have nothing to do with how the content of the educational programs was developed. "There's no connection between the funder and the people who are actually providing the content . . . We're confident that these two elements meet and exceed any expectations from any observer."[26] Others were not so reassured. The opinion of Dr. Arnold Relman, a past editor of the *New England Journal of Medicine*, was "that the pharmaceutical industry has no business at all educating doctors . . . It's simply a matter of common sense that if Pfizer is going to pay the Canadian Medical Association for medical education to doctors, Pfizer expects to get something in return."[26]

THE COLLEGE OF PHYSICIANS AND SURGEONS OF ONTARIO

The Canadian Medical Association has to rely on moral suasion but the colleges, the provincial regulatory bodies that license doctors, have the power to discipline doctors who break the rules that they set. In the late 1980s, the provincial colleges were all over the map when it came to how they dealt with the relationship between doctors and the pharmaceutical industry. New guidelines in Manitoba allowed doctors to accept gifts and hospitality worth token amounts. The guidelines said that payments from drug companies for physicians' lectures should be consistent with the usual payments for such talks and doctors should make appropriate inquiries to ensure that any research or clinical trial proposed by a drug company has a valid scientific and ethical framework.[27] In Alberta, on the other hand, doctors were warned about accepting holidays, gifts and cash incentives that might lead to increased prescribing of a company's products.[28]

The College of Physicians and Surgeons of Ontario regulates the largest number of doctors in Canada. The initial foray of the college into developing guidelines was triggered by a series of headlines in the *Globe and Mail* that revealed that Squibb was offering doctors the permanent use of computers that they had been given in order to take part in a Squibb-sponsored marketing study.[29] (See Chapter 8 for more about Squibb and computers.) The realization that something needed to be done was also spurred forward by the report of the Pharmaceutical Inquiry of Ontario that recommended "that, by 1991, the College of Physicians and Surgeons of Ontario . . . develop and publicize ethical guidelines for physician/industry interaction, which also deal with the industry's involvement in continuing medical education."[30] The result of the confluence of these events was that

in 1990 the college set up a task force to produce a set of
guidelines with representation from the medical profession
(including me), the generic and brand-name pharmaceutical industry and the public. A draft guideline was circulated
to about one hundred different individuals and organizations in early 1991 and twenty-nine responded. The most
controversial part of the guidelines was the section dealing
with continuing medical education, although the four points
hardly seemed radical: physicians should not accept any
benefits or honoraria to attend continuing medical education
conferences, seminars or meetings; physicians should assure
themselves that continuing medical education be free of any
possibility for commercial bias; the organization, content
and choice of speakers must be determined by healthcare
professionals, independent of a pharmaceutical company;
and where physicians render a legitimate service they are
entitled to fair compensation. A secondary concern was the
requirement that doctors had to disclose the nature and
source of funding received to any patient enrolled in any trial
or surveillance study.[31,32] The Ontario Medical Association
did not have any major concerns with the draft being used as
the basis for future discussions, but did propose changes to
soften the language around accepting benefits at continuing
medical education events, hospitality and promotional gifts.
Ciba-Geigy (now part of Novartis) was not so agreeable,
calling the guidelines inflammatory and the pharmaceutical industry association strongly objected to the prohibition
on payment for doctors to travel to and attend continuing
medical education events.[32] By June 1991 the Task Force
had come out with a final version of the guidelines, but in
the end the college opted to adopt the guidelines that had
recently been passed by the Canadian Medical Association.[33]

Following the college's decision to follow the medical association's guidelines, there are only scattered anecdotes about how
much attention either companies or the college itself paid to them.
In the summer of 1997, Bristol-Myers Squibb planned to hold a
weekend event for doctors to learn about recent advances in the
treatment of AIDS at a rural resort that featured a golf course,
horseback riding, tennis courts and an assortment of other leisure
activities. The site of the event was changed after Dr. Philip
Berger, then chief of family medicine at the Wellesley Central
Hospital, complained to the college. Dr. John Bonn, registrar of
the college, sent a letter to Berger stating that "perhaps it is time
for the College to revisit these guidelines, which are now five
years old, to see if they are still relevant, fair and enforceable."[34]
There is no indication that there was a review and three years later
Berger sent another letter to the college, this time regarding an
invitation sent by Glaxo Wellcome (now merged with SmithKline
Beecham and called GlaxoSmithKline) and BioChem Pharma
to some HIV physicians inviting them to attend an international
conference on the treatment of HIV infection. In Berger's words,
it was "an illustration of the industry asking Ontario physicians to
breach a [college] policy."[35] As a consequence, Bonn wrote to Dr.
Anne Michelle Phillips at Glaxo Wellcome pointing out that the
invitation was in violation of the Canadian Medical Association's
guidelines.[36] Phillips must have sent the letter on to the industry
association because subsequently Berger got a letter from the
association saying that they were investigating his complaint as
a violation of the organization's marketing code.[37] There is no
record of what happened next. What is even more important is
that neither of these two episodes resulted in the college taking
any action against any of the doctors involved. In fact, according
to research done by one of my former PhD students, Adrienne
Shnier, the college has never disciplined any doctor for violation

of its policy about physician-industry interactions[38] and there is no information about how rigorously the code is monitored.

The College of Physicians and Surgeons of Ontario eventually did begin the process of revising its policy starting in 2014. The draft policy inviting comments drew 318 submissions, the majority from physicians but also from the pharmaceutical industry association and drug companies like AstraZeneca.[39] When the college did an online survey there were responses from a total of 201 people, including 155 doctors and 26 members of the public. There was general support for the provisions in the policy, including one that doctors should be allowed to accept "modest" meals provided by drug companies.[40] The pharmaceutical industry association supported a number of sections of the draft but also raised objections to others. The draft said that "Decisions regarding the content, faculty, educational methods, and materials are made without influence from industry sponsors";[41] the industry association felt that this clause would preclude industry from "making suggestions based on sound evidence."[42] It also felt that the section that prohibited physicians who sit on industry advisory or consultation boards from providing any promotional or educational activities on behalf of the company was too restrictive.[41,42] The Canadian Medical Association did not send in a submission although the Ontario Medical Association did, but for unstated reasons the feedback was redacted so its views are unknown. The Ontario chapter of the College of Family Physicians raised an especially relevant point about how any new policy would be monitored and whether there was a mechanism to report industry activities that do not conform to the code.[43]

After hearing the feedback, the College of Physicians and Surgeons of Ontario retained a section that prohibited physicians from accepting industry funding to attend continuing medical education events, but it also made a number of concessions. Specifically, the final policy permits doctors to organize and/or present at educational events directly organized and/or funded by industry, including "drug dinners"; physicians can engage in education by sitting on industry consultation or advisory boards; and physicians can accept meals of modest value, patient teaching aids and free drug samples.[39]

Is this new policy, adopted on September 4, 2014, an improvement on the college's previous one? Adrienne Shnier compared the two for part of her PhD thesis and I gratefully draw on her analysis with her kind permission. There were a couple of favourable additions to the 2014 policy that were missing from the 1992 one. One of the key ones is the definition that a conflict of interest is "created any time a reasonable person could perceive that a physician's personal interest or relationship with industry is at odds with the physician's professional responsibilities. It is important to note that a conflict of interest can exist even if the physician is confident that his or her professional judgement is not actually being influenced by the conflicting interest or relationship."[44] The other potentially key change is the sentence, "Physicians must comply with the expectations set out in this policy when interacting with industry."[44] This very clearly gives the college the authority and the responsibility to actively monitor compliance with its policy. However, as Chapter 5 shows, it failed to exercise its regulatory power to enforce its previous policy, so whether it will do any better with the new one is an open question.

The new 2014 policy is significantly weaker than its 1992 counterpart in a number of important ways. As Shnier explains, "A clear difference [between the two] is that the 1992 policy repeatedly refers to the 'primary obligations' of physicians, which is language that is consistent with the literature defining and analyzing conflict of interest relationships between physicians and the pharmaceutical industry. In the 2014 policy, this language is absent not only in the Principles quoted above, but also throughout the remainder of the policy. The removal of this language from the 2014 policy is important to highlight because the absence of discussion about the primary obligations of physicians weakens the way that relationships with industry are presented to, and conceptualized by physicians who are governed by this policy . . .

"The 1992 policy also includes statements . . . about physicians' participation in surveillance studies and accepting gifts. Where the 1992 policy states that '[p]hysicians are encouraged to participate only in surveillance studies (i.e., phase IV research studies) that are scientifically appropriate for drugs relevant to the area of practice' . . . the 2014 policy broadens the acceptable roles of physicians in clinical studies by stating that '[p]hysicians must only participate in research involving human participants, including postmarketing surveillance studies (phase IV clinical research), that has the approval of a research ethics board.'

"The 1992 policy clearly states that it is ethically acceptable for physicians to receive remuneration for participation in approved surveillance studies only if the participation exceeds their normal practice pattern. This remuneration should not constitute enticement . . . The amount of remuneration should be approved by the relevant review board, agency, or body mentioned previously . . . In contrast, remuneration is mentioned twice in the 2014 policy and in both cases, it is stated that '[r]emuneration must only be accepted if it is at fair market value and commensurate with the services provided' . . . The 2014 policy mentions nothing about requiring the amount of remuneration to be approved by a relevant committee and also does not set parameters for when this remuneration is acceptable.

"The 2014 Principles and the remainder of the policy no longer state that physicians' relationships with the pharmaceutical industry are also constrained by the [Canadian Medical Association's] Code of Ethics. An additional important omission from the 2014 policy that was present in the 1992 policy is that '[m]edical curricula should include formal training that is based on [the 1992] guidelines.' The 2014 policy contains nothing regarding the inclusion of any formal or informal conflict of interest training within the medical curricula. Another area of weakness in the 2014 [College of Physicians and Surgeons of Ontario] policy, as compared with the 1992 policy, is [continuing medical education]. The 1992 policy states that ' . . . [continuing medical education] clearly distinguishes between education, training . . . and product promotion', while the 2014 policy makes no such statement."[38]

Other provincial regulators are not necessarily doing a better job of regulating interactions than Ontario. The College of Physicians and Surgeons of New Brunswick decided not to develop a specific policy on physician participation in post-marketing studies sponsored by pharmaceutical companies. Therefore, according to the college, it was acceptable for physicians who enrolled patients into these studies to receive compensation ranging from equipment to trips to meetings held to discuss study findings.[45] While some provincial colleges have adopted the Canadian Medical Association's guidelines, others have their own and some have no guidelines at all listed on their websites. (See Table 6.1.) Regardless of whatever regulations they have developed or borrowed, as of 2013, none of them have publicly ever used them to actually regulate the activities of doctors.[46]

Table 6.1: Provincial regulatory bodies' policies on physician-industry interactions

Province	Policy
Alberta, Manitoba	Related principles to those in CMA* guidelines referenced (independent judgment, distinction between continuing medical education and marketing)
British Columbia	CMA guidelines referenced
New Brunswick, Newfoundland and Labrador, Prince Edward Island, Saskatchewan	No relevant guidelines or policy available on website
Nova Scotia	CMA guidelines adopted
Ontario	Independent guidelines adopted
Quebec	Guidelines from Conseil québécois de développement professionnel continu des médecins

*CMA = Canadian Medical Association

Source: Adapted from Reid and Herder[46]

CONTINUING MEDICAL EDUCATION: ROYAL COLLEGE OF PHYSICIANS AND SURGEONS OF CANADA, CONSEIL QUÉBÉCOIS DE DÉVELOPPEMENT PROFESSIONNEL CONTINU DES MÉDECINS AND COLLEGE OF FAMILY PHYSICIANS OF CANADA

By now it should be apparent that one of the key issues driving the creation of guidelines was that continuing medical education had been sorely in need of regulation for a long time. Industry funding for continuing medical education in Canadian medical schools in 2008 ranged from a low of 5 per cent to a high of 50 per cent of total continuing medical education funding and for most schools was in the 5 per cent to 20 per cent range. (Funding from faculties of medicine generally accounted for about 10 per cent of the revenue. The remainder came from program fees, contracts with governmental and nongovernmental agencies and research grants.[47]) Seventy percent of programs accredited by the

College of Family Physicians of Canada in the period from 1998 to 2004 had pharmaceutical company funding, either by direct sponsorship or through exhibit fees. (The college's director of continuing professional development was not troubled by that figure.[48])

Besides the excesses often associated with continuing medical education (see Chapter 8) there are three additional reasons for regulating industry's involvement: first, both the College of Family Physicians of Canada, the Royal College of Physicians and Surgeons of Canada and the Conseil québécois de développement professionnel continu des médecins require doctors to accumulate a certain number of continuing medical education hours in order to maintain their certification as family physicians and specialists. Second, when asked what their preferred source of information for prescription products is, doctors consistently name continuing medical education in various forms — meetings, print and online at or near the top of their choices.[49-54] Similarly, when doctors were asked what they would like to see pharmaceutical companies provide as educational support when new drugs become available, 65 per cent answered continuing medical education.[55] Like the regulatory colleges, these bodies have real power, in their case the power to establish policies for which continuing medical education programs to accredit and which not to accredit. Only accredited continuing medical education counts for what doctors are required to accumulate.

ROYAL COLLEGE OF PHYSICIANS AND SURGEONS OF CANADA

There is little written information about the development of the guidelines by the Royal College of Physicians and

Surgeons of Canada apart from a 1990 discussion paper from its Biomedical Ethics Committee. The paper focused on three main unethical activities that could result from the interaction of doctors and drug companies: the inducement of physicians to use certain pharmaceutical products rather than others, regardless of their therapeutic effectiveness or cost; the undue reliance on company promotional literature for information about the effectiveness of pharmacological agents; and physician participation in industry-sponsored research studies of dubious scientific and ethical stature.[56]

An editorial in the *CMAJ* in 2008 called the current system of continuing medical education "unacceptable to self-regulated health professionals" and said that "[i]t is time to stop the pharma-driven 'free lunch' approach and place our continuing medical education system firmly in the hands of unbiased and qualified people, not corporations whose main concern is the bottom line."[57] Responding to that editorial, Dr. Craig Campbell, the Royal College's director of professional affairs, said that "the editorial's call for the creation of an arm's-length institute to provide oversight would appear to be premature . . . [and that] the Royal College will continue to develop and implement standards for effective continuing professional education . . . in collaboration with multiple partners."[58] Two years later, in 2010, Campbell was confident that Canada has "among the highest [continuing medical education] standards in the world today."[16] The Royal College does permit industry to be on the planning committee for a continuing medical education event with physician organizations, but prohibits industry representatives from being involved with deciding on the scientific content of those events.[59]

By early 2016, the Royal College had a total of twenty-nine different policies, guidelines or interpretive documents dealing primarily with continuing medical education and these policies were collectively referenced by twenty medical associations and adopted by fifteen. (The Canadian Medical Association guidelines were referenced or adopted by thirty and twenty-two associations, respectively.) With Adrienne Shnier taking the lead, she and I evaluated the strength of the Royal College's policies in particular, and more generally, the strength of the policies of a total of fifty-eight specialty associations in twenty-one separate categories. Each category was scored between zero and three, depending on the strength of the relevant policy or policies of the organization. (One category could be covered by more than one policy.) Therefore, the maximum score that any one organization could get was sixty-three. The score for the college was 28/63 (41 per cent); twenty-six organizations received an overall score of 0/63 (0 per cent), indicating that these associations either had no policies that were publicly available or that their policies did not address the items in the scoring tool. The remaining thirty-four medical associations received scores that ranged from 1/63 (1.6 per cent) to 33/63 (52.4 per cent) with a median of 25.0 (41.7 per cent). None of the twenty-one items achieved a mean score of greater than 1.1/3 and three items had scores of 0.1/3.[38]

CONSEIL QUÉBÉCOIS DE DÉVELOPPEMENT PROFESSIONNEL CONTINU DES MÉDECINS

Up until the start of 2016, the Code of Ethics for Parties Involved in Continuing Medical Education was a joint product of the Conseil and the pharmaceutical industry association, but after that the Code of Ethics belonged to only the Conseil québécois de développement professionnel continu des médecins, although the industry association continues as one of eleven members of the Conseil.[60] Most of what is in the code from the Conseil is similar to that in other guidelines and codes. It states that: commercial biases have no place in continuing medical education; healthcare professionals who have ties to funding organizations must disclose them as must organizers and resource people; and that advertising for a commercial organization associated with a topic, a lecturer or the educational material distributed to the participants is not permitted. Like the Canadian Medical Association's guidelines, the Conseil's code permits the use of trade names accompanied by generic names. It is somewhat stronger than the association's guidelines when it comes to social events at continuing medical education functions. The medical association says that subsidies are allowed for social events that are held as part of a conference or meeting; in contrast, the Conseil's code states that the relative cost of social activities must be entirely paid for by the participants. The Conseil's code has a section about penalties for violations of the code, also in contrast to the guidelines from the Canadian Medical Association and College of Physicians and Surgeons of Ontario, but despite the fact that the Collège des médecins du Québec, the licensing body, is a member of the Conseil, the penalties apply only to medical organizations, not to individual physicians.

COLLEGE OF FAMILY PHYSICIANS OF CANADA

The College of Family Physicians of Canada has been involved in setting guidelines for continuing medical education for decades and has been criticized for its lax guidelines for just as long. Often the college agreed with the criticisms, sometimes it defended its accreditation process, but similar problems seemed to keep arising.

In 1976, Dr. Donald Bates wrote to the *Canadian Family Physician* (*CFP*) about a one-day conference on sexual problems in medical practice, sponsored by Pfizer, where the company was covering both the registration cost and paying for a luncheon. The course was approved by the college for six hours of continuing medical education credit. Bates urged the college to re-examine both its policy regarding continuing medical education and its relation to the promotional activities of pharmaceutical companies.[61] (Pfizer also received further endorsement of its promotional practices through affiliation with the Department of Family Practice at the Queen Elizabeth Hospital in Montreal.) In 1982, it was the turn of Dr. Christine Bourbonniere to write about the First National Gynaecologic Grand Rounds, held in London, Ontario, that were accessible to thousands of physicians across Canada through television satellite communication and that were approved for two hours of continuing medical education credit by the college. These rounds were sponsored by Ortho Pharmaceuticals.[62] In 1985, I attended a college-approved national interactive satellite symposium entitled "Benzodiazepines Today: New Advances in Research and Clinical Practice." The conference was financed by an educational grant from Hoffmann-La Roche, the world's largest manufacturer of benzodiazepines. Attendance at the conference was free and it was also telecast live to medical audiences in ten major Canadian cities. None of the speakers at that conference were critical of the way that benzodiazepines were being prescribed.

In the mid-1990s, a rural family doctor wrote to *Canadian Family Physician* saying that he felt that the college's requirements for continuing medical education did not take into account the concerns of physicians who were living in rural areas where, according to this doctor, continuing medical education would be very infrequent (e.g., Corner Brook, Newfoundland, where he lived) without the support of pharmaceutical companies.[63] In response, Dr. Calvin Gutkin, executive director of the college and Dr. Richard Handfield-Jones, director of Continuing Medical Education, acknowledged that they were aware that the college's accreditation criteria had not been consistently applied across the country for years. They said that the college had recently been developing accreditation criteria that were clearer and more solidly based on sound educational principles.[64] Does that mean that the college's leadership believed that pharmaceutical sponsorship is more acceptable in some circumstances?

In early 2004, I complained to the college about material distributed through mdBriefCase, a commercial continuing medical education provider, that was approved for continuing medical education credit. This material came with an issue of the *Canadian Medical Association Journal* (*CMAJ*) in the same plastic wrap so a copy of the complaint also went to the Canadian Medical Association. The case concerned a man who was supposedly suffering from andropause, a decrease in his level of testosterone. At that point there had not been any long-term randomized controlled trials showing the benefits of androgen replacement in men who met the description of the patient in this case. (There still have not been any convincing studies.[65]) The doctor in charge of reviewing the case before it was distributed was Peter Pommerville, who was on the advisory board for Solvay Pharma, the company that funded production of this material. Pommerville's conflict of interest was not disclosed in the material. One of the questionnaires mentioned in the case, "Androgen Deficiency in Aging Males," was developed in part by Solvay. This potential commercial bias was also not disclosed. Finally, the therapy given to the patient in this case fit the description of the product that Solvay was currently promoting. The association responded that it had requested immediate clarification on the accreditation process used for the material and all other mdBriefCase resources. In addition, it sent urgent communications to the producers of the material, in this case mdBriefCase, and the accrediting academic centre. In the meantime, the association placed a hold on all distribution of mdBriefCase materials in *CMAJ*.[66] Dr. Bernard Marlow, the director of Continuing Medical Education and Continuing Professional Development for the college, initially wrote to me saying that the college takes the integrity of its accredited programs very seriously, and it also valued the opinion of its members who review these programs, as the college did not have a systematic method for auditing programs after they are accredited. He went on to say that he was forwarding my letter to the associate dean of Continuing Medical Education and Professional Development for the Faculty of Medicine at the University of Calgary, where the program had been accredited.[67] A month later he again wrote to me outlining measures that were being taken to correct the problems that I had identified.[68]

Twenty months later, I complained about another case distributed by mdBriefCase, this time one that had been approved through McGill University. In this instance the case concerned a hypothetical patient with high blood pressure who was going south for the winter and the material recommended a medication that was made by the company paying for the distribution of the material. Again this case came wrapped in the plastic envelope with the *CMAJ*.[69] Marlow once again agreed that there was commercial bias.[70] (Interestingly, neither the associate dean for Continuing Education at McGill,[71] the chair of Family Medicine at McGill[72] nor the president of mdBriefCase thought that the material was biased.[73])

In between the two complaints that I made, there was an editorial in the *CMAJ* regarding continuing medical education from mdBriefCase. The editorial said that the *CMAJ* would no longer distribute these continuing medical education inserts with the journal (however, based on the one that I received in 2005 this was a short-lived promise) and went on to say that whatever benefits came from allowing continuing medical education to be orchestrated by pharmaceutical companies were "dwarfed by the harm of masquerading inadequate content as adequate and by the damage to the reputation of the profession and its governing bodies caused by deficient and ambivalent oversight." The editorial concluded that continuing medical education should be funded from the public purse and that if continued to be "left to the marketplace we'll find we have Continuing Product Education, not Continuing Medical Education."[74] Marlow responded to the *CMAJ* that "the fact remains that the pharmaceutical industry in Canada has been a major contributor to innovative, ethically conducted, continuing education programs and health education research."[75] He was concerned that tougher restrictions on financing continuing medical education would result in reductions (and perhaps even withdrawal) of commercial sponsorship, thereby increasing tuition fees for quality educational offerings and "adding to the burden on physicians who are trying to maintain their skills."[75] He went on to defend the way that the College of Family Physicians of Canada accredits continuing medical education and said that he anticipated that new auditing procedures would be put in place soon by the college. (He also advocated a model of continuing medical education funding that would combine paying physicians for lost income, giving government grants to universities and professional associations to create programs and continuing to allow industry to pay for unbiased education.) About fifteen months later, after my second complaint, he said that the college was awaiting the publication of the Canadian Medical Association's new policy on physicians and the pharmaceutical industry before updating its continuing medical education guidelines and the organization was working to address ongoing challenges, including disclosure, conflict of interest, peer selling and co-sponsorship.[15]

In 2007, Marlow made the claim that "All [continuing medical education] and [continuing professional development] programs accredited by the College are unquestionably balanced, free of bias, and not being used by pharmaceutical companies to market their products,"[76] and that whatever problems existed with continuing medical education in the United States didn't exist in Canada.[48] The next year, responding to the *CMAJ* editorial referred to in the paragraph above, Marlow said that "the College of Family Physicians of Canada rejects the notion that continuing health education in Canada is 'a truly broken system'" and that the college has "strict rules governing commercial support that incorporate the [Canadian Medical Association's] ethical guidelines, and we mandate full disclosure and review of content for bias and balance before a program receives accreditation."[77] In 2010, Marlow said that the college felt "relatively comfortable accepting funding from industry"[16] and that he didn't "think there's much getting through with the College of Family Physicians seal on it that one would declare as biased."[78]

In some respects, the policies of the College of Family Physicians of Canada are stricter than those of the Royal College of Physicians and Surgeons. Starting in January 2013, the College of Family Physicians prohibited industry from attending continuing medical education content planning meetings and from having any role in continuing medical education program content development.[79] By 2014, Dr. Jamie Meuser had taken over from Marlow and asserted that the college's "absolute, beginning obligation is to ensure that education trumps promotion." Meuser also maintained that "there are three potential benefits to corporate sponsorship of [continuing medical education] . . . It pays for the development of education programs that otherwise wouldn't exist . . . communication companies that offer [continuing medical education] also take care of all of the logistics involved in delivering the programs. And if corporate money were shunned, drug companies . . . would likely start offering more unaccredited programs, which wouldn't be held to the same standards as those approved by accrediting bodies."[80] That same year, doctors gathered at a high-end Toronto restaurant to hear a leading specialist talk about diabetes treatments. They "were given their choice of a Californian red or Italian white. For the starter, they had either butternut squash soup, a fried green tomato dish or arugula salad garnished with cumin cashews, grapefruit, toasted coconut and rhubarb citrus vinaigrette. That was followed by an entrée of Cornish hen, organic BC Chinook

salmon, pasta, or artisanal beef tenderloin. The meal ended
with a pineapple confection or a milk-chocolate mousse."
The 2014 dinner, sponsored by drug company Boehringer-
Ingelheim, was approved by the college for one credit. "I
honestly don't know how that (menu) would have gotten past
our ethical review," Dr. Meuser told the *Toronto Star*.[81] In
the same article, the *Star* reporters also talked about another
event at ORO restaurant in Toronto where appetizers are
in the $15–20 range, main courses cost about $30, desserts
are about $10–$12 and wine runs from $10–$24 per glass.[81]
Before the event started the speaker told the audience about
a "new and exciting" drug for diabetes made by Actavis, the
company sponsoring the event, and, said the *Star*, "Within
a week of the dinner, an Actavis sales rep visited the clinic
of one of the doctors who attended. 'Just stopped in to say
hi & drop off Constella samples,' the rep wrote in a note."[81]

All of the above should not imply that the college has
been unconcerned about its relations with industry. Indeed,
in 2010 it established a task force to review and make recommendations about the relationship and the task force's
recommendations were highlighted and approved at the
November 2013 meeting of the college's board. In addition, the board initiated an analysis of the effect of complete
dissociation from industry and those results were presented
at the board's November 2014 meeting.[82] However, the task
force report was released only in late 2015, over two years
after it was approved by the college's board. This release took
place after I and two other doctors wrote an article criticizing the college for the long delay.[83] The report contained
some promising recommendations, such as rejecting industry
sponsorship of any food, emailing stations or other "gifts"
at accredited educational activities and other college-related

meetings; creating an unrestricted fund for continuing medical education within three years that would support the development, dissemination, and evaluation of accredited educational activities (industry would be allowed to contribute to the fund); and banning industry funding of educational elements in accredited residency training programs and medical student training programs.[84] However, in other respects it showed a lack of vision. For example, the college was required only to "be aware of the relationships between individuals associated with the College" and industry, "requests to initiate or continue a sponsorship relationship must be assessed for impact on the [college's] reputation" and only members will be able to access information on the college's website relating to the disclosure of relationships with the industry.[84] There was also nothing in the report about disclosing the sources of revenue for the *CFP* or how much money industry contributes to continuing medical education events that the college accredits. When *Pharmalot*, a section of the website statnews.com, asked why the college "will not require its members to disclose financial relationships with industry," a spokeswoman for the college "wrote that its task force 'believed that the spectrum of such input was too broad . . . It's an honor system based on the trust we have in our members and our health care system."[85]

In responding to the critique of the college's failure to release the task force report, Dr. Jennifer Hall, the college's president, and Dr. Francine Lemire, the executive director and chief executive officer, asserted that it was not the financial impact on the college as an organization that prevented it "from moving immediately to eliminate health care and pharmaceutical industry sponsorship of continuing professional development programming." Rather it was

the college's concern that were it not for industry funding, program development/dissemination for all members,
particularly those who practise in more isolated parts of
the country, would be negatively affected. Again, there is
the appearance that the college's leadership is adopting
the principle of moral relativism and believes that industry sponsorship is acceptable under certain circumstances.
Moreover, according to Hall and Lemire, the college did
not want to be seen as dictating physician behaviour.[86]
(Does that also mean that the college does not want to
provide leadership on this question?) They also pointed out
that the college has "started to take steps to mitigate the
influence of pharmaceutical companies on the annual scientific program at Family Medicine Forum as well as clearly
articulate what is education and what is marketing . . . We
also clearly describe the Exhibit Hall as the 'marketplace' so
that the Family Medicine Forum attendees are acutely aware
that this affords exhibitors the opportunity to market their
products and services. To ensure registrants do not have to
be subjected to marketing should they so choose, we have
adopted a direct access route to meals offered at Family
Medicine Forum, which have traditionally been available in
the Exhibit Hall. The Exhibit Hall passport contest [doctors
who get their "passports" stamped by enough exhibitors are
eligible for a prize] and ancillary sessions will be reviewed
and opportunities to limit influence and gain additional
financial independence will be examined for implementation at the Family Medicine Forum in 2016."[86] Why it had
taken the college until 2015 to address these issues was not
mentioned in the article.

The evaluation of the college's dependence on financial
support from industry still has not been released as of October

2016. Lemire's rationale for continuing to keep the analysis secret was two-fold. First, the Family Medicine Forum and the *Canadian Family Physician* "would be strongly affected by a complete dissociation from the health care and pharmaceutical industry" and second, an admittedly nonscientific survey of college members found that "nearly half of respondents said that the [college] should maintain relationships with the pharmaceutical industry with the current level of diligent management. About 30 per cent said that we should have more stringent management in place, and 20 per cent agreed with complete dissociation."[87] When reporters from the *Toronto Star* asked Lemire if the report would eventually be made public, her response was, "We are not a public organization . . . Our accountability is to our members," and that the results may be released to member doctors who ask for it.[81]

A NEW NATIONAL STANDARD FOR CONTINUING MEDICAL EDUCATION

In late winter 2016, there was an announcement that the College of Family Physicians of Canada, the Royal College of Physicians and Surgeons of Canada and the Collège des médecins du Québec had combined to develop a single national guideline for accredited continuing medical education. The guideline is going to be phased in over a twenty-two–month period leading to its official adoption on January 1, 2018.[88] Like the guidelines that have preceded it, this new one is a mixed bag. The scientific planning committee needs to review all disclosed financial relationships of speakers, moderators, facilitators and authors in advance of the event, but there are no criteria outlined regarding what is and is not acceptable, thereby virtually ensuring that this sub-element will be subject to multiple different interpretations. The new guideline prohibits social activities associated with an event from occurring at a time or location that interferes or competes with or takes precedence over accredited activities but nothing is said about the amount of time for social activities relative to academic activities.[89] Will this new guideline prove to be a floor or a ceiling for other medical societies? Just as important as the content of the guideline is whether the three organizations are willing to go beyond just publishing it and actually enforce it.

CONCLUSION

Up until the mid-1980s, the relationship between individual physicians and industry did not seem to concern the regulatory colleges, suggesting a laissez-faire attitude on their part. Since then, the colleges, especially the Ontario College of Physicians and Surgeons, have developed codes of conduct and engaged in widespread consultation with their membership and other individuals and organizations, but the strength of their codes is variable. The previous policy on continuing medical education from the Quebec Conseil was jointly developed with the pharmaceutical industry and although that is no longer true of the current policy, the pharmaceutical industry association is still one of eleven members of the Conseil. The College of Family Physicians continues to refuse to publicly disclose the reports that it has produced about its relationship with industry and how much money it receives directly or indirectly from pharmaceutical companies. It hides behind the claim that as a private organization it has no obligation to the public to do so.

Beyond just promulgating guidelines, organizations need to aggressively educate their membership about their content, monitor whether the guidelines are actually being respected and, if necessary, levy sanctions for noncompliance. None of the five organizations that have been examined in this chapter has been publicly willing to take these steps. Their reluctance to monitor compliance and to discipline doctors who violate their codes may stem from a recognition of the underlying ambivalence that many individual physicians have towards the industry and a desire to not antagonize a large portion of their membership. But their role is not to please their members. They have a regulatory function to ensure that physicians practise evidence-based medicine and by not monitoring compliance they are failing. Unfortunately, the costs of non-action or partial action on how doctors learn and practise do not seem to enter into the equation.

CHAPTER 7
MEDICAL STUDENTS AND PHYSICIANS-IN-TRAINING (RESIDENTS): GET THEM WHILE THEY ARE YOUNG

Francis Xavier, one of the co-founders of the Society of Jesus (Jesuits) was alleged to have said "Give me a child until he is seven and I'll give you the man."[1] In the case of medicine, the children are the medical students and physicians-in-training (residents) and the men are practising doctors. Women and men go into medical school relatively ignorant of medical culture but are immersed in it for a minimum of six years (four years of medical school and two years of training for family practice and at least four years for a specialty) and come out as doctors with the cultural attributes that being a physician implies. How they are taught, what kind of exposure they have to the pharmaceutical industry and how they see their teachers and those above them on the medical hierarchy relating to the industry will, in large part, determine their own relationship once they are independent doctors.

MEDICAL STUDENTS AND MEDICAL SCHOOLS — THE WILD WEST

The 1970s were the wild west when it came to controls over interactions between medical students and the pharmaceutical industry. Martin Shapiro went to medical school at McGill in the early 1970s, and writes about his experiences in *Getting Doctored*.[2] At the end of the first year, Eli Lilly offered the students a stethoscope, reflex hammer, tuning fork and doctor's bag, all free of charge. Some students made an attempt to have the entire class reject the offer, but in the end most of the students were indifferent, and the boycott effort failed. At the University of Toronto, where I attended medical school between 1973 and 1977, education about the pharmaceutical industry consisted of twenty pages of readings that were mildly critical of certain aspects of the industry and a one-hour session in the first year. Until I enrolled in 1973, this hour was divided between two speakers, a representative of the pharmaceutical industry association and a government spokesperson who discussed Ontario's public drug program. I, along with a few other students, objected that we did not think that this was a well-balanced panel, and the lecturer agreed to add me to the panel. The industry association representative sat through most of the session with a gaze of incredulity on his face, clearly unprepared for the "unfriendly" comments. He answered my points with personal innuendos directed at me. Interestingly, the industry association did not send a representative the following year.

Since the 1970s there have been continuing anecdotal reports about student concerns with industry involvement in medical education. As medical students at the University of Manitoba in the early 2000s, Elia Abi-Jaoude and Shannon

Wiebe circulated a petition to protest drug company donations of free textbooks. For example, the main textbook used
for teaching about the gastrointestinal system was published
by AstraZeneca. Their petition read, "It is important to
guard the quality and integrity of our medical education
from targeting by parties with a vested financial interest."
The petition proved to be very controversial and resulted
in a four-hour debate on the question, "Does the pharmaceutical industry have too much input in the education of
doctors?" that drew three hundred medical students and
health professionals. The depth of the feelings about the
issue can be gauged by the comment from one student who
told Abi-Jaoude that he would rather pass a kidney stone
than attend the event. Murray Elston, a former Liberal
Ontario cabinet minister, and then the president of the
industry association, spoke on behalf of industry and said
that Dr. Gordon Guyatt, one of the other panelists and
an early and articulate critic of industry practices, was "on
a bit of a crusade to get pharmaceutical companies away
from providing the latest and most interesting information
about their products." He assured the students present that
they can be "absolutely assured that material [provided by
the pharmaceutical industry] is as scientifically based as the
material in any text."[3] According to Abi-Jaoude, who is now
a psychiatrist at Toronto's Hospital for Sick Children, Dr.
Sunil Patel, then president-elect of the Canadian Medical
Association, was announced as being on the panel to speak in
support of the pharmaceutical industry. Very shortly before
the event, he emailed to say that he could no longer attend
due to a conflict. When Abi-Jaoude contacted him, Patel
said that he could not present his personal views as he was
a Canadian Medical Association official. Abi-Jaoude then

suggested that Patel participate as an association official and represent the association's views. Patel then said he could not do so as the medical association had been in contact with the industry association and that the two organizations agreed that the medical association would not take part in the event.

The question of the quality of information provided by the pharmaceutical industry and conflict of interest became highly public issues at the University of Toronto. Since 2000, the university has given a one-week course on pain management to all of its health science students. Between 2002 and 2006, the course was funded by $117,000 in unrestricted educational grants from four pharmaceutical companies, including Purdue Pharma, makers of OxyContin (extended-release oxycodone). Up until 2010, students were given a book on pain management, *Managing Pain: The Canadian Healthcare Professional's Reference*, that was funded by Purdue. The book contained a "modified World Health Organization analgesic ladder" that listed oxycodone among weak opioids. In fact, oxycodone is at least 1.5 times more potent than morphine and the original World Health Organization pain ladder does not mention oxycodone. Dr. Roman Jovey was one of the coauthors of the book, an unpaid guest lecturer for the course and on the speakers' bureau for Purdue.[4,5] One of Jovey's slides included an alleged direct quote from a 2006 *Canadian Medical Association Journal* (*CMAJ*) article saying placebo controlled trials showed "strong" and "consistent" evidence that opioids relieve pain and improve function for patients with chronic, noncancer pain. However, the article in question did not contain the quote, nor did it use the words "strong" and "consistent" to describe the evidence. In addition, Jovey did not disclose his conflicts in his slides, although he said that they were verbally disclosed. He characterized the *CMAJ* misquote as an "inadvertent error."[6] Jovey has not been involved with the course since 2010. (See Chapter 5 for more about Jovey and OxyContin.)

Public knowledge of this controversy started with a student complaining to the authorities at the University of Toronto and then that complaint being taken forward by two doctors at St. Michael's Hospital, Philip Berger and Rick Glazier. Eventually, an informal inquiry into the management of the course was established under the direction of Dr. Lorraine Ferris, Associate Vice Provost, Health Sciences Policy and Strategy at the university. Ferris concluded: "Last, making available or distributing a book (not available on the retail market) to students free of charge for which copyright is held by a pharmaceutical company that manufactures opioids raised serious concerns about possible financial conflicts of interest. It is my opinion that our academic community (and the public more generally) would find making this available to students objectionable, regardless of it being assessed by those delivering the Interfaculty Pain Curriculum as a useful and quality resource. In response to a concern brought forward about students receiving such a gift, the 2010 Interfaculty Pain Curriculum did not make the book available to students. I strongly support the 2010 decision and my recommendation includes prohibiting such gifts in the future."[7]

According to Dr. Barbara Mintzes, who previously taught in the Faculty of Medicine at the University of British Columbia, as recently as 2010, sessions for second-year medical students on pharmaceutical promotion at the university would have an industry representative to provide balance. Since then, medical students have sessions on drug promotion and ethics of interactions with industry without an industry representative necessarily being present. The university also now requires all speakers to declare conflicts of interest, which previously did not necessarily occur.

STUDENT ATTITUDES AND REACTIONS

Kelly Holloway explored how a select group of Canadian and American medical students, who were critical of the pharmaceutical industry, negotiated its presence in the course of their medical education through a series of interviews as part of her PhD at York University. Based on these interviews, Holloway reports that there is a clear and pervasive influence of the pharmaceutical industry in medical education. Her interviewees said that "when their ideals [were] challenged by an approach to medicine that they [found] troubling, they [made] a genuine attempt to address this both in their ideas about medicine and in their practice of medicine . . . At an everyday level, they negotiate[d] complex and conflicted feelings about the presence of industry as they attempt to meet the rigorous requirements of medical school . . . [Canadian students] extensively discussed their efforts to manage the conflict industry presence represented for them, possibly because they lacked an outlet in a broader movement for change."[8] In contrast, in the United States, the American Medical Students Association has organized a national campaign to raise awareness about industry influence in medical education.

Holloway concluded that "Contrary to the idea that these students have simply accepted that ideology, participants demonstrated that they register unease quite regularly. When students addressed their unease about industry influence,

they had to confront not only the hierarchy of medical training, but the extent to which the superiors of that hierarchical
relationship had accepted industry presence in the clinic
as normal and necessary."[8] One student talked about her
reluctance to voice concerns about her supervisor's relationship with pharmaceutical industry personnel: "Like to me
this would be tantamount to going to someone's house and
insulting their food. I don't feel like I'm on neutral ground?
And because of that I felt uncomfortable. And also at the end
of the day I also have an evaluation that needs to be filled out
by one of the physicians at the clinic and if they think I'm a
difficult person to get along with because of my views that
would certainly color the evaluation."[8]

However, as Holloway herself acknowledges, her results
are not necessarily generalizable across medical students
and this becomes apparent in the results of a survey
of students at the University of Western Ontario (now
Western University). Eighty-one percent "of students were
not opposed to interacting with drug companies in medical
school. Medical students felt comfortable accepting gifts
of low monetary value, such as lunches (75 per cent) and
penlights (74 per cent), but were willing to accept gifts of
higher monetary value if the gifts served an educational
purpose, such as textbooks (65 per cent) and drug company
sponsored educational seminars (66 per cent). [Seventeen]
per cent of students said that if presented with a choice of
drugs identical in terms of price, efficacy, and effectiveness, they would prescribe the drug from the company that
provided them with financial incentives."[9]

The Canadian Federation of Medical Students started to
address industry involvement in medical education in 2011
when it produced a position paper.[10] In the aftermath of

that report, one recent graduate from McMaster medical school said that there was definitely room for improvement in teaching about how to relate to industry and that he was working with medical students and other physicians to explore whether the federation could sponsor an annual survey of policies at Canadian medical schools similar to the one done by the American Medical Students Association (amsascorecard.org). The 2013 head of the Canadian Federation of Medical Students said that "When it comes to relationships with industry, students pretty universally across the country have really strong opinions . . . They want their decisions to be uninfluenced. They want to make the best decisions with their patients."[11] A search of the federation's website as of August 2016 could not find any evidence of further activity on this initiative.

MEDICAL SCHOOLS AND THE ASSOCIATION OF THE FACULTIES OF MEDICINE OF CANADA

None of the stories about what was happening in medical schools seemed to generate an interest in teaching students about interactions with the pharmaceutical industry in the mid-2000s. Health Action International, a nongovernmental organization based in Amsterdam, the World Health Organization and the European Union commissioned a survey to examine the extent to which medical and pharmacy students were being educated about drug promotion.[12] There were responses from six faculty members at four Canadian medical schools. Overall, they were fairly pessimistic about how successful the education being offered was, with no one saying it was very successful. Two respondents mentioned the lack of support from the medical faculty as a barrier to success. One said that teaching in this area was actively undermined because companies were allowed to promote their products and subsidize events (especially in postgraduate education). The second said that the lack of positive role models was a problem. There was one example given where sales representatives were invited to present and discuss the role of the industry in providing information — with promotion addressed secondarily. There were also some examples of informal teaching, for example, the involvement of a "no free lunch" student group and informal teaching at rounds, while doing clinics and seeing drug representatives (Barbara Mintzes, personal communication, November 9, 2006).

The attitude of various officials in medical schools across the country towards the end of the 2000s still seemed to be that not much needed to be done, sometimes on the basis that things in this country were not as bad as they were in the US and sometimes because the medical schools felt that they needed the income that they received from industry. Policies varied widely across the country, with some schools having no policies at all. Dr. Gavin Stuart, dean of medicine at the University of British Columbia, felt that subsidies and handouts were not "of the [same] order of magnitude" as in the US. (At that time, the medical school at the university allowed financial payments from industry up to 20 per cent of a faculty member's salary.) Dr. David McKnight, associate dean of equity and professionalism at the University of Toronto, added another twist to why policies shouldn't be uniform, saying that if the Association of Faculties of Medicine of Canada took a stand, schools would be resentful of a top-down approach: "Each university likes to keep its individuality." As an article in the *CMAJ* reported, Canadian medical schools were also very reluctant "to adopt anything like a prohibition on handouts, primarily because they now rely entirely on registration fees or industry subsidies to pay for continuing medical education programs . . . Administrators at several other schools, speaking on condition of anonymity, said they simply 'could not afford' to wean themselves of industry monies for continuing medical education, or wouldn't dare to do so, for fear of a physician backlash . . . Other institutions flatly refused to even disclose whether they have policies governing industry handouts or like McGill University and the University of Ottawa, indicated only that they are in the midst of reviews."[13] Some, like Queen's University senior associate dean for medical education, Dr. Lewis Tomalty, were a bit more skeptical: "My sense is that we don't see abuses in the system so that we're comfortable where we are at." Although most medical schools were influenced by the guidelines on interactions from the Canadian Medical Association, Tomalty's position was that those guidelines didn't go as far as many wanted.[13] The editors at the *CMAJ* were not happy about what was going on in Canadian medical schools and in an editorial criticized the lack of policies on conflict of interest. The *CMAJ* was particularly critical about the fact that the profession failed to protect students, the least experienced members of the profession, and failed to mandate disclosure about whether the information being taught is subject to external influences. The editors laid the blame for this failure squarely on the medical schools.[14]

The Association of Faculties of Medicine of Canada was not quite as blasé about the relationship between medical schools and industry as its individual members, but it was also not willing to make any direct recommendations to its membership. Its Board of Directors passed a resolution endorsing the principles underlying a report from the Association of American Medical Colleges on industry funding of medical education. The resolution urged all academic medical centres to accelerate their adoption of policies that better manage, and when necessary, prohibit, academic-industry interactions that can inherently create conflicts of interest and undermine standards of professionalism.[15] The Association of Faculties of Medicine of Canada said it was not structured to compel individual schools to bring their policies in line with the report, but since the resolution to support the principles was passed unanimously by its board it was confident that its membership would work to ensure that their individual policies were in line with the adopted resolution.[16]

The association reaffirmed the role of industry involvement in medical education and acknowledged that it had been working with industry representatives regarding implementation of the principles of the Association of American Medical Colleges report. Dr. Nick Busing, the president and CEO of the Association of Faculties of Medicine of Canada, was extremely positive about industry involvement in medical education. "There is no question that industry plays an important role in supporting all aspects of our healthcare system, including medical education."[17] Having industry sit at the table to help develop policies about its role in medical education seems to be a questionable practice when industry doesn't agree with the rules. In September 2010, the Association of Faculties of Medicine of Canada devoted the entire issue of its newsletter to the question of industry and conflict of interest. One of the contributors was Russell Williams, president of the pharmaceutical industry association. (Williams retired from his position in June 2016.)

Williams began by saying that "the definition of [conflict of interest] is often a matter of debate," a position that is at odds with most of the literature on the topic, including the United States Institute of Medicine report that clearly defined conflict of interest as "a set of circumstances that creates a risk that professional judgment or actions regarding a primary interest will be unduly influenced by a secondary interest."[18] Williams went on to say that "[Conflict of interest] guidelines must also be reasonable and balanced. We live in an increasingly complex world where talented people are in great demand in their specialized field. If Canada is to fully embrace innovation in health care, we need the expertise of the best people with divergent backgrounds and perspectives to get the best possible results. Limiting the participation of a qualified scientist or a health care professional on the basis of some connection with an industry does not in our view, serve the public interest."[19] While superficially what Williams was saying may sound reasonable, what he was advocating was a position that would allow virtually unlimited interaction between researchers, educators, clinicians and industry and would ignore the conflict of interest implications of those interactions.

Busing may not have been troubled by what Williams had to say, but others were not as starry-eyed about bringing industry in. Illustrating the diversity of opinion within the Association of Faculties of Medicine, Dr. Chris de Gara, the University of Alberta medical school's associate dean of the Division of Continuing Medical Education, posed the question, "What possible interest could the pharmaceutical instrument manufacturers (for example) have in the continuing education of physicians, except that it increases sales of product? Can they really claim to be interested in our education? . . . Industry always wants to fund things that are very close to their needs and the marketing of their products. If I go to industry and say, 'Please can you put on an event on statins?' they're lining up to help. If I say, 'I want one on gout' — there hasn't been a new treatment for gout for decades — I'm deafened by the silence."[20]

Dr. Gordon Guyatt, who led the development of guidelines for interaction between residents and industry in the early 1990s at McMaster University (see later in this chapter) was not optimistic that industry's role would be restrained. Dr. Jerome Kassirer, a former editor of the *New England Journal of Medicine*, told the Canadian Press that the endorsement of the Association of American Medical Colleges report by the Association of Faculties of Medicine of Canada would help with the issue of conflict of interest, but "the problem will persist as long as medical schools don't get tough with their faculty. 'I think that the notion of having students be more aware of the dangers of physician-industry involvement is a good thing. But we haven't cleaned up the Augean stables,' he said, referring to one of the tasks placed before Hercules."[21]

The Association of Faculties of Medicine of Canada may have been confident that medical schools would institute strict policies about industry involvement and conflict of interest, but that was not the case, as demonstrated by three separate studies[22–24] on policies at Canadian medical schools. Although there were some differences in their conclusions, all three found that, in general, policies were relatively weak or in many cases nonexistent. The paper by Shnier and colleagues (of which I was one of the coauthors) found that, of the seventeen medical schools in Canada, over half (ten) received summative scores of five or less out of the maximum score of twenty-four for the strength of their policies, indicating that in most of the categories they had either no policy or a permissive policy.[24] (Since these three studies were published a number of schools have gone on to review and modify their policies — Dalhousie University, University of Toronto and Western University. Queen's University produced a draft of a revised policy in 2014 but as of the date of writing this chapter — October 2016 — the draft has not been enacted. There has not been any reevaluation of the strength or breadth of medical school policies since the last of the three reports appeared in 2013.)

When Shnier and I (and others) did our survey, the Northern Ontario School of Medicine did not yet have a conflict of interest policy (it later developed one in 2014) and according to its dean, Dr. Roger Strasser, one of the main reasons for the absence of a policy was the question of funding for continuing medical education. Government money for continuing medical education is almost nonexistent, and to a large extent medical schools rely on industry funding for the events that they sponsor. When the school first circulated a draft policy prohibiting industry-sponsored education, Strasser said, "quite a few physicians who are faculty members said, 'If I can't have dinner with a drug rep or attend a guest speaker organized by a drug rep, then how am I going to have [continuing medical education].'"[11] What applied to the Northern Ontario School of Medicine regarding continuing medical education funding at medical schools seems to be widespread. Russell Williams, the industry association president, said he was told that the vast majority of medical schools need industry money to maintain their programs.[20]

David McKnight, from the University of Toronto, offers three additional reasons medical schools may have been reluctant to embrace the idea that they needed strict policies. First, "Under the federal funding laws, there are a set of grants that can only be obtained if there's an industrial partner" and therefore, it is essential that some faculty enter into relationships with industry. Second, "People everywhere like freebies" and, finally, "No one believes they are being influenced . . . We know they are being influenced — why else would the companies do it if it didn't work? — but none of [the faculty] believe it."[11]

Events in New Brunswick in 2009, when Dalhousie University was establishing a satellite medical school on the Saint John campus of the University of New Brunswick, provide another example of how money can intrude on medical education. Just before the satellite school opened, the New Brunswick Medical Education Trust was established with a goal of raising enough money to pay for the education of ten students per year, to help attract and retain doctors in the province. AstraZeneca Canada was first off the mark to give money with a donation of $500,000. Dr. Donald Craig, chair of the Medical Staff Organization in the Saint John area, was enthusiastic about the donation and said, "I hope the donation encourages other pharmaceutical companies."[25] Others were not quite as positive. Dr. Adam Hofmann, a clinical fellow in the general internal medicine program at McGill, wrote to the *Telegraph-Journal* "to express his strong reservations against New Brunswick accepting a donation from a pharmaceutical industry sponsor to fund medical education." His point was that "indenturing the students or schools to the pharmaceutical or biotech industry is unethical, and perhaps unwise."[26] Not surprisingly, Russell Williams did not agree with Hofmann. According to Williams, if Hofmann's position was accepted it "would negate the many beneficial effects for Canadians and especially patients of the ongoing dialogue between health-care professionals and those in the public and private sectors."[27]

ACADEMIC HEALTH SCIENCE CENTRES AND PHYSICIANS-IN-TRAINING

Once medical students graduate they move into academic health science centres for their training as either family physicians or specialists. These centres are the primary place where physicians-in-training (residents) translate their classroom knowledge into how to actually deal with patients in real life. As such, these centres need to not only teach residents the clinical skills that they will need when they go out into the real world, but they also need to teach them the values that doctors should uphold. There was a set of recommendations offered in 1993 by two individual physicians for how residents should interact with industry within the confines of the teaching hospital environment. Some of the recommendations were relatively restrictive, for instance: direct support of drug lunches (lunches provided by drug companies) and other rounds (discussion of medical topics) by the pharmaceutical industry should not be accepted; residents should not accept honoraria to give talks during working hours; and the postgraduate education committee should control all funds obtained from pharmaceutical companies. However, the guidelines also allowed companies to sponsor social events provided that they were approved by the postgraduate education committee. Perhaps most surprising was that the authors recommended that similar recommendations be developed for the staff that taught the residents.[28] There is no evidence that there was any uptake of these recommendations either for residents or teaching staff.

PSYCHIATRY

In the mid-1990s, the need for a program to teach psychiatric residents about interactions with industry seemed obvious. Residents doing a rotation on a psychiatry ward or in a psychiatric hospital in Toronto were surveyed about their relationships with drug companies over a one-year period. The median number of drug company lunches that residents attended was ten, and they had received gifts with a median value of $20 but ranging up to $800. As reported in *CMAJ*, "Fewer than one third felt that pharmaceutical representatives were a source of accurate information about drugs; however, 71 per cent (52/73) disagreed with the statement that representatives should be banned from making presentations. Although only 15 per cent (11/73) felt they had sufficient training about meeting with pharmaceutical representatives, 34 per cent (25/73) felt that discussions with representatives would have no impact on their prescribing practices, and 56 per cent (41/73) felt that receiving gifts would have no impact on prescribing."[29] Seven years later, another survey was done of chief psychiatry residents and psychiatry residency program directors, this time at all sixteen training programs in Canada. Three-quarters of the respondents were either unaware of, or noted an absence of, policies or guidelines regarding interactions with the pharmaceutical industry in their training programs and an equal number "were unaware of any structured teaching regarding potential conflicts of interest between psychiatry and the pharmaceutical industry. A significant number of respondents perceived occasional excessive influence by the pharmaceutical industry on residents' training."[30]

Psychiatry residents at the University of Calgary also described limited training in how to interact with industry, but in this case it seemed to be due to an active effort by faculty to shelter them from the effects of pharmaceutical industry biases. Residents felt that this lack of training made them vulnerable when they transitioned from residency to practice because they lacked the skills to effectively interact with drug companies. When industry did try to influence them it was through a variety of tactics such as gifting-reciprocity, control of the information regarding products, active efforts to engage in the delivery of healthcare, provision of education to medical personnel and integration of pharmaceutical representative agents into the healthcare system.[31]

In some cases, psychiatry residents took action on their own to try to deal with the influence that the pharmaceutical industry had on their education and practice. Residents in the psychiatry training program at McGill, with the aid of experts and a literature review, set out to systematically evaluate areas of concern and to develop guidelines around educational activities, training, fundraising, and other specific resident–industry interactions. Their guidelines addressed limitations on fundraising activities, restriction of direct gifts to residents, the appropriateness and awarding of industry fellowships, and the handling of drug samples, meals and other presentations to residents. While those who developed the guidelines felt that they were useful adjuncts in guiding their interactions with pharmaceutical companies, they also recognized that they needed to be reinforced with education and sensitization by faculty.[32]

PEDIATRICS

An ad hoc committee of residents and two staff physicians developed a set of guidelines and a proposed system for handling funds from pharmaceutical companies in the pediatric residency program in Montreal in the late 1990s. Under this system, each residency program would develop a common fund for money donated by pharmaceutical companies, which would then be administered by a committee with defined priorities. In addition, the presence of residents on this committee, under staff preceptorship, would serve as a springboard for education on the subject of relationships with industry. The ad hoc committee also developed guidelines for acknowledgement of sponsorship, the solicitation of funds, gifts for the care of patients and ongoing education. At the time that the article describing the work of the committee was written, the system for handling company donations had not been implemented and there is no documentation that I can find about whether this process was actually completed.[33]

FAMILY MEDICINE

The situation in family medicine training programs in the late 1980s to late 1990s was no better than it was in psychiatry or pediatrics. Promotional material was present in all the offices and examining rooms of clinicians in a Canadian family practice teaching centre, with an average of 10.5 promotional items in each individual patient care area.[34] At the same time, many residents were quite happy to partake of industry largesse, and few training programs had taken steps to address this issue. Fewer than a quarter of the Ontario family practice residents who responded to a survey stated that they had read the Canadian Medical Association's policy statement on appropriate interactions between physicians and the pharmaceutical industry. (See Chapter 6 for more about the association's policy.) Over half said that they would attend a private dinner paid for by a pharmaceutical

representative, and that proportion did not change regardless of whether residents had or had not read the Canadian
Medical Association's guidelines that prohibit the receipt of
personal gifts. A large majority reported that they would like
the opportunity to interact with pharmaceutical representatives in an educational setting, even though several programs
discouraged these interactions. Finally, approximately three-
quarters of the residents indicated that they planned to see
pharmaceutical representatives in their future practice.[35]

Only four of the sixteen family practice training
programs in Canada had formal policies or guidelines
about doctor-industry relationships in the mid 1990s. Five
programs addressed what factors affected prescribing,
five had sessions on the Canadian Medical Association's
guidelines on physician-industry interaction and four
looked at marketing techniques used by companies. All
programs allowed some level of industry sponsorship and
nine used industry-sponsored speakers, tapes and videos,
while five allowed lunches paid for by drug companies.[36] In
Montreal, almost half of the doctors and nurses surveyed in
the sixteen family medicine teaching units associated with
the University of Montreal did not know if their unit had
a policy governing contact between residents and pharmaceutical industry sales representatives.[37]

Residents in some family medicine programs also took
the initiative to try to expand teaching about relationships
with industry. At McMaster University's family practice
residency, they developed a curriculum that consisted
of two parts: a faculty-led debate and discussion of a
systematic review of physician–pharmaceutical industry
interactions, and an interactive workshop that included a
presentation highlighting key empirical findings, a video

illustrating techniques to optimize pharmaceutical sales representatives' visits, and small- and large-group problem-based discussions. Before and after the intervention, residents were asked about their attitudes toward drug samples, industry-sponsored continuing medical education, one-on-one interactions with sales representatives, free meals and gifts worth less than $10. After the intervention residents had more cautious attitudes and rated marketing strategies as less ethically appropriate compared to before they participated in the curriculum.[38]

In another program, a faculty initiative accepted as a given that once residents graduated and were practising independently they would be interacting with drug industry representatives. Therefore, faculty developed a program with four objectives: to help residents understand the role of industry sales representatives, to practise communication between residents and sales representatives, to practise residents' critical appraisal of advertising and promotional material provided by the drug industry and to practise residents' communication skills when presenting drug information to preceptors.[39] Residents were generally supportive of the initiative. In a survey about their attitudes towards promotion, most residents indicated that they regarded journal advertising as having little value. The authors of an article on the program speculated that this finding was an indication that residents were developing a critical attitude towards promotion, but another explanation for the response may have been that residents did not realize the effect that journal advertisements had on them. The program was funded by Astra Canada and Boehringer Ingelheim (Canada) Ltd. The source of funding may be why most sales representatives liked the program and urged its expansion.

DR. GORDON GUYATT AND MCMASTER UNIVERSITY

The most ambitious and radical attempt to reorient a training program, briefly mentioned earlier in this chapter, took place in the early 1990s in the general internal medicine program at McMaster University under the leadership of Dr. Gordon Guyatt. (Full disclosure here, Gordon Guyatt and I have been friends since the late 1970s.) Guyatt, with the expressed agreement of the residents, reorganized the general internal medicine training program at McMaster University to restrict contact between pharmaceutical industry sales representatives and medical residents. Policies included obtaining and screening educational materials from the industry before residents were exposed to them, proscribing "drug lunches" and accepting industry sponsorship only when the residency program maintained complete control of the educational event being sponsored.[40] Guyatt summarized the results of a poll of twenty-four pharmaceutical companies about the guidelines.[41] Of the eighteen who responded, half found the guidelines acceptable and the other half found them not acceptable and indicated that their funding for the residency program at McMaster would be negatively affected. Guyatt also recounted a visit he received from a senior official in the marketing arm of the pharmaceutical industry association who suggested that research funding at McMaster might be compromised. When Dr. David Sackett, also from McMaster, requested funding from the industry to help with research done by medical residents, the response from a senior official with a Canadian subsidiary of a multinational company was, "Recently, access to many of these key people [healthcare professionals at McMaster] has become limited, including the medical residents. Without this contact, it is very difficult for a partnership to develop. Consequently, it is not easy for [our company] to justify philanthropic donations to research when there is limited or no access to researchers, and no hand in the type of research project selected for support. Unfortunately, at this time we will have to decline your request."[41]

Judy Erola, the president of the industry association, responded to Guyatt by stating that "I must admit that had I not known the identity of the author, I would have immediately assumed that it was written by someone from another time and place, and certainly not by a physician operating in the health care environment of the 1990s."[42] She went on to say that "attempting to restrict unduly the access of physicians-in-training to an industry whose medicines and supporting information will play a critical role throughout their careers will neither enhance their knowledge nor contribute to the health of their patients, either now or in the future."[42]

Guyatt and the guidelines were praised by some, and one of those letters recounted a story about when the author, Dr. Ernest Stearns, appeared before the House of Commons Committee on the Status of Women in May 1992. At that appearance, he made the point that "the pharmaceutical industry profits from the manufacture of drugs and biologicals used [to treat] breast cancer and, counter to its newspaper and television ads, its contribution to research is disgraceful." About two months later, he received a letter from Gordon Postlewaite, the executive director of the industry association, in which Postlewaite called his remarks "disparaging" and "uninformed." Postlewaite also sent copies of the letter to the dean of the medical school at Queen's, the associate dean of research and the two scientists funded by the industry association.[43] Guyatt was also severely criticized by a number of doctors, including ones associated with other Ontario medical schools.[44,45]

CONCLUSION

One of the earlier pieces of advice that I got about how to function as a doctor was "see one, do one, teach one." What medical students and residents see when they look around at the position of industry in the medical schools that they attend or the academic health science centres where they work will inform what they do and what they tell others to do. What they see now is a permissive attitude towards industry that for many makes interacting with industry part of the norm of being a doctor. That's the message that they will take forward in their own interactions with industry and when they in turn become teachers. The evidence shows an overall lack of strong policies about conflict of interest and an absence of any sustained efforts at teaching medical students how industry promotes its products or how students might manage this interface with industry. Studies also show that residency programs tend to disregard the issue of these relationships.

Surprisingly, relatively little has been done to investigate the attitudes of residents towards industry, but the few surveys that do exist often show that their attitudes are lax. On a positive note, whatever initiatives have been taken to develop policies about interacting with industry have come largely from the residents themselves. In particular, Guyatt's move to limit interactions between residents and industry in the general internal medicine program at McMaster in the early 1990s was explicitly endorsed by the residents.

The question is, what message do we want to impart to future doctors about their relationship with the pharmaceutical industry? Do we want to teach them that industry and medical education share the same values or that the two may not be compatible?

CHAPTER 8

DOCTORS, SALES REPRESENTATIVES, SAMPLES, GIFTS, TRIPS AND DINNERS

Until now, this book has primarily focused on how medical organizations, societies, institutions and schools relate to the pharmaceutical industry, but ultimately it is the individual doctor who writes the prescription for her or his patient. That action is the end of the chain, the one that is the most important and the one that companies try to influence through their interactions with doctors.

In the late 1980s, the Pharmaceutical Inquiry of Ontario documented that doctors in that province had much more extensive contact with drug companies than they had with professional sources of information. For high-volume prescribers that level of contact was even greater. "They are . . . more likely to have contacts with the pharmaceutical companies, and these latter contacts are substantially more numerous. On average, physicians who write more than 70 prescriptions per week are visited by pharmaceutical company representatives once each week."[1] Although the activities of sales representatives within hospitals is not the focus of this chapter, companies devoted considerable efforts in that area as well.[2]

Companies bombard doctors with offers to engage with them. Over the span of a single year from November 1999, an Alberta doctor received 120 invitations (ninety for dinner) from multiple companies to attend various continuing medical education events.[3] By 2005, brand-name companies were spending over $1 billion a year to reach the seventy thousand doctors in Canada (see Table 8.1) primarily through detailing, the practice of company sales representatives visiting doctors individually in their offices or in groups, funding meetings and leaving behind samples of their products for doctors to give to patients. Complete figures about all forms of promotion for 2015 are not publicly available, but according to the 2015 annual report from IMS Brogan, companies were spending a total of $563 million on sales representatives and journal advertising.[4] In a 2016 survey, 46 per cent of physicians said that they had been retained by a pharmaceutical company in some capacity at some point in their career and the majority of that 46 per cent agreed with the statement, "I would not be able to serve my patients as well without the information provided to me by the pharmaceutical companies I have professional relationships with."[5] But trust in the industry by doctors is not a given. In 2015, doctors gave the industry a score of 5.3 out of 10 in terms of how trustworthy it was in providing guidance on ethical business practices when it came to the relationship between pharmaceutical companies and Canadian healthcare professionals.[5] (The Canadian Medical Association scored 7.4 on the same survey, while the generic drug companies got a score of 4.6.) Paradoxically, although

doctors didn't think that industry association member companies were trustworthy in the guidance they gave, 73 per cent
still thought that the industry followed a strict code of ethical practices when it came to its relationship with Canadian
healthcare professionals, although only 40 per cent thought
that the industry was transparent.[5]

Table 8.1: Promotional expenses, 2005

Category	Amount ($)
Detailing*	648,753,377
Meetings	154,498,089
Samples	152,268,010
Print advertising	75,034,866
Clinical trials	13,482,591
Mailing	12,325,430
E-promotion	9,890,499
Total	1,066,252,862

*Detailing is the practice of drug company representatives visiting
doctors either individually in their offices or in groups to promote
products that their companies make.
Source: CAMMCORP International (Marc-André Gagnon, personal
communication, January 15, 2011)

After first looking at how companies have, over the
years, promised to reform their interactions with doctors,
the rest of this chapter will investigate the various forms of
interactions — visits by sales representatives, leaving behind
samples and offers of gifts, trips and dinners.

PROMISES OF CHANGE

For a long time, companies have claimed that they are
changing how they interact with doctors. In 1977, Guy

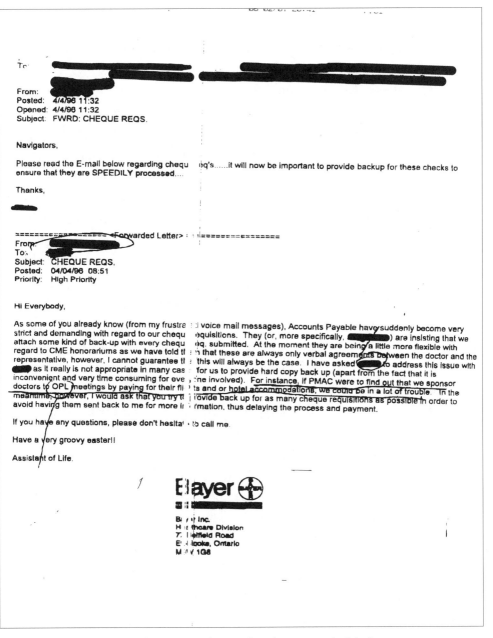

To:

From:
Posted: 4/4/96 11:32
Opened: 4/4/96 11:32
Subject: FWRD: CHEQUE REQS.

Navigators,

Please read the E-mail below regarding chequ eq's......it will now be important to provide backup for these checks to ensure that they are SPEEDILY processed....

Thanks,

=========-========= <Forwarded Letter> ==================
From:
To:
Subject: CHEQUE REQS.
Posted: 04/04/96 08:51
Priority: High Priority

Hi Everybody,

As some of you already know (from my frustra d voice mail messages), Accounts Payable have suddenly become very strict and demanding with regard to our chequ quisitions. They (or, more specifically,) are insisting that we attach some kind of back-up with every chequ eq. submitted. At the moment they are being a little more flexible with regard to CME honorariums as we have told tl n that these are always only verbal agreements between the doctor and the representative, however, I cannot guarantee tl this will always be the case. I have asked to address this issue with as it really is not appropriate in many cas for us to provide hard copy back up (apart from the fact that it is inconvenient and very time consuming for eve ne involved). For instance, if PMAC were to find out that we sponsor doctors to OPL meetings by paying for their fli ts and or hotel accommodations, we could be in a lot of trouble. In the meantime, however, I would ask that you try t ovide back up for as many cheque requisitions as possible in order to avoid having them sent back to me for more ii rmation, thus delaying the process and payment.

If you have any questions, please don't hesita to call me.

Have a very groovy easter!!

Assistant of Life.

Bayer 🜨

B y Inc.
H thcare Division
7. lotfield Road
E looke, Ontario
M V 1G8

Figure 8.1: Bayer admits to violating the pharmaceutical industry
association's marketing code

Beauchemin, executive vice-president of the pharmaceutical industry association, said that the pharmaceutical industry was reorienting its promotional activities and that his organization was extremely interested in continuing medical education, which "must be entirely divorced from marketing."[6] In 1994, Gerry McDole, president of the Canadian subsidiary of Astra Pharma, said that his company was altering the way that it related to doctors and would tone down advertisements directed at them and devote more resources to continuing medical education courses and patient information. Under its new policy, Astra was only going to advertise a new product for a couple of years, until the company felt knowledge of the medication had spread and was going to devote a bigger portion of spending to continuing medical education for doctors.[7] In the same year, Searle said it was attempting to change its marketing to better meet physicians' needs; for instance, by giving money for a conference on echocardiography that was run independently by the University of Toronto. The company said it had also retrained sales representatives to put less emphasis on the product and more on understanding physicians and how they work.[8] Also in 1994, Judy Erola, president of the industry association, said that brand-name drug companies were working with New Brunswick to set up a training program for doctors who are overprescribing drugs. "Many of the problems are with older drugs that doctors are no longer getting information about," she said.[7] At the start of 2003, the industry association eliminated payments by companies for expenses, grants and honoraria to physicians attending continuing medical education events, other than those participating in the role of faculty (i.e., speaking at or moderating programs) or having a significant organizational responsibility for events.[9] (See Chapter 6 for more on this particular change to the industry association's code.)

As of January 2005, the industry association overhauled its marketing code to outlaw handing out tickets to physicians for drug company–sponsored tables and activities at charity events and explicitly required employees of member corporations to offer drinks and food "that are modest in content and cost." Previously, it had been left to the discretion of individual companies to decide what a "modest" meal was,[10] but the revised code also did not define what "modest" meant. To counter perceptions that drug firms can improperly influence doctors' prescribing habits, Julie Lamatrouille, speaking for the industry association, said that there would be no expenses-paid trips to medical meetings in tropical locales, no more lavish meals at high-end restaurants and, specifically, no more golf tournaments.[11] In January 2006, the code was updated again, expanding three guiding principles to eleven, with changes to the infraction process and resolution system. For instance, the Industry Practices Review Committee was going to expeditiously review and adjudicate complaints and impose strict penalties for violations of the code.[12] A few years later, Russell Williams, the president of the industry association, was confident that "we [industry and those involved in continuing medical education] can work together to develop a 'Made in Canada' collaborative approach [to conflict of interest] that will improve the quality of care and the health of our citizens."[13]

COMPANIES AND BREACHES OF THE CODE OF ETHICAL PRACTICES

At times, companies are caught in gross violations of the provisions of the industry association's code about interacting with doctors. By way of example of how embarrassing those infractions are to the companies that get caught see Figure 8.1, where in a series of emails Bayer officials in 1996 openly admitted that they needed to hide their wining and dining of doctors. One person who termed herself "Assistant for Life" said "if [the industry association] were to find out that we sponsor doctors to . . . meeting by paying for their flights and or hotel accommodations, we could be in a lot of trouble."

A 2001 *Globe and Mail* story enumerated a series of violations of the industry association's marketing code by a number of companies: "Bayer Canada treated doctors to four hours of golf, a brewery tour and dinner with their spouses at Dartmouth's Grandview Golf and Country Club last year. There was less than an hour of educational content. Janssen-Ortho and Schering Plough paid for doctors' Friday-to-Sunday stay, including meals, at the Manoir Saint-Saveur, a four-star ski resort in Quebec's Laurentian mountains this February [2000], in exchange for their attendance at about six hours of workshops and presentations on women's health. Smithkline Beecham feted doctors with a fancy meal and a Royal Winnipeg Ballet performance in Vancouver, salsa lessons and food at a trendy bar in Toronto in the name of diabetes education late last fall."[14]

AstraZeneca, in 2004 the second-largest drug company in Canada, had its membership in the industry association put on probation and was fined for an "unprecedented" number of violations of the group's code of ethical conduct. In one case, the company paid for doctors to attend an educational session at the Ritz-Carlton Hotel in Jamaica. In another case, the company provided airfare and accommodation for physicians to go to a conference on the French Riviera and AstraZeneca provided doctors with form letters to request funding for the trip.[15]

The pharmaceutical industry association's Code of Ethical Practices has penalties for violating the code starting at $25,000 and escalating to $100,000 for a fourth breach in a year.[16] However, with companies spending upwards of $30 million on promotion (see Table 8.2), a fine of $100,000 may be seen as just the price of doing business.

Table 8.2: Company spending on sales representatives and journal advertising, 2015

Company	Amount spent ($ 000)	Number of products promoted
AstraZeneca	34,411	5
GlaxoSmithKline	26,645	3
Servier Laboratories	20,759	2
Merck Canada	18,441	5
Takeda Pharmaceuticals	17,901	4
Janssen Inc.	16,839	2
Boehringer Ingelheim	16,523	4
BMS Pharma	14,669	2
Pfizer	12,178	2
Lundbeck Canada	12,146	1
Bayer Healthcare	11,486	1
Abbott EPD	8,104	1
Astellas Pharma	8,094	1
Valeant Pharma	7,782	2
Warner Chilcott	7,699	1
Lilly	7,592	1
Purdue Pharma	7,414	2
Forest Laboratories	6,786	1
AA Pharma	6,515	1
Novartis Pharma	5,376	1
Sunovion Pharma	3,660	1
Novo Nordisk Canada	3,517	1
Shire Canada	3,287	1
Paladin	3,113	1
Galderma	2,905	1
Actavis Specialty	2,753	1
Biosyent	2,752	1

Source: IMS Brogan[4]

SALES REPRESENTATIVES AND DOCTORS

In the early 1960s, Canadian doctors, on average, were seeing 11.5 detailers per month and spending thirteen minutes with each of them.[38] A member of a Canadian Medical Association delegation to a House of Commons committee in the mid-1960s said, "I have always had an open office to them . . . They bring information on new drugs and perform a service."[17] At that time, the vast majority of both general practitioners and specialists were more likely to hear about new drugs from sales representatives than from any other source of information, either commercial or non-commercial,[18] and they were seen as by far the most informative and acceptable form of promotion.[19] The majority of doctors also rated them as good or excellent on their personality, honesty and reliability but were not as convinced about their level of general knowledge, knowledge of drugs in particular and usefulness.[19]

A decade later, in the mid-1970s, there seemed to be even more skepticism about sales representatives' knowledge and their motivation for visiting doctors. A 1976 survey of Maritime specialists and general practitioners found that only 13 per cent used sales representatives "frequently" as a source of drug information and a further one-quarter used them "sometimes."[20] By the 1980s, sales representatives were behind medical journals and discussions with colleagues as a source for changing the prescribing behaviour of Canadian internists, surgeons and gynaecologists[21] and were considered a useful source of information by only 36 per cent to 56 per cent of family doctors.[22,23] In 1989 to 1990, that figure was down to under 19 per cent of doctors in Ontario[24] as well as nationally.[25] By the mid-1990s, 80 per cent of doctors believed that sales representatives overemphasized their products' effectiveness, 45 per cent thought that they did not fairly present the negative aspects of the drugs that they were promoting and over 90 per cent thought that they had product promotion as a goal,[26] and this downward trend has continued.[27-29]

But other data makes it clear that there is a fair degree of confusion about how doctors actually relate to sales representatives. In the early 1990s, sales representatives were the second most frequently used source of information about medications.[25] From 1998 to 2002, the number of sales representatives in Canada grew from 3,000 to 5,100.[30] In the mid to late 2000s anywhere from 75 per cent[31] to over 90 per cent[32] of doctors continued to see sales representatives, some doctors as often as one a day,[31] and a third of doctors would see them at any time of the day.[32] In 2009, 88 per cent of doctors who saw representatives said that they did so for the information that they provided.[32] In 2015, just over a third of doctors were not seeing sales representatives, but 11 per cent saw six or more a month[5] and in that year there was a total of 3,720,000 visits, including 111,000 for Coversyl (perindopril, used for high blood pressure), 100,000 for Breo Ellipta (fluticasone furoate/vilanterol, used for asthma) and 73,000 for Invokana (canagliflozin, used for diabetes).[4]

Drug companies spent almost $650 million paying the salaries and expenses associated with sales representatives in 2005. (See Table 8.1.) Why? In the words of Paul Levesque, vice-president of marketing for Pfizer Canada, "One-on-one interaction is still the most effective way to get our [the industry's] message across."[14] In 2015, companies were still spending almost $550 million on sales representatives.[4]

Elements of the leadership of the Canadian medical profession have been supportive of sales representatives. As late as the mid-1980s, influential Canadian family doctors, including the chairman of the Department of Family and Community Medicine at the University of Toronto and family physician-in-chief at the Toronto General Hospital, were telling family physicians to use sales representatives, among other sources of information, when they were considering introducing a new drug into their practice.[23] In the early 1980s, officials with the Canadian Medical Association denied that sales representatives engaged in a "hard sell."[33] This attitude from the leadership of the association was repeated in 2006 when its then president, Dr. Robert Ouellet, saw no need for action on how doctors interacted with sales representatives because, according to Ouellet, "I don't think there is much influence [on prescribing]. I'm not sure doctors will change their mind each time they see a rep."[34]

Sales representatives usually come into doctors' offices knowing more about their prescribing habits than the doctors themselves by virtue of the information that the companies buy from IMS Brogan. The company collects prescriptions from thousands of pharmacies across Canada. Although it removes patients' names from the prescriptions, the names of the doctors who wrote the prescriptions are recorded along with a variety of other information about the drug and the doctor. This data is then aggregated into groups of ten or more doctors, but individual physicians can be identified within these groups, along with their level of prescribing.[35,36] (The practice of buying prescription data is not allowed in British Columbia as a result of an amendment to the bylaws of the College of Pharmacists of British Columbia by the government in 1997.[37]) This information, along with notes about doctors that sales representatives make when they visit physicians, is then used to target doctors individually. The CBC TV news show *Disclosure* interviewed a former sales representative in 2002 who explained how this process works: "What that [the information from IMS Brogan] tells a rep is how many prescriptions Dr. X is writing of my specific drug. It's very, very detailed . . . I think a lot of companies, what they try to do is to target their efforts . . . So I am selling an antibiotic and I know doctors in the 'A' class tend to prescribe a lot of antibiotics — that's where I want to focus all of my efforts."[36] Two drugs that had tens of thousands of sales representatives visits in 2000 — Vioxx (rofecoxib, used for pain and inflammation) and Baycol (cerivastatin, used for high cholesterol) — were pulled from the market by 2005 because of safety issues.[38] Judy Erola defended the sale of prescribing profiles on the grounds that companies were using them to help guide doctors in proper medication management. Although she thought that doctors should be informed that drug company sales representatives had detailed information about their prescribing practices, she could not say whether she would recommend to industry association members that they tell doctors about possession of this information.[39]

COMPANIES' DEFENCE OF SALES REPRESENTATIVES

The industry's view about the role of sales representatives has been consistent for the past fifty years. Companies justify them because of their supposed educational role, but in reality because of their value in increasing sales. In his 1966 testimony to the House of Commons Special Committee on Drug Costs and Prices, the president of the industry association referred to these people as "highly-trained professional representatives."[40] All of the various versions of the marketing code or code of ethics from the pharmaceutical industry since the 1960s have contained passages about how sales representatives are supposed to conduct themselves and the quality of information that they should provide to doctors.

The brand-name industry founded the Council for the Accreditation of Pharmaceutical Manufacturers Representatives of Canada (now the Council for Continuing Pharmaceutical Education) in 1969. (It is currently a requirement that sales representatives complete the accreditation course offered by the council within two years of commencing their employment.[41] There are currently 250 to 300 hours of study in two units: anatomy and physiology, and pathophysiology and pharmacology, at the end of which there is a multiple-choice exam with a minimum passing grade of 60 per cent.) Initially, the course was one year with final exams held in a Canadian university "setting." The result, in the opinion of the director of the council, was supposed to be a graduate who "provide[s] accurate information supported by adequate documentation on all topics of the physician's concern as they relate to drugs."[33] In the *CMAJ* of December 9, 1978, Dr. Kenneth O. Wylie, then president of the Canadian Medical Association, issued a blanket endorsement of detail men — at that time virtually all were men — who had taken the accreditation course. His endorsement was in the form of a letter, written on the official stationery of the president of the Canadian Medical Association, and gave the impression that Wylie was stating an official association position rather than his personal opinion.[42]

Dr. Norman Eade from McGill University investigated the council in the 1970s. He reported that the council had no teachers and conducted no classes; all coursework was done by mail. The functional staff consisted of one administrator and a secretary. The "Canadian university setting" where the exams were written was a room rented at a university. The council refused to make a copy of the text or core material available for Eade's inspection. A representative exam was largely of the true-false variety, including questions on the rates of profit of various industries and other matters unrelated to the safety or efficacy of drugs.[43] Eade concluded: "This program is a ploy to make the detail men more convincing in their presentations. Doctors are often very naïve and they don't have much time to review data on drugs."[33]

In the early 1980s, multiple companies were touting the virtues of their sales forces. David Brand, vice-president of marketing at Smith, Kline & French (now part of GlaxoSmithKline), said most of his company's fifty sales representatives were science or commerce graduates and a few were pharmacists.[44] Percy Skuy, president of Ortho Pharmaceuticals, said in 1982 that the image of pharmaceutical sales people had changed in the past decade. They were more professional, better educated and bound by a strict code of ethics established by the industry association.[45] Also in 1982, the position of John Stewart, associate director of scientific affairs at Purdue Frederick, was that "the role of the detail man [sic] [was] to provide accurate information supported by adequate documentation on all topics of the physician's concern as they relate to the company's drugs."[33] About a decade later, Carol Southcombe, manager of sales training and development for Glaxo, said that "The level of training that we provide [to our sales force] in the pharmaceutical industry generally is much higher than other industries because of the type of product we're selling."[46] In the late 1990s, Lee Marks, the industry association's director of policy development, said that as far as she was aware, there had never been a complaint about a sales representative giving misleading information about a drug.[47] The 2010 word from the industry association about sales representatives was, "**Detailing helps improve patient care** [emphasis in the original]. Provider-supported detailing generates awareness about new treatments and provides science-based and Health Canada approved advice on how to administer these medications. Conversations between health care providers and representatives of Canada's research-based pharmaceutical companies focus on the appropriate use of medicines, but represent just one of the many factors that doctors consider when making their prescribing decisions."[48]

The following three examples, over a period of almost three decades, show that reality often does not match the industry rhetoric about its sales force. In an interview in *Maclean's* in 1980, a sales representative for McNeil Pharmaceutical candidly acknowledged that his job entailed "perceiving needs, or creating them." McNeil hired this representative at the age of twenty-one, when his work experience amounted to three years of driving an ambulance. One of the drugs he sold was Haldol (haloperidol), an antipsychotic medication. However, his company training did not deal with what mental illness is. "Diagnosis is the doctor's job," he believed. "Besides, I can't see how that would help us sell."[49] Between 1989 and 2006, one Victoria-area sales representative distributed gifts like pens and notepads (now no longer allowed under the industry association's code), brought in meals or took doctors and clinic staff out for meals. He organized luxurious weekend "medical education" events featuring drug company–paid speakers in locales like Whistler. Another Victoria-area representative who worked between 2002 and 2009 once met with a physician who was heading an institute. They discussed the drug company possibly funding research chairs in return for its drugs being prescribed by all the institute's doctors.[50]

The 2016 version of the Code of Ethical Practices says:

- "4.2.1 Member employees must act in accordance with the highest professional and ethical standards at all times. They are expected to understand and abide by the Code whenever they are acting in a professional capacity.

- "4.2.3.1 All employees should have sufficient knowledge of their subject matter, reflecting the requirement of their professional practice. Employees interacting with Health Care Professionals must have sufficient knowledge of general science and product specific information to provide accurate and up-to-date information."[16]

Whether the representatives do this in practice was recently investigated in a study led by Dr. Barbara Mintzes that I was involved with. General practitioners in Montreal and Vancouver were asked to fill in survey forms after they had seen a representative. The primary outcome measure was presence of "minimally adequate safety information," defined *a priori* as mention of one or more of the following: approved indications, serious adverse events, common non-serious adverse events and contraindications *and* no unapproved indications or unqualified safety claims (e.g., "this drug is safe"). "Minimally adequate safety information" was provided in five of 412 (1.2 per cent) promotions in Vancouver and seven of 423 (1.7 per cent) in Montreal. Representatives did not provide any information about harms (a serious adverse event, a common adverse event or a contraindication) in two-thirds of interactions.[51] In a promotion of the drug Avandia (rosiglitazone) in August 2009, one Vancouver doctor reported that the sales representative's key message was that the drug was "safe in patients not in congestive heart failure." Another doctor, in Montreal, reported in December 2009 that the sales representative said that "Avandia is safe even in patients with heart disease as long as they don't suffer from heart failure" (Barbara Mintzes, personal communication, October 17, 2016). The sales representatives were delivering these messages despite a 2007 meta-analysis that linked the use of Avandia to a significant increase in the risk of heart attacks and a borderline significant increase in the risk of death from cardiovascular causes.[52]

DRUG SAMPLES

Providing drug samples to doctors has long been a way for sales representatives to see doctors. One company official testified before the Restrictive Trade Practices Commission in the early 1960s that "A representative [of the company] must usually 'bribe' his way into the doctor's presence by the offer of free samples in generous volume,"[53] and this point of view was confirmed in a 2009 survey where 85 per cent of doctors in Ontario and Quebec said that they saw sales representatives in part for the samples that they received.[32] Many doctors feel that samples are a way of providing therapy to patients who are unable to afford the cost of a prescription[54,55] and companies give away huge volumes of samples to doctors. In 2015, there were over fourteen million samples distributed for the top fifty drugs (as measured by the amount of money spent promoting them).[4]

In the mid-1960s, companies justified the use of samples on the grounds that "it is important for a doctor to be personally acquainted with a new drug and its results before he prescribes it with confidence."[53] This is still the position of the pharmaceutical industry association in the 2016 version of its Code of Ethical Practices where it says, "When used appropriately members believe [drug samples] are an important tool for Health Care Professionals and provide benefit to patient health outcomes . . . Their main use is to, when appropriate; determine a patient's clinical response to drug therapy before a full course of therapy is prescribed."[16] Some doctors also express essentially the same rationale for accepting samples. Here is the view of one Maritime pediatrician: "[I]f there are new things on the market that are supposed to be better, I'd rather have patients trying them first — and seeing if they are of any use to them — before asking them to go out and buy them."[56]

In the past, there were widespread reports of doctors receiving unwanted samples. A study of drug sampling in 1967 discovered that about one-quarter of all samples received by doctors were unwanted. One doctor who had requested no samples received samples of thirteen different drug preparations.[57] In July of 1973, Dr. Murray Katz wrote in the *Montreal Star* that in one month his mail included twelve different unsolicited samples.[58] This type of delivery is no longer an issue as doctors need to sign a receipt every time they receive a sample, but problems with samples persist.

224 DOCTORS IN DENIAL

All sixteen family medicine teaching units at the University of Montreal were surveyed in 2013 about their use of samples. Only half of the units had written institutional policies governing the management of samples. Most of the doctors and nurses who dispensed samples did not know if their units had written policies about how to manage samples, or if they had guidelines for the selection of samples or a list of acceptable samples. Three-quarters of the healthcare professionals who dispensed samples reported that sometimes they were unable to find the medications they sought; half of those said they ended up giving the patient another drug.[55]

GIFTS, TRIPS AND DINNERS

The industry association revised its marketing code in 2004 to prohibit its membership from offering doctors "any gift — in cash or in kind, or any promotional aid, prize, reward, or any item intended for personal/family benefit, or pecuniary advantage"[59] and as we have already seen in Chapter 6, that same year it also prohibited companies from offering to pay for travel costs and accommodation for doctors attending conferences within Canada. But while these changes to the code changed the nature of the inducements offered to doctors, the inducements themselves continued more or less unabated. What follows is a chronological list of gifts, trips, dinners and other blandishments that were offered to doctors over almost four decades that either I personally know of or that became public knowledge through the media.

In September 1978, I was at a major Canadian family practice conference in Charlottetown at the time that Muhammad Ali was fighting Leon Spinks for the heavyweight boxing title. One of the large multinational companies rented a suite in the hotel and set up a large-screen television so that any doctor attending the meeting could drop by to watch the match while drinking a beer or some wine. I declined to go, but many other attendees were in the suite.

Here is how Dr. Philip Berger, at that time a Toronto family physician, described what went on at one Toronto conference in 1983. He said, "the participants' educational materials included lottery cards. If doctors spent their time usefully (as judged by detail men) in interactions at drug company booths, they received one red dot for good performance. The red dot was then affixed to the lottery card. After collecting 25 red dots (there are usually 50 company booths at medical conferences) the physicians deposited their cards in a lottery bin. At the end of the conference, several cards were drawn with the winners receiving $100 from the companies represented at the conference." At another company booth "a sleeping-pill manufacturer challenged doctors to press a button in the shortest time possible after a detail man said go. The leaders' scores and names were prominently posted, with a winner declared at the convention's end."[60]

Towards the end of the 1980s, a number of examples of gifts came to light. Perhaps the most publicized was the provision of computers by Squibb (now part of Bristol-Myers Squibb) as part of a postmarket study the company was carrying out. (A postmarket study is one that looks at a product after it has been approved for sale.) Two thousand doctors across Canada received computers valued at $2,000 if they enrolled ten patients into the drug trial. At the end of the trial, Squibb would retain ownership of the computers but doctors would be allowed to keep them in their offices and continue to use them.[61] The College of Physicians and Surgeons of Ontario eventually reached an agreement with Squibb under which the computers remained the property of Squibb, although they remained in the doctors' offices indefinitely, as long as they were participating or planning to participate in future Squibb studies, or studies approved by Squibb. Linda Franklin, a spokeswoman for the college, said that the college would rely on doctors to abide by the agreement they signed with the company regarding use of the computer.[62]

At the same time as Squibb was offering computers to doctors, one Calgary doctor received a free trip to Rome and accommodation at a luxury hotel to attend an international conference on gastroenterology. His estimate was that the trip cost the drug company about $5,000. A southern Alberta representative for a drug firm recounted other similar, if not quite as expensive, examples in the late 1980s: "'Lending' a VCR to doctors to view an educational tape promoting their product. The rep 'forgets' to collect the VCR from doctors who switch patients to that company's drug . . . Doctors given $50 a head by a drug company for each patient switched to a new slow release drug which has no competition."[63]

At the 1989 Alberta College of Family Physicians Chapter Annual Scientific Assembly, "Meals, funspiels and other 'happenings' sponsored by pharmaceutical companies . . . helped draw the crowds back from the slopes" to the hotel where the conference was being held.[64] Around the same time, 57 per cent of Ontario doctors were accepting meals from drug companies, 48 per cent accepted stationery such as prescription pads, 10 per cent accepted conference fees, almost 3 per cent took computer hardware or software, and nearly 2 per cent took office services. Compared to other physicians, the highest prescribers accepted significantly more benefits: 68 per cent accepted meals, 60 per cent accepted stationery,

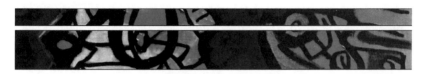

You are invited to attend

New Long-acting Injectable Antipsychotics - Considerations in the Homeless and Underserved Population

At the end of this program, participants will be able to:

- Discuss challenges common to treating schizophrenia in patients who are homeless or living in supportive housing
- Update on the use of new long-acting injectable antipsychotics (including demonstration)
- Interactive group discussion on the audiences' case examples and questions

SPEAKER: **Jorge Soni, MD, FRCPC**
Psychiatrist, Centre for Addiction and Mental Health (CAMH)

DATE: **Thursday, November 15th, 2012**

6:00pm reception

6:30pm dinner and presentation/discussion

LOCATION: Morton's, The Steakhouse

4 Avenue Road (at Prince Arthur), Toronto, ON

To RSVP to this program (or for any Risperdal Consta or Invega Sustenna questions): contact Eunice Youhanna at 416-382-5000 ext. 3091 or EYouhann@its.jnj.com

This program is sponsored by Janssen Inc.

Figure 8.2: Janssen invitation to Morton's, The Steakhouse

You are cordially invited to attend an evening presentation on:

PSA testing (latest recommendations)
followed by **Testosterone Deficiency Syndrome**

Dear ████,

We are very pleased to invite you to participate in an upcoming CME entitled:

PSA testing (latest recommendations) followed by Testosterone Deficiency Syndrome

Speaker:	████
	Urologist, University of Toronto
Location:	The Ruth's Chris Steak House, 145 Richmond Street West, Toronto, ON M5H 2L2
Date:	Tuesday, March 26, 2013
Time:	Registration at 6:30 pm / Meeting commencing at 6:45 pm

At the conclusion of this educational program, participants should have a better knowledge of:

- PSA Testing, latest recommendations
- Prostate Health
- Testosterone Therapy, is there an impact on the prostate?
- The diagnostic approach to testosterone deficiency syndrome
- Available treatments options and the benefits and risks of therapy
- How to monitor patients on testosterone replacement therapy

We would be most pleased to count you among our participants. Please note, in accordance with the Rx&D Code of Conduct, this event is only open to healthcare professionals.

Places are limited; please kindly RSVP before Tuesday, March 19, 2013 to ████ by:
Fax: 514-340-7836, e-mail: ████@paladinlabs.com, or phone: 1-888-376-7830 Ext. 5448.

REGISTRATION FORM

Yes, I will attend ☐   No thank you, I cannot attend ☐

Participant:	████
Address:	Davenport Perth Community Health Centre , 1900 Davenport Rd
City:	Toronto
Tel.:	14166586812
Fax:	14166584611

**PLEASE CONFIRM YOUR ATTENDANCE by fax, e-mail or phone
by March 19, 2013**

paladin

RECEI████
FEB 20 ██3

Figure 8.3: Paladin invitation to The Ruth's Chris Steak House

and 7 per cent accepted computer hardware or software. As the authors of this survey pointed out, these figures did not measure the total number of benefits received, only whether physicians received at least one benefit in a category; many would have received multiple benefits.[24]

In 1991, Dr. Philip Berger "was offered $5,000 unconditionally by a drug company to attend an international AIDS conference." Berger declined to go but later discovered that without his knowledge or consent the company had paid his $600 conference registration fee. Five years later, another company offered him $1,000 to attend an AIDS conference. Another example Berger gave of industry largesse was that "AIDS physicians and AIDS activists [we]re regularly appointed to so-called company advisory committees at honoraria of up to $1,000 a day — advisory sessions consisting of elegant dinners and a day of listening to company presentations."[65]

In 2000, the *Globe and Mail* reported how Glaxo Wellcome (now merged with SmithKline Beecham and called GlaxoSmithKline) flew Dr. Stephen Barron, a family physician in Port Coquitlam, from Vancouver to Montreal for a day of work, paid for his meals and hotel bill and gave him $1,500. He was "under the impression he was taking part in developing influenza education for Quebec's licensing authority for doctors . . . [but in fact] he was being asked to design an educational presentation for Relenza [zanamivir, a drug for the treatment of influenza]."[14]

The CTV public affairs show *W5* in 2002 followed a group of doctors to Montego Bay in Jamaica where they were staying in rooms costing more than $600 per night, all expenses paid courtesy of Boehringer Ingelheim. In return, all the doctors had to do was attend some seminars about arthritis drugs and hear about the benefits of a Boehringer product. One rheumatologist, Dr. Wally Pruzanksi, justified taking the trip on the basis that he had sacrificed some of his income to go to the meeting in order to be educated. He denied that he felt obligated to the drug company.[66]

In spring of 2005 the *National Post* ran a series of articles about the pharmaceutical industry. The first one opened with the story of how in February of that year a group of Montreal doctors enjoyed food free of charge at Canada's top new restaurant of 2004 courtesy of Biovail, and in addition took home a $350 honorarium. "Cardiologist Colin Rose, who was there, describes the session as a thinly veiled 'sales job' for [the company's] new hypertension drug. Later that night, the company handed out invitations to another event a few weeks later, at the Casino de Montreal, this time to evaluate training of the company's sales representatives. It was to be capped with free admission to the casino's 'souper spectacle' show, doctors' spouses welcome. The honorarium was $400."[67] (A year earlier, the same Dr. Rose was offered an honorarium of $6,000 for referring patients for a trial of two cholesterol drugs.[67])

In 2012 and 2013, Toronto doctors were invited by Janssen (Figure 8.2) and Paladin (Figure 8.3) to eat, drink and hear lectures about long-acting injectable antipsychotics and testosterone deficiency syndrome at two upscale steakhouses, Morton's and Ruth's Chris, respectively, so it seems that doctors are still able to avail themselves of fine food courtesy of the pharmaceutical industry. According to Russell Williams, head of the industry association, these meals should never have taken place. "We [the industry association] do not allow for lavish dinners . . . Those are banned."[68] (Williams retired from his position in June 2016.)

CONCLUSION

How do doctors who accept various perks from drug companies really feel about these companies? Do some doctors think that they are "putting one over on the companies" by eating their food and drinking their wine? Since most doctors accept samples, does that translate into an affinity for the companies or merely the belief that samples are necessary in a country where many people cannot afford to purchase prescriptions?[69]

Companies spend hundreds of millions each year to reach Canadian doctors by sending their sales representatives to their offices or the hospitals where they work, using samples to ease their way in when personal relationships are not enough and enticing doctors with free meals, gifts and trips. The industry marketing code is an inadequate tool for controlling what goes on. Although the industry association has disciplined companies that have violated its Code of Ethical Practices, the effectiveness of the sanctions is highly questionable. The organization does not actively monitor compliance with the code but instead relies on complaints, often from other companies. Four of the six permanent members of the committee that adjudicates complaints are either company or industry association employees and the two healthcare professionals are appointed by the organization's Board of Directors.[41] Perhaps most critically, the industry association regulates itself through its own internally developed code. As Kawachi and I have previously written, the mission of trade associations is primarily to increase sales and profit. From the business perspective, self-regulation is mostly concerned with the control of anti-competitive practices, not to protect public values. Therefore, when industrial associations draw up their codes of practice, they deliberately make them vague or do not cover certain features of promotion, in order to give companies wide latitude, thereby allowing misleading advertising tactics that are typically good for increasing business.[70]

Nor does it seem that we can rely on the medical profession to regulate itself. One previous president of the Canadian Medical Association, Dr. Henry Haddad, acknowledged that it is wrong for doctors to accept gifts, because a gift implies obligation: "Your dealings with the pharmaceutical industry must not come between you and your patient and we [the association] feel that accepting gifts, accepting trips, whatever order is wrong." But the medical association is powerless to stop doctors from taking drug company perks. As Haddad said, "The [Canadian Medical Association] is not a police. [The association] has no role in enforcement. We can't sanction physicians."[66]

CHAPTER 9
DON'T WORRY, BE HAPPY?

The preceding chapters have laid out the evidence for a set of interactions between the pharmaceutical industry and the Canadian medical profession that have resulted in a comingling of interests. These interactions take many forms and are not just seen in one element of the medical profession but involve all of medicine's organizations and institutions as well as individual doctors. In some cases, anecdotes are the only evidence for these interactions, but in many instances there is high-quality systematic research establishing that the interactions are real, long-standing and deeply entrenched. At the same time they are also dynamic, reflecting changes in public attitudes and professional values.

The task of this chapter is to see whether there is any reason to be concerned about these interactions and relationships. The major question is whether patient care is negatively affected in any one of a number of dimensions: do drugs cost more than they otherwise would have, has the interaction between medicine and the industry led to a bias in the way that doctors prescribe, do the interests of society come first and do patients get the correct medications such that serious side effects are minimized and the maximum benefit is realized? Before moving on to address these questions, it is important to note that the relationship that I have been describing is not one-sided. The material that I have presented clearly indicates that the medical profession has been a willing and active participant with the pharmaceutical industry and, therefore, if any reforms are going to be necessary, they need to come from the medical profession.

CANADIAN MEDICAL ASSOCIATION SUPPORT FOR INDUSTRY POSITIONS

Chapter 2 looked at the Canadian Medical Association's support for industry positions on a couple of issues: compulsory licensing and direct-to-consumer advertising of prescription medications. Prior to the introduction of compulsory licensing, a series of reports in the early to mid-1960s established that Canadians were paying among the highest prices for drugs in the world. The response from the government of the day was to bring in compulsory licensing to import generic drugs. This move was deeply opposed by the pharmaceutical industry; organized medicine, primarily the Canadian Medical Association, allied itself with industry.

Compulsory licensing was successful in reducing overall drug expenditures. According to the Eastman Commission report, it saved Canadians at least $211 million in a 1983 market for pharmaceuticals of $1.6 billion.[1] Compulsory licensing was replaced by a federal agency, the Patented Medicine Prices

Review Board, that sets a maximum introductory price for new patented medications and then limits increases in prices to the rate of inflation until the patent expires. Under the review board, Canadian prices are once again near the top of the industrialized world. Average per capita spending per year on pharmaceuticals for the thirty countries in the Organization for Economic Cooperation and Development in 2013 was $515 US. Canada was fourth from the top at $713 US. (The United States was in first place at $1,026 US.[2]) The Canadian Medical Association was an active but secondary participant in getting the government to first limit compulsory licensing and later eliminate it, and therefore must assume some of the blame.

One of the motivations behind the medical association's actions (and those of other medical societies and institutions) was the desire to encourage pharmaceutical research and development (R&D) in Canada. The industry promised more R&D in exchange for getting rid of compulsory licensing and initially kept that promise. But as of 2015, drug company spending on R&D as a percent of sales was 4.4 per cent, compared to 6.1 per cent in 1988.[3] The Canadian Medical Association cannot be held accountable for the fact that the industry did not keep its promises, but perhaps it can be held accountable for being unduly naïve about how likely it was that the industry would live up to its commitments.

Although it later reversed its position, initially the medical association was quite supportive of allowing direct-to-consumer advertising in Canada on the grounds that patients would benefit from the additional information that they would get. The push by industry to change the government's position on direct-to-consumer advertising was ultimately not successful, but the federal government did make changes to allow partial direct-to-consumer advertising. Currently, Canadians can see television ads telling people that there is a new drug for a particular condition and that they should consult their doctor for more information, and ads that mention the name of a drug and provide broad hints about what it is used for.[4] Did the medical association's position on direct-to-consumer advertising in the mid-1990s make it easier for the government to justify the changes it made in how that advertising was regulated?

CANADIAN MEDICAL ASSOCIATION JOURNAL (AND OTHER JOURNALS)

Dr. Alan Klass made the point in his 1975 book, *There's Gold in Them Thar Pills*, that regardless of the content of the advertisements, their mere appearance in prestigious medical journals implies apparent approval. The top people in medicine publish in such journals, which lends the journals a special cachet that even extends to the advertising. The implicit approval of the ads is further reinforced by the fact that advertising in journals is generally limited to items associated with medical practice, primarily pharmaceutical products. Klass went on to say: "In a curious way . . . because of the disciplined habit of obedience to the guidance of leaders . . . the imprint of the drug manufacturer's advertisement obtains a subtle and persuasive impact on the professional reader. As a result of sophisticated insight by the advertiser, the trick in the advertising message is not only the message itself but the media."[5] Or, in the words of Marshall McLuhan, "the medium is the message."[6] The same point was echoed in 1992 when Dr. Bruce Squires, the *CMAJ* editor, insightfully said that "pharmaceutical firms need the journal's integrity so they can say, 'Yes, we are putting our advertisements in a highly respected journal.'"[7] Yet the *CMAJ* does not seem to have taken Squires's message to heart, as it continues to run ads for medications. Until the *CMAJ*, and other medical journals, recognize that the medium is the message, the drug ads that appear in them will go on influencing doctors, if not through their content then through the legitimacy that the journal confers.

PARTICIPATION IN INDUSTRY-FUNDED RESEARCH

Industry funds virtually all clinical trials before drugs are marketed and the vast majority of those in the postmarket stage.[8] As we have seen in Chapter 4, academic health science centres are eager to get industry involvement in order to increase the amount of research that takes place within them, especially as federal money is increasingly difficult to get. Total health R&D funding from the federal government barely moved from 2003 to 2009, going from $1.031 billion to $1.339 billion; and the Canadian Institutes of Health Research budget has remained essentially static, going from $993,663,000 in 2007 to 2008[9] to a planned $1,008,584,000 in 2015 to 2016.[10]

However, industry funding comes with a serious downside. My colleagues and I did a meta-analysis that showed that when drug companies pay for clinical trials, those trials are much more likely to have both positive results and positive conclusions than if any other source provides the money for them.[11] We concluded that "industry sponsorship should be treated as bias-inducing."[11] The implication of our meta-analysis is that doctors' understanding of how effective and safe drugs are may be distorted and many drugs might be less effective and less safe than we assume. The ones that directly suffer from these false assumptions are the patients and, in a publicly funded healthcare system, taxpayers.

KEY OPINION LEADERS, CONFLICT OF INTEREST AND CONTROL OF INFORMATION

Information that doctors receive can be manipulated by drug companies in a number of ways — through the talks that key opinion leaders give, through the development of clinical practice guidelines, in the choice of topics that are covered by continuing medical education and through the content of those education courses. In each of these forms, conflict of interest can play a key role in shaping the information that doctors get. When authors have a conflict of interest, research has shown that their publications are associated with a more positive image of the product(s) that they are writing about than when a conflict is absent. This finding comes from research about the conclusions of clinical trials in general[12] and original research in a variety of specific subject areas[13] such as calcium channel blockers (a group of drugs used to treat high blood pressure and various heart problems),[14] hormone replacement therapy for postmenopausal women[15,16] and rosiglitazone (Avandia, used for treating diabetes).[17]

Key opinion leaders are not hired because of the number of prescriptions they write as individuals but, in the words of one firm that specializes in managing key opinion leaders for drug companies, because their talks, research, publications, positions in professional societies and other actions can influence the prescribing habits of a very large proportion of practising doctors.[18,19] One way of judging the importance that pharmaceutical companies place on key opinion leaders is the fact that roughly one-third of companies' marketing budgets are spent on them.[20,21] In the US, this amounts to an average of about $38 million US on each product as it moves from clinical testing to launch.[22] The decision to spend this amount of money is not haphazard, but is based on corporate research into the prescribing behaviour of doctors. According to an internal Merck document, US doctors who attended a lecture by a key opinion leader on Vioxx (rofecoxib) each wrote an additional $623.55 worth of prescriptions for the drug over a twelve-month period compared with doctors who didn't attend. "After factoring in the extra cost of hiring a doctor to speak, Merck calculated that the 'return on investment' of the doctor-led discussion group was 3.66 times the investment, versus 1.96 times for a meeting with a sales representative."[23] Whereas in 1998, in the US, the number of talks by sales representatives and key opinion leaders were about equal at just over sixty thousand each annually, by 2004 there were almost twice as many talks by key opinion leaders compared to sales representatives[23] — a reflection of the economic benefits that key opinion leaders bring.

Clinical practice guidelines have the potential to play an important role in directing clinical practice and informing quality improvement initiatives.[24] However, in the area of psychiatry, Dr. Lisa Cosgrove has found that there is an association between conflict of interest and poor use of evidence. All of the members of the committee of the American Psychiatric Association that developed the organization's Practice Guideline for the Treatment of Patients with Major Depressive Disorder had conflicts of interest; members on average reported 20.5 relationships each. Fewer than half (44.4 per cent) of the studies supporting the recommendations met criteria for high quality and 17.2 per cent did not measure clinically relevant outcomes. One-fifth (19.7 per cent) of the references were not congruent with the recommendations.[25] What's true of guidelines in psychiatry is also likely to apply to guidelines in other areas.

Committees developing clinical practice guidelines in Canada have significant numbers of members with conflicts. As noted in Chapter 5, in fifteen out of twenty-eight guidelines at least one author, and in eight guidelines over half of the authors, disclosed conflict of interest with manufacturers of drugs that they recommended.[26] Should the US findings about the use of evidence by committees where members have conflicts of interest apply to Canadian clinical practice guidelines, then many of those may be based on a poor interpretation of the evidence.

Should we be concerned about how well various professional bodies develop and regulate continuing medical education? When the Canadian Medical Association cooperates with companies such as Pfizer to deliver education, it lends an air of legitimacy to Pfizer's role as an information provider, thereby distancing Pfizer's message from the company itself and making it more credible to doctors. Both the College of Family Physicians of Canada and the Royal College of Physicians and Surgeons of Canada only accredit continuing medical education when company money comes in the form of unrestricted educational grants, i.e., companies are not supposed to have any direct role in the design of the content or in the choice of speakers — but they definitely do decide on what events they are willing to fund.

There has not been any systematic analysis of the actual content of Canadian continuing medical education courses that have received industry funding, so it is necessary once again to fall back on literature from the US, some of it relatively old. At one conference sponsored by industry, the policy was that the content had to be controlled by the institution (and not the company), generic names had to be utilized and alternate therapies had to be appropriately identified and addressed. Despite this policy, products made by the company sponsoring the conference were mentioned much more often than comparable products made by non-sponsoring companies.[27] A second study looked at three conferences at the same institution that were each heavily subsidized by a single, but different, company. The policy at the institution stated that the program director was responsible for all course content and speakers, generic names were to be used at all times and drug company representatives attending the course needed to be identified by a name badge. All the same, when prescribing was monitored after the courses, the sponsoring drug company's products were favoured over equivalent products.[28] A third study looked at the range of topics offered through continuing medical education when the education was directly supported by industry compared to when the funding came from multiple sources including industry and the course director was shielded from direct contact with industry. There were 221 talks with multiple funding sources and 103 where industry provided all the funding. The former group covered 133 separate topics whereas the latter group focused on thirty topics, most of which were linked to recently approved new therapeutic products manufactured by the funders.[29]

The Accreditation Council on Continuing Medical Education, the body that accredits continuing medical education in the US, claims that the results of these three studies are no longer relevant. The organization makes the point that all three were conducted before the latest revision to its standards and that when these new standards are followed, there is no evidence that industry sponsorship leads to bias in the content of continuing medical education.[30] However, there are questions about how objective the accreditation council is in the way it interprets bias in continuing medical education.[31] Moreover, research into the effects of bias is often coloured because doctors deny that they personally will be influenced by attending industry-sponsored events.[32]

Finally, industry-sponsored continuing medical education may encourage off-label prescribing, i.e., prescribing for uses not approved by Health Canada. In the US, Kesselheim and colleagues found that off-label prescribing of medications by physicians was encouraged through teaching and research activities, including continuing medical education. In over half of the cases in their study, speakers chosen for continuing medical education were known to promote off-label medication use.[33] Also in the US, Steinman and colleagues found that drug companies use continuing medical education activities as a venue for direct-to-physician promotion in order to convince both current prescribers and non-prescribers to increase new prescriptions.[34]

GUIDELINES FROM MEDICAL ORGANIZATIONS

Medical organizations that speak for the bulk of Canadian physicians, such as the Canadian Medical Association, regulatory bodies that license doctors to practise and groups that certify doctors as family physicians or specialists have all devoted considerable time and effort to developing guidelines for how doctors should interact with industry. One could argue that these are largely public relations efforts and that is why the policies have serious flaws and why they are not enforced in any meaningful way, but I believe that what we are seeing is the conflicted nature of these bodies and a reluctance to challenge existing patterns of behaviour. The important question is whether the strength of these guidelines, and how well they are publicized and monitored, really effects two groups — the doctors to whom they apply, and the public at large.

Doctors outside of leadership positions in medical organizations may not even be aware of the existence of guidelines. In one survey of active clinical investigators at the University of California San Francisco and Stanford University in the US, fewer than half of the interviewed investigators could accurately describe their campus's conflict-of-interest policy.[35]

Maintaining (or restoring) public confidence in the medical profession is often cited as one of the main reasons organizations develop policies, but this assertion has never been actually tested by surveying the public. As an analogy, have the policies of licensing bodies about sexual relationships between doctors and their patients made a difference in either doctors' behaviour or how the public views the medical profession? The answer seems to be that no one has ever looked into the question. So, in short, while it makes sense to think that strong policies about conflict of interest that are widely disseminated and that are actively monitored would be beneficial, there is no hard data to back up that assertion.

MEDICAL STUDENTS AND DOCTORS-IN-TRAINING (RESIDENTS)

While we may not know how conflict-of-interest policies affect the behaviour of practising doctors, there is evidence from Canada and the US that they affect the way that medical students and residents practise once they get out into the real world, i.e., stronger policies are associated with

244 DOCTORS IN DENIAL

more skeptical future relationships with drug companies. Attending a US medical school with a restrictive policy on accepting gifts from companies was associated with a reduced risk of prescribing a newly introduced psychotropic medication once doctors were out in practice.[36] Psychiatry residents in the US who graduated after their residency programs adopted maximally, moderately and minimally restrictive conflict-of-interest policies were all much less likely to prescribe heavily promoted, brand reformulated and brand antidepressants than those who graduated before their programs adopted the policies. Differences were greatest in those who went through the program with the maximally restrictive policy.[37] Canadian internal medicine residents who graduated after their program adopted a restrictive policy about interactions with pharmaceutical companies were less likely to find information from sales representatives useful, compared to residents who either graduated before the policy was introduced or residents who graduated from another program that had no such policy.[38]

Based on the conclusions of these three studies, it should be concerning that policies in most medical schools and residency programs in Canada are relatively weak or are nonexistent.

INDIVIDUAL DOCTORS

In a survey of Canadians,[39] whether the public was concerned about the relationship between individual doctors and the pharmaceutical industry clearly depended on the type of interaction being described. Overall, one third of 1,041 participants reported a prior concern about physician–pharmaceutical industry relationships. The acceptability of interactions was high when doctors requested information from drug companies about a particular drug or when doctors accepted small gifts of obvious educational value to patients. It was mixed when doctors took free meals in exchange for listening to pharmaceutical industry personnel or accepted payment to attend a conference, and it was low when doctors took money for entering patients into research studies or when they made personal use of medication samples.

If the public is not overly worried about certain types of interactions, specifically small gifts or requests from companies for information about medications, does that legitimatize them and mean that we shouldn't worry about them affecting patient care? The answer comes from studying what is known as the gift relationship. The Introduction described what happened when people were approached by members of the Hare Krishna Society as one example of how the gift relationship works. Other, more formal research, demonstrates the effects of gifts on personal attitudes. In one such study, half of a group of university students were given coffee mugs, worth about $6 at the university bookstore, emblazoned with the university logo, and half did not receive a mug. Those given a mug rated its value more than twice as high as those not given one.[40]

Subtle exposure to promotional items, i.e., gifts, has been associated with changing perceptions about the value of equally effective drugs. Medical students at two different schools in the US were asked to take part in a survey about their attitudes towards two similar drugs used to treat high cholesterol — Lipitor (atorvastatin) and simvastatin. In one group, students signed in on a clipboard that had a Lipitor logo and completed the questionnaire on a form with a Lipitor logo, while in the other group the clipboard and the questionnaire form had no logos. Students who were exposed to the Lipitor logos had much more favourable attitudes towards that product than did students who had not been exposed.[41]

Samples are an entry strategy for sales representatives. Even doctors who would not normally see sales representatives are willing to do so to get samples for their patients. Doctors rationalize the acceptance of samples on two grounds — testing the value of new drugs and saving people money — but both rationales have serious flaws. In the first case, the idea that doctors can make a judgment about the therapeutic value of a drug by using it on a couple of patients flies in the face of why companies are required to conduct large-scale clinical trials before they can market their products. The benefits of drugs can only be determined through rigorously conducted trials where the experimental therapy is compared to either a placebo or an existing therapy. In addition, because new drugs have only been tested on a few hundred to a few thousand highly selected patients before they reach the market, knowledge about their safety is very limited and safety problems only become evident once the drug has been in use for three to five years. It is in this period that drugs start to acquire serious safety warnings due to problems that may not have been recognized when they were first marketed.[42–44] Research also strongly suggests that samples distort the way that doctors prescribe. When drug samples are available, doctors dispense them even though the particular drugs are not their preferred choice for the patient's problem.[45] Similarly, when distribution of samples of drugs used to treat high blood pressure was prohibited at a US family practice clinic, prescriptions for first-line drugs for the treatment of this condition increased;[46] i.e., in the absence of samples patients got better care.

Second, the common practice of companies is to give doctors samples of the newest and usually most expensive products. When doctors in turn give those samples to patients, they may save people money in the short term. But unless those samples will get people through a full course of treatment, and this only applies in a small minority of cases, e.g., antibiotics for infection, then when those patients need a renewal of their prescription they will be purchasing products that may be no better, but are virtually certain to be more expensive, than drugs that have been on the market longer. Doctors who take samples tend to prescribe those drugs. Since most samples are for new, more expensive drugs, it makes sense that the prescriptions written by doctors who work in clinics that use samples are more costly than prescriptions written by doctors who work in clinics that don't accept samples.[47] After samples were removed from one US family medicine clinic, doctors were three times more likely to prescribe generic drugs to patients who lacked insurance for drug costs than when samples were available.[48] Ironically, it is exactly for this group of patients that doctors accept samples, but the availability of the samples ends up costing the patients more.

In Canada, even though generic drugs are more costly than in other countries,[49] savings from getting a prescription for a generic drug can still be substantial: the average 2015 cost of a generic prescription was $20.92 versus $91.92 for a brand-name prescription.[50] Doctors tend to believe that giving out samples increases patients' satisfaction with therapy,[51] but it is questionable how satisfied patients are when they find out how much they will need to pay in the long term. Doctors are not in a position to even be able to answer the question about costs. Doctors' guesses about the cost of a prescription are only within 25 per cent of the actual amount one-third of the time, and they consistently overestimate the cost of inexpensive products and underestimate the cost of expensive ones.[52]

I was part of a group that looked into how exposure to information that comes directly from pharmaceutical companies — reading journal ads, seeing sales representatives, attending pharmaceutical sponsored meetings, receiving mailed or emailed information, using industry-generated prescribing software and participating in industry-sponsored clinical trials — affects prescribing patterns. What we wanted to know was what happens to the quality of prescribing, the cost of prescribing and the frequency of prescribing. What we found when we examined the results of fifty-eight studies was that there was only one example of prescribing getting better. Otherwise, there was either no effect on prescribing or it got worse — quality deteriorated, prescribing was more frequent and more expensive.[53]

CONCLUSION

At the start of this chapter I posed the question about whether or not we should be concerned about the interactions and relationships between the Canadian medical profession, collectively and individually, and the pharmaceutical industry. In some cases, the answer is clear; the relationship has contributed to negative effects, e.g., on drug prices and overall expenditures, the quality of continuing medical education and the exposure of medical students and residents to conflicts of interest, and far-reaching reforms are necessary. In other cases, such as advertising policies of medical journals, government policy about direct-to-consumer advertising and guidelines from various organizations about how to relate to industry, evidence is lacking or it is unclear. Finally, at times — e.g., effects on the quality of research and prescribing and the evidence base for clinical practice guidelines — I am relying on international, mainly American, experience, in concluding that there are negative effects.

In the Introduction, I said that this is a book about Canada and therefore, it seems only fair to ask if relying on American material is appropriate. My answer is a tentative, but still reasonably firm, yes. The companies are the same on both sides of the border — American multinationals in the US and their Canadian subsidiaries here — and while there may be some differences in the way that they operate, to a significant extent the policies of Canadian branch plants are determined in the US. Medical culture is the product of many forces, including "the historical evolution of a distinctive set of institutionalized relationships among the state, industry, physicians, and disease-based organizations,"[54] but there is substantial cultural overlap between Canada and the US. While we cannot map what happens in the US between doctors and industry directly onto Canada, the relationship in that country can point to what may be going on here and, at the very least, should serve as a basis for a much more thorough analysis of the Canadian situation when evidence is currently lacking.

In cases where there is no Canadian evidence, should we be introducing major changes in the relationship even before we have undertaken enough research to definitely establish that there is a problem? Here I turn to the precautionary principle that states that behaviour should be framed and enforced to emphasize safety rather than risk when present-day scientific knowledge alone cannot provide clear answers.[55] In the case of medications, safety writ large means the way that drugs are researched and knowledge about them is transmitted to doctors and using medicines in the most cost-effective way, both for individual patients and society as a whole. Risk is the reasonable chance that safe use of medications will not be respected. Based on the precautionary principle, I advocate taking action even though we will sometimes be acting on information from another country. The final chapter will outline what actions I think need to be taken.

CHAPTER 10

REFORMING THE COMFORT ZONE SO THAT DOCTORS ARE NO LONGER IN DENIAL

The preceding chapter showed that there is good evidence that interactions between the pharmaceutical industry and the medical profession have a negative effect on the way that doctors prescribe and on the quality of therapy that patients receive. Here I examine what can be done to either end the interactions or to change their nature such that they are no longer a major cause for concern and that doctors no longer remain in denial about the effects of their relationship with the pharmaceutical industry on their patients.

The text in this chapter lays out the general principles behind the needed reforms, drawing on experiences from Canada and other jurisdictions. Table 10.1 then translates these principles into concrete recommendations for what should be done.

NEOLIBERALISM AND ITS RELATIONSHIP TO THE INTERACTION BETWEEN THE MEDICAL PROFESSION AND INDUSTRY

Front and centre, we need to acknowledge that what we have seen are not examples of a "few bad apples" in an otherwise well-functioning system, but a systemic failure to constructively manage the relationship between the medical profession and the pharmaceutical industry. This failure extends to the three main actors in this relationship — industry, government and the medical profession itself. The final party involved, that suffers the consequences of this relationship is, of course, the general public.

The alliance started well before the onset of neoliberalism in the early 1980s, but neoliberalism exacerbated the problems that already existed and shaped the form that the alliance now assumes, and limited the range of responses that are acceptable to deal with the consequences of the alliance.

Broadly speaking, neoliberalism's core philosophy is a belief in the superiority of unregulated markets.[1] Neoliberal theory claims that a largely unregulated free market economy achieves optimum economic performance with respect to efficiency, economic growth, technical progress and distributional justice. Applying these basic tenets, the conclusion is that corporate self-regulation is superior to government regulation and that, to the extent possible, governments should set out broad regulatory objectives but leave the actual regulation to corporations. Or, to use a metaphor, government should steer the boat, not row it.

As neoliberalism gained increasing momentum in the mid-1980s, federal and provincial governments in Canada began to "withdraw from direct intervention and responsibility in the health sector, encouraging private corporations and the 'market' to take increasingly greater roles in organising the design and delivery of health care."[2] At both levels of government this withdrawal is seen in privatization, e.g., Air Canada and the ongoing privatization of Hydro One in Ontario. In the healthcare area, it is evident in the opening of private for-profit MRI clinics,[3] a private blood collection service[4] and in the adoption of public-private partnerships. Public-private partnerships "are contractual arrangements between government and a private party for the provision of assets and the delivery of services that have been traditionally provided by the public sector."[5] They are predicated on the notion of combining what each sector does best. The government is supposed to guard the public interest by deciding what is necessary in the way of infrastructure or services. The financing, construction, operation and maintenance is turned over to the private sector that is allegedly more efficient in these areas, thereby guaranteeing efficiency and economies of scale. The underlying assumption that the private sector is superior or even equivalent to the public sector when it comes to healthcare delivery is difficult to accept given the history of public-private partnerships failures when it comes to hospital construction and management both internationally[6] and here in Canada.[7,8] Mayes and colleagues point out that "The increasing commercialisation of health care, through neoliberal policies of privatisation and rhetoric of funding cuts, creates a scenario where commercial influences, and associated conflicts of interest, are simultaneously pervasive and increasingly accepted as a normal part of contemporary medical education and medical care."[2]

The alliance between medical organizations and the pharmaceutical industry can be seen as analogous to the ideology behind public-private partnerships. There is the acceptance that the medical profession and industry are necessarily interdependent, and that the former needs the resources of the latter to effectively serve the public and that any resultant conflict of interest can be managed. Drawing further from the analysis by Mayes and colleagues, the normalization of conflicts of interest at the organizational level "can be seen in the role of professional societies and codes to monitor and guide the conduct of individuals."[2] The use of professional codes of ethics is central to the illusion that there is an attempt to resolve the incompatibility between public service and conflict of interest. These codes appear to demonstrate concern, and enable an evaluation of the behaviour of both the organizations that have developed them and the physicians whose practice they are meant to govern. However, these codes have no real power, as they are rarely publicized, monitored or enforced. "When it becomes known to a public that professional conduct is not adhering to these codes of behaviour — for example by interacting with private industry — the role of the professional society or leaders is to 'periodically make speeches reaffirming the profession's resolution to sustain high ethical standards of performance that justify the public's trust.' Statements of apparent ethical commitment and self-critique made by professional societies serve to normalise certain behaviours and activities and inoculate the profession against loss of public trust and protect against more drastic interventions such as external review or regulation . . . Closely related to normalisation is the individualising effect of neoliberalism. Neoliberal reforms and policies tend to undermine collective thinking, action and responsibility. Instead, the individual comes to be seen as the basic unit of society. The individual is responsible for their own actions and is encouraged to work on and develop their self as if it is an enterprise."[2]

Piecemeal changes are not sufficient to make fundamental changes in the way that the medical profession and industry interact. Neoliberalism is not simply manifested in the subject matter of this book, but is intimately woven into the fabric of contemporary society and as such its effects on the medical profession cannot be overturned simply by trying to change the relationships that this book has been describing. However, even in the absence of calling for a complete overthrow of the current political/economic system, major changes to make the comfort zone less comfortable are an achievable objective.

INDUSTRY'S ROLE

Out of the three actors, we should expect the least from industry as its allegiance is first and foremost to its shareholders, not to the public interest. In the late 1970s, a representative of the British pharmaceutical industry was quoted regarding why drug companies were operating in developing countries: "I would just be talking rubbish if I were to say that the multinational companies were operating in the less developed countries primarily for the welfare of those countries . . . They are not bishops, they are businessmen."[9] What was true of developing countries forty years ago is still true of developed countries today. Companies often preach about acting in a socially responsible way but, when scrutinized, there is little to back up that talk. According to Consumers International, within the European Union, companies "have embraced the concept of corporate social responsibility . . . as an appropriate response to the mounting pressures to live up to their social and ethical responsibilities. Many companies proudly flaunt their [corporate social responsibility] objectives in their annual reports, on their websites and their public relations activities."[10] A Consumers International investigation of the actual European promotional practices by twenty large multinational pharmaceutical companies found that corporate social responsibility was honoured more in the breach than in the practice. Of these only two, GlaxoSmithKline and Novartis, reported the number of confirmed marketing code breaches and resulting sanctions. Consumers International could not find any information about the European marketing policies for eight companies. According to Consumers International, "[t]he absence of clear marketing policies for these companies is remarkable, given that irresponsible marketing practices form a serious, persistent and widespread problem among the entire pharmaceutical industry . . . A particularly worrying trend shown by our research is that the difference between policies and practices is often striking."[10]

Chapter 8 showed how Canadian industry-generated codes cannot be relied upon to control the behaviour of individual companies. Recently, the industry association has been touting a new set of ethical standards called the Canadian Consensus Framework for Ethical Collaboration. The Framework is meant to guide collaboration among patients, healthcare professionals and the pharmaceutical industry and is a Canadian version of a parallel international initiative. Besides industry, the Framework is endorsed by Best Medicines Coalition, Health Charities Coalition of Canada, the Canadian Medical Association, the Canadian Nurses Association and the Canadian Pharmacists Association.[11] According to the industry association, "The Framework provides guidance on activities like clinical trials, continuing health education, conferences, accountability and funding, and sets out four overarching principles: Ensures patients' best interests are at the core of activities; Promotes transparent and accountable conduct; Sets clear rules on gifts, funding and conferences, continuing health education and clinical research; and Guides national ethical leadership." The Framework is not meant to replace the codes of individual organizations but rather to enhance credibility, increase public confidence and create an environment that will improve patient outcomes.[12] As of late 2016, beyond being a vague statement of aspirational goals, what this Framework actually means in practice or the extent to which its principles have made any impact is unknown.

GOVERNMENT'S ROLE

The medical profession would never accept direct government interference in what is typically termed the practice of medicine or clinical freedom, and that is why governance of doctors has been turned over to independent regulatory professional colleges. On the other hand, government does have a legitimate role in controlling corporate activities (product promotion and the money that companies give to doctors through gifts, trips and dinners). It also has a duty to help ensure that doctors are getting reliable and objective information about the drugs that they prescribe (without dictating the contents of that information), to provide funding for research into the effects of medication (again without directly controlling that research) and to ensure that everyone has access to the drugs that they need without any financial barriers. It should not be acceptable for provincial health ministers to deny any responsibility for dealing with questions such as gifts and benefits from industry to doctors.[13] Measures to address these issues are sorely called for, to diminish the need for the medical profession, collectively and individually, to interact with industry.

Control Medicines Promotion

The promotion of medicines by the companies that make them and the resulting misuse of those medicines by doctors is a long-standing problem, but promotion continues because it works. Pierre Garai, an advertising executive and staunch supporter of the pharmaceutical industry and the free enterprise system in general, in 1964 wrote: "As an advertising man, I can assure you that advertising which does not work does not continue to run. If experience did not show beyond doubt that the great majority of doctors are splendidly responsive to current [prescription drug] advertising, new techniques would be devised in short order. And if, indeed, candor, accuracy, scientific completeness, and a permanent ban on cartoons came to be essential for the successful promotion of [prescription] drugs, advertising would have no choice but to comply."[14]

What was true in the mid-1960s is equally true now and is probably worse as the regulation of promotion has been increasingly turned over to industry as a result of the deregulatory trend that is part of neoliberalism. The material in Chapters 3 and 8 has made it clear that deregulation is ineffective and leads to doctors receiving misleading information. All promotion should be governed by an independent, government-funded agency established in legislation, so that it has the legal authority to monitor and, if necessary, enforce compliance with sanctions.

Organizations connected with drug therapy, e.g., health professional bodies, patient and consumer groups and guideline creation groups, provided that they are independent of revenue from pharmaceutical promotion, could nominate representatives to this agency, but with the final selection being made by government.

In particular, there needs to be more control over the actions of sales representatives, since they are by far the most influential method that drug companies have of changing prescribing behaviour. The ideal solution would be for doctors not to see sales representatives, but it is probably inevitable that some doctors, particularly those in private practice, will continue to do so. (See later in this chapter for a discussion of doctors working in hospitals.) Other countries have recognized this problem and implemented changes. In France, the national Health Products Payment Committee has co-signed a legally-sanctioned contractual agreement with the pharmaceutical industry association referred to as the Sales Visit Charter. The stated goal of the Charter is to reinforce the role of the sales visit in encouraging appropriate use of nationally reimbursed drugs, and to improve the quality of information disseminated. The Charter mandates the provision of approved product information and evaluations of drug efficacy issued by the national health authority, and sets standards for sales representatives' practices. All gifts, including free samples, are banned. In cases of noncompliance, the French National Agency for the Safety of Medicines can ask the manufacturer to revise promotional materials, stop their dissemination or impose fines of up to €10,000. If the agency judges that a company has promoted a product illegally, the Health Products Payment Committee may also impose fines up to

10 per cent of the product's annual sales revenue. However, as of November 2015, no such fines had been levied.[15]

Although the Sales Charter seems to have increased the frequency with which French sales representatives mention harmful effects of their drugs, compared to Canadian and American sales representatives, there is no difference in how often serious adverse effects are mentioned in any of the three countries.[16] The relative ineffectiveness of the Sales Charter may be due to a lack of compliance monitoring. This deficiency could be overcome by recruiting a national sample of doctors who already see sales representatives, and having them complete survey forms after the visits, detailing what information they did or did not receive. This sample could be rotated every six to twelve months to avoid putting undue strain on any individual doctor. Such a survey was carried out in France on a volunteer basis over a fifteen-year period by the independent drug bulletin *La revue Prescrire*. The survey results clearly indicated that there was a strong bias in the information that sales representatives gave to doctors and that doctors can refuse to see sales representatives without jeopardizing the quality of their work.[17] (*Prescrire* discontinued its survey in 2006 because it felt that its fifteen-year history had made it quite clear that sales representatives were not a source of useful information for healthcare professionals and the journal staff planned to move on to projects looking at other forms of promotion.[17])

Require Companies to Declare Payments to Doctors
Even if companies are prohibited from offering gifts to doctors there are still other forms of payment to them that will continue, e.g., speakers' fees, meals, money for serving on advisory boards. These payments to doctors come from

companies' earnings on the sales of their drugs, and under a national pharmacare system (see the section on sampling later in this chapter) most of those earnings will come from the public system. One could argue, therefore, that if it is public money that is paying for the drugs, then the public has a right to see how its money is being spent. In the United States, under the *Physician Payments Sunshine Act*, enacted as part of the *Affordable Care Act*, any manufacturer whose products are paid for by the US government must annually report transfers of value to licenced physicians or teaching hospitals exceeding $10 per instance or $100 per year, along with the recipient's identity and the purpose of the payment. This information is made available in a publicly accessible database.[18] Doctors are free to continue to accept payments but their names, what companies paid them and how much are now public knowledge.

Many doctors claim that their prescribing is not influenced by such payments but by linking prescribing databases and information in the database set up by the *Sunshine Act*, researchers have shown that industry payments to physicians are associated with higher rates of brand-name prescribing when elevated cholesterol is diagnosed.[19] Receipt of industry-sponsored meals with a value as low as $20 US was also associated with an increased rate of prescribing the brand-name medication promoted at the meal and the more meals doctors received the more they prescribed.[20]

Since the Canadian federal government operates a number of public drug plans for groups such as First Nations (aboriginal Canadians) and the military, it could require disclosure as a condition for payment, and these company payments could be linked to provincial prescribing databases in a manner similar to what is being done in the US.

Ten members of the pharmaceutical industry association have announced that starting in 2017 they will voluntarily disclose statistics on their overall payments to health professionals, though stopping short of releasing figures for individual physicians. Forty other members of the organization had yet to announce whether they would also join this initiative as of the end of March 2016.[21] In a radio interview, Russell Williams, the head of the industry association until June 2016, justified this type of approach based on provincial privacy laws. He went on to add, "Now, will there be progress in this area when we see what we can learn together as a society in 2017? We're open to continually improving and monitoring this . . . Society is moving towards this movement of disclosure. We think this is a helpful offering to help show the value of these relationships between our industry and health care professionals."[22] He neglected to say that under this proposal it will be impossible to link payments to prescribing behaviour.

Ensure that Doctors are Getting Objective Information about Drugs
One of the reasons that doctors often give for seeing sales representatives and for going to industry-funded continuing medical education is to learn about new drugs and get updated about drugs that they are already prescribing. However, even when sales representatives leave out significant information about drug safety, doctors often rate the quality of the scientific information that they have received as either good or excellent and say that they intend to increase the number of prescriptions that they write for the drugs mentioned.[16] Seeing academic detailers instead of sales representatives is a much better way of helping doctors

to prescribe appropriately. Under this system, pharmacists (or other healthcare professionals) are trained in educational techniques and visit doctors to talk about ways to improve prescribing. This method, when introduced in a coherent and judicious way, has been shown to be successful in optimizing prescribing behaviour.[23] However, provincial governments need to be much more willing to fund such programs. Presently, there are province-wide programs in only three of ten provinces (British Columbia, Nova Scotia and Saskatchewan) and the one in Alberta closed in 2010 because of lack of funding.[24]

Funding academic detailing is only one measure that governments can take and these programs can be part of something larger, such as the Therapeutics Initiative in British Columbia.[25] In Australia, the independent organization NPS MedicineWise, formerly the National Prescribing Service, gets about $50 million annually from the Australian federal government to help provide evidence-based continuing medical education to twenty-four thousand participating general practitioners.[26] Programs sponsored by NPS MedicineWise have improved prescribing in a number of areas including secondary stroke prevention.[27] As Spithoff points out, at present the public already pays the higher drug costs passed on from industry sponsorship of continuing medical education. Public funding of continuing medical education should lead to drug cost savings for the public.[28] Some of that public money could come from a tax levied on industry to fund education programs, such as the 1.6 per cent tax in France.[29]

Provincial governments could also give money to medical schools to help underwrite the cost of continuing medical education that they provide and could directly subsidize doctors for part of their continuing medical education expenses in a manner similar to that of Ontario and other provincial governments, whereby they rebate most of the money that doctors have to pay for their malpractice insurance.

Provide More Funding for Research Facilities and Clinical Trials

Academic health science centres take money from pharmaceutical companies in part because it is not readily available from other sources. In late July 2016, the federal and Ontario provincial governments announced that they would provide $83.7 and $14.3 million respectively to upgrade hundreds of medical laboratories scattered across the University of Toronto.[30] However, government can do much better. The US population is about nine times that of Canada, but funding for the National Institutes of Health in 2016 was US $32.3 billion,[31] thirty-two times larger than the Canadian Institutes of Health Research's budget of $1.01 billion:[32] therefore, on a per capita basis, US government funding for research is about 3.6 times greater than Canada's. Canada has the capacity to do very good science but the federal government's funding of biomedical research is paltry compared to what happens south of the border, as well as in the UK and Australia.[33] When it comes to clinical trials the entire investment from the pharmaceutical industry in 2015 was $331.1 million.[34] If the federal government directed this amount of money specifically for clinical research, then at least some of the incentive for researchers to ally themselves with drug companies would be reduced and the objectives of the research would be reoriented to be more in line with the real needs of medical practice and public health.

Make Samples Unnecessary

Doctors claim that they see sales representatives to get samples for patients who cannot afford to purchase medications or to see if they respond better to a new drug. A tax-financed national pharmacare plan that provides medically necessary medications at no cost to patients[35] would mean that doctors would no longer need to accept samples for low-income patients. The need to give out samples to see if patients are able to tolerate side effects could be overcome with a program of trial prescriptions whereby patients could get an initial prescription for a short period and then be able to renew it if side effects were acceptable. The argument against trial prescriptions is often that they add to overall expenditures on medications because they increase the dispensing fees payable to pharmacists. This problem can be overcome if the pharmacist is paid one standard "fee for all dispensing related services connected with the trial prescription, and a separate 'cognitive service' fee for the additional monitoring and assessment required to determine whether the balance of the prescription should be dispensed."[36]

THE MEDICAL PROFESSION'S ROLE

Over a hundred years ago, Sir William Osler warned the medical profession about getting in bed with the pharmaceutical industry: "Far too large a section of the treatment of disease is today controlled by the big manufacturing pharmacists, who have enslaved us in a plausible pseudo-science."[37] It is time that doctors paid heed to that warning. As a self-regulating profession, doctors can define for themselves how they do or do not relate to the pharmaceutical industry. If those interactions mean that doctors, individually and collectively, cannot perform the functions that society entrusts them with, then the medical profession has an obligation to reform itself.

Conflict-of-Interest Policies

At the heart of many of the negative effects arising from interactions between the medical profession and industry are the conflicts of interest that are unavoidable. Some people, such as Boston oncologist Dr. Thomas Stossel, take the position that all that is necessary is to declare one's conflicts, and that armed with this knowledge people can then decide for themselves about the validity of the research that doctors produce, the journal articles they write and the talks that they give.[38]

The other side of the argument is that there is no evidence that disclosure is sufficient to resolve problems. "First, physicians differ in what they consider to be a conflict, which makes the disclosure of conflicts incomplete. Because declarations of conflict are usually unverified, their accuracy is uncertain. Second, recipients of information who are not experts in a particular field often find it impossible to identify a biased opinion that they read or hear about in that field. Third, disclosure may be used to "sanitize" a problematic situation, suggesting that no ill effects will follow from the disclosed relationship."[39] A controlled trial has shown that people generally do not discount advice from biased advisors as much as they should, even when conflicts are disclosed. Furthermore, once people have disclosed their conflicts and their audience has been warned, then they feel morally licenced and strategically encouraged to exaggerate their advice.[40]

In order to be acceptable to the medical profession,

policies on conflicts of interest need to come from dialogue within the profession, and its leadership needs to be committed to them, not merely paying lip service or seeing them as window dressing. These policies must apply to institutions and organizations and not just to individuals. Enacting even strict policies is not enough; they need to be publicized and widely discussed so that doctors know what they contain. Finally, compliance needs to be monitored and, if necessary, sanctions levied. To this end, policies need to have clear definitions regarding who will monitor them, how they will be enforced and what the consequences are for violating them. Developing appropriate sanctions is a difficult issue — if sanctions are too weak then they have no deterrent effect, if too strong then they are unlikely to be applied. For these reasons, Ayres and Braithwaite argue in favour of an explicit enforcement pyramid.[41] Using a pyramid approach, the sanctions could range from a simple warning letter for minor violations up to more severe measures such as suspension from a faculty position or the imposition of significant financial penalties. Warnings are more likely to be effective if everyone understands that if noncompliance continues then the individual or the institution will inevitably receive a sanction that will significantly disturb their functioning.

Academic Health Science Centres and Conflict of Interest

Dr. Troyen Brennan and colleagues, in an article in the *Journal of the American Medical Association*, one of the world's leading medical journals, make the case for putting a major focus on academic health science centres, including medical schools and their affiliated teaching hospitals, for being places for developing effective conflict-of-interest policies.

These are places where medical students and residents are trained, major research is performed and the public looks to for the most specialized medical care — and as such are seen to represent the pinnacle of the current medical system. Brennan et al. argue that "Objectivity and scientific integrity should be central tenets of physician training"[39] and in the research that they perform. Academic health science centres "are also in a position to take immediate action [on conflicts of interest] . . . Moreover, independent research into the impact of medications . . . on population health is concentrated in [them]; therefore, unwarranted influence by manufacturers must be avoided. For these reasons, academic medicine should take the leadership in reforms."[39] Conflict-of-interest policies developed for these centres need to address "relatively small items, including meals; payment for attendance at lectures and conferences, including online activities; [continuing medical education] for which physicians pay no fee; payment for time while attending meetings; payment for travel to meetings or scholarships to attend meetings; payment for participation in speakers' bureaus; the provision of ghostwriting services; provision of pharmaceutical samples; grants for research projects; and payment for consulting relationships."[39] Avoidance of visits by sales representatives should be the de facto position. Specifically, these centres should prohibit faculty from serving on speakers' bureaus for companies, or being listed as authors on ghostwritten articles and any and all investigations into allegations of ghostwriting should be made public.

For more than a decade now the Permanente Medical Group, which serves 3.4 million members in Northern California and employs approximately seven thousand doctors, has prohibited doctors from interacting with sales representatives while at work, and banned them from accepting anything of value from a vendor, serving on speakers' bureaus, or being paid to consult with drug and device companies. After the adoption of this policy, only two of the seven thousand physicians left the medical group.[42]

When it comes specifically to medical schools, all of these items in conflict-of-interest policies for academic health science centres are important and, in addition, policies should cover onsite education activities, industry support for scholarships and funds for students and the medical school curriculum. Industry should not be permitted to provide financial support for educational activities, including continuing medical education, either directly or through a subsidiary agency. Any policy must either prevent industry from earmarking or awarding funds to support the training of particular individuals (recipients must be chosen by the school or department). Students and residents need to be trained to understand institutional conflict-of-interest policies.[43] Most importantly, all medical schools should provide education about how industry promotion can influence clinical judgment.[44] Health Action International, an Amsterdam-based nongovernmental organization, and the World Health Organization have combined to develop a manual for teaching medical students about promotion[45] and this should form the basis for a curriculum examining relationships with industry. (Full disclosure: I wrote one chapter in this manual and co-wrote another.)

Medical Societies and Conflict of Interest

Most doctors are members of one or more medical societies and these societies should be providing leadership on questions of conflict of interest. All officials and employees within medical societies should be completely free of conflicts during their employment or tenure in office and for three years before. Medical societies should post a comprehensive annual financial statement that gives all of their sources of income along with the amount from each source. There should be a maximum percentage of total revenue that comes from industry and from any individual company, and the financial statement should provide details about how industry money was used. Organizations that accredit continuing medical education, such as the Royal College of Physicians and Surgeons of Canada, the Conseil québécois de développement professionnel continu des médecins and the College of Family Physicians of Canada, should also develop and make publicly available policies about conflicts and income statements similar to those for medical societies.

Medical Journals and Conflict of Interest

Medical journals are a major source of information on both healthcare news in general and medical advances in particular and are also seen as the voice of organized medicine. They should require editors, editorial teams, editorial boards and managers to be free of conflicts while working at the journal and for three years before; specifically, these people should not have any direct financial ties (for example, stock ownership, speaker's fees, sitting on advisory boards) to any healthcare business advertising in the journal that they edit or work for. Journals should emulate what the *BMJ* already does and publish earlier versions of manuscripts along with reviewers' and editors' comments on the Internet so that readers can see the forces that went into revisions in the tone and content of published articles. This evidence of the lineage of an article could help detect the origin of any biases.[46] In addition, for articles based on original research, journals should require the publication of the data so that others can confirm (or refute) the conclusions of the article. Journals should publish detailed information about their sources of income, including the amount that they get from the sale of reprints, supplements and advertising, and produce detailed financial analyses to show why it is necessary to continue to accept industry money. Smaller specialized journals such as *Emergency Medicine Australasia* have decided to forgo drug advertising completely. According to the journal's editors, "It is time to show leadership and make a stand, and medical journals have a critical role to play in this . . . At *Emergency Medicine Australasia* we have, therefore, drawn a line in the sand, and have stopped all drug advertising forthwith . . . We invite other journals to show their support and follow suit by declaring their hand and doing the same."[47]

If journals find that individuals have signed on to ghost-written articles as "guest" authors, those people should be banned from publishing in the journal for a long enough period of time to make the penalty meaningful (say five years), the relevant article(s) should be retracted and the penalty and the retraction should be made public. Alastair Matheson, himself a former independent consultant in the pharmaceutical, marketing and medical communications sectors, points out that the problem with ghostwriting goes far beyond just the "wholly secret production of texts for sign-off by academics but is also evident in the extensive role of commercial teams in planning and crafting this literature being recognized only in a footnote." He argues that "ICMJE [International Committee of Medical Journal Editors, representing most of the major medical journals in the world] authorship criteria should be changed, such that writers contributing to manuscript composition or revising the manuscript for intellectual content are required to be coauthors." Further, the committee "should develop guidance on author order, corporate coauthorship, and, most importantly, clear commercial labelling" and that "whenever industry instigates and finances research and owns the data, publications must be presented to readers as industry projects with academic contributions, not spun as academic led ventures."[48]

Finally, the *CMAJ* and other Canadian medical journals should emulate the *BMJ* and refuse to publish certain types of articles from authors with conflicts of interest. Starting in 2015, the *BMJ* only published clinical education articles — editorials, clinical reviews and most practice series — from authors without any financial ties to industry. By the end of 2016, the journal hoped to have extended this policy to the rest of its education section: its specialist state-of-the-art reviews and diagnostics and therapeutics series.[49]

Clinical Practice Guidelines and Conflict of Interest

There have recently been a series of articles dealing with conflicts of interest in clinical practice guidelines, and the following recommendations draw from some of these to ensure that clinicians will regard them as being evidence-based and unbiased. "Individuals should be invited to join guideline panels through an open, transparent application process centred on [rational, public] selection criteria"[50] that should be publicly disclosed in the resulting guidelines. Wherever possible, panelists should be free of any conflicts, and chairs and co-chairs of committees should always be free of conflicts.[51] If it is not possible to include only panelists who are conflict-free, then "nominated panelists must disclose all industry-related professional activities, including research grants and speaker support, and for the duration of guideline development, divest themselves of direct financial interests (stock ownership, board positions, consultancy agreements) in commercial companies with an interest in any guideline recommendation."[50] Panelists should primarily be experts at reviewing scientific evidence and not content experts, since the first task of any guideline panel is to review the evidence to decide if there is an uncontested "best" answer. "To assure guideline readers that panels are not stacked, panelists should declare their a priori beliefs about a proposed intervention at the time they are nominated, and again at the conclusion of the panel's term."[52] Because content experts are generally conflicted when reviewing topics in their own specialty, for the most part, they should be consulted for content/topical issues, but should not be the authors of the guidelines themselves.[52] "Only conflict-free panelists . . . [should be] involved in determining the direction (for or against a specific clinical action) and strength of recommendations [and] lack of consensus around evidence quality or recommendations [should be] resolved by explicit democratic processes involving conflict-free panelists."[50]

Currently, the Canadian Medical Association Infobase (www.cma.ca/En/Pages/clinical-practice-guidelines.aspx) lists guidelines that meet the following criteria: include information to help patients and physicians make decisions about appropriate healthcare for specific clinical circumstances; are produced by an authoritative Canadian organization, or if produced outside of Canada, be officially endorsed by such an organization; have been developed or reviewed in the last five years; and have evidence that a literature search was performed during guideline development.[53] The association should expand those criteria for listing and include the ones about conflicts of interest listed above.

Finally, it's expensive to produce guidelines, but it is possible to do so without drug company money. The budget for a guideline for monitoring the effectiveness and safety of antipsychotic use among children was about $35,500 and Dr. Tamara Pringsheim, an assistant professor in the Faculty of Medicine at the University of Calgary, was able to secure a grant from the Canadian Institutes for Health Research for this guideline rather than going to drug companies. When she was offered an unrestricted grant from a drug company for another guideline, she and her collaborators turned it down, for fear that it might influence their work.[54]

Continuing Medical Education and Conflict of Interest
In late 2007, the Josiah Macy Jr. Foundation, a private philanthropy dedicated to improving the health of individuals and the public, hosted a conference on continuing education in the health professions. (Continuing medical education applies just to physicians, whereas continuing education applies to all healthcare professionals.) Summing up the message of the conference, its chair, Harvard professor Dr. Suzanne Fletcher, wrote that when it came to continuing education, the responsibilities of pharmaceutical companies and healthcare professionals were "fundamentally incompatible" and that "No amount of strengthening of the 'firewall' between commercial entities and the content and processes of [continuing education] can eliminate the potential for bias."[55] Her summary emphasized that "Commercial support for [continuing education]: risks distorting the educational content and invites bias; raises concerns about the vows of health professionals to place patient interest uppermost; endangers professional commitment to evidence-based decision making; validates and reinforces an entitlement mindset

among health professionals that [continuing education] should be paid for by others; [and] impedes the adoption of more effective modes of learning."[55] She concluded by recommending a five-year phase-out of commercial sponsorship for continuing education.

Around the same time, in a controversial editorial, Dr. Paul Hébert, the editor of the *CMAJ*, reinforced Fletcher's messages and called for the creation of an independent Institute of Continuing Education that would be funded through a combination of money from a portion of the profits from each new patented medication, government and the medical profession. His rationale for advocating a new institute was multifold, starting with the observation that industry funding of continuing medical education has built up a culture of entitlement amongst doctors who receive the benefits of free or low-cost education. In his view, industry focuses "primarily on treatments and treatment-related issues at the expense of the larger therapeutic picture, including quality of care and patient safety not involving drugs, determinants of health, prevention and health promotion and other modalities of treatment . . . Physicians are seen as being aligned with the pharmaceutical industry and with its commercial priorities . . . Many of [the] heavily subsidized events use lectures and emphasize counting hours of credit, rather than measuring improved knowledge, competence, performance and, most importantly, clinical outcomes."[56] Hébert's proposed institute would help eliminate conflict of interest by setting guidelines and standards for efficacious, unbiased continuing education. Funding sources would be monitored and accreditation standards set for continuing education providers, with continuing education grants given only to accredited institutions.

Dr. Sheryl Spithoff, in a commentary in the *Canadian Family Physician*, advocated that both the College of Family Physicians of Canada and the Royal College of Physicians and Surgeons of Canada should take up this message of phasing out accrediting continuing medical education funded from industry money.[28] (The same should also apply to the Conseil québécois de développement professionnel continu des médecins.) In the meantime, she strongly recommended that an independent medical body disperse any industry continuing medical education money, and that industry not be allowed to "participate in the planning, development, or delivery of [continuing medical education]" and that both colleges "should prohibit industry involvement in the planning, development, and delivery of [continuing medical education], not just the educational component." She went on to say that the colleges should also "explicitly state in their guidelines that industry is not permitted to suggest speakers or content to the planning committee."[28]

Are these goals possible? In 2008, the 1,300-member Oregon chapter of the Academy of Family Physicians decided to no longer accept any grants — restricted or unrestricted — for its continuing education seminars or to allow drug companies to have booths in its exhibit hall during conferences.[57] Here in Canada, the Yukon Medical Association has banned pharmaceutical industry sponsorship from its annual joint general meeting and continuing medical education weekend since 2007. The move also meant that sales representatives could no longer set up booths at the event.[58] Since November 2014, the Ontario College of Family Physicians no longer accepts funding from the pharmaceutical industry for exhibits or booths at its Annual Scientific Assembly.[59] Dr. Chris de

Gara, the University of Alberta medical school's associate dean of the Division of Continuing Medical Education, was a key driver in the push to reduce his division's reliance on pharmaceutical industry support of continuing medical education. As a result, the university has reduced its continuing medical education offerings by about two-thirds and now runs mostly educational events that are based on its undergraduate curriculum and that have received funding from provincial groups, or for which the university charges tuition fees. The benefit, according to de Gara, was that "we have much greater control over the content and the way in which things are delivered."[60]

Decreasing the frequency of large continuing medical education conferences is not necessarily a bad thing. Research into adult education has shown that the best methods for improving not only knowledge retention but actually changing practice are multiple interventions, active interventions, longer interventions and/or interventions delivered and reinforced over a period of time rather than short, passive, single-event types of continuing medical education such as sitting in a large lecture theatre.[61] Spithoff viewed cutting the ties with industry money as a way for medical organizations to develop educational objectives or a standard curriculum, as currently the development of continuing medical education is haphazard and often determined by industry funding.[28]

Individual Researchers and Conflict of Interest

Financial conflict of interest can occur at multiple stages during a project and investigators may not recognize when they have such a conflict. Bias can creep into a study without anyone being consciously aware of it, but nonetheless it is still present and can distort the findings of a study and how those results are applied in clinical practice. To counter this potential problem, Rochon and colleagues, of whom I was one, developed a standardized checklist that researchers can use to report different aspects of conflict of interest.[62] Such a tool is useful not only to researchers individually, but also to those who fund research, journal editors and those supervising research in academic health science centres, so that conflict of interest can be recognized, recorded and dealt with when it cannot be avoided.

Community Physicians and Conflict of Interest
Doctors working in a community setting are not immune to the problems associated with conflict of interest nor, if they are motivated, are they helpless to do something about it. For example, they can and should refuse to accept samples for the reasons outlined in the previous chapter — such samples distort prescribing choices and end up costing uninsured patients more money. At one family medicine clinic associated with St. Michael's Hospital in Toronto, all twelve doctors voted unanimously to no longer accept drug samples. Dr. Nav Persaud, a spokesperson for the group, said that the decision was taken because accepting samples set a bad example for medical students and residents who do rotations at the clinic as part of their training. According to Persaud, "A lot of younger trainees get into the practice and see it as normal." Persaud also felt that "There is something unseemly and inappropriate about their [sales reps] presence in a clinical setting," as sales representatives would make sales pitches to doctors in areas of the clinic where patients are seen.[63]

Similarly, doctors should refuse to see sales representatives. These people are not objective sources of good information and relying on them, even if other sources of information are used, means at best wasting time checking out their claims and at worst poorer prescribing. Already, in Canada, over a third of doctors say that they do not see any sales representatives.[64] All staff at one Australian general practice clinic agreed to adopt a policy that significantly limited access of sales representatives to doctors: reception staff stopped making appointments for sales representatives to see doctors and stopped accepting promotional material.[65] Sales representatives were not able to access the cupboards where samples were kept and if doctors wished to see sales representatives they had to do so outside of office hours. Nine months after the policy went into place, all staff, on average, were satisfied with its impact, doctors were spending less time with sales representatives, there were no sales representatives' visits booked into the patient appointment diaries and there were no reported visits with sales representatives in the clinic's corridors. In addition, the number of samples was down by 70 per cent and generic prescribing went up. Since 2012, pharmaceutical representatives cannot stop by any of the twenty Kelsey-Seybold medical clinics in the Houston area or meet with its 370 doctors unless a physician requests an appointment for guidance in prescribing certain drugs.[66]

Finally, doctors should refuse to accept any gifts of any kind. The Wisconsin Medical Society has passed a policy that physicians should not accept any gifts from pharmaceutical companies such as textbooks, patient aids, office supplies, food, travel and time costs, or payment for participation in online continuing medical education. The basis for this blanket policy is that it "eases the burdens of compliance, biased decision making and patient distrust."[67]

THE PUBLIC'S ROLE

The final group that has a role to play is the general public, a group that has been largely ignored and is mostly uninvolved in discussions about the relationship between the medical profession and the pharmaceutical industry. However, the public is intimately connected to the economics of medications. Almost all payments to doctors, who do the prescribing, come from tax revenue; the Canadian Institutes of Health Research get over $1 billion annually from government, some of which goes to basic research that is the origin of new drugs; and the public pays $12.5 billion per year for prescription drugs.[68] Even more importantly, members of the public are on the receiving end of the prescriptions that doctors write. For these reasons, the public not only needs to be supportive of any reforms but it should also play a leading role in driving them.

One of the major reasons that so little is heard from the public is the lack of knowledge regarding the extent of the interactions, so the first step is public education. This begins with the disclosure of information that earlier recommendations in this chapter called for — how much money do individual doctors, medical societies and professional regulatory bodies such as the Royal College of Physicians and Surgeons of Canada and the College of Family Physicians of Canada get from drug companies and where does that money go (e.g., meals, trips, funding of educational events, etc.)? How much revenue do medical journals get from advertisements that they run? How often do doctors see sales representatives? How much research that is done in academic health science centres is funded by drug companies and are there any restrictions on whether the information that comes from that research can be published? How often, if at all, do medical bodies such as the Canadian Medical Association or the College of Family Physicians of Canada meet with industry representatives? Rather than wait for academics like me to survey medical schools about their policies regarding relationships with the pharmaceutical industry, medical schools should proactively be releasing this information. How many members of the public are even aware of the various codes, guidelines and policies that organized medicine has developed for relating to industry? The College of Physicians and Surgeons of Ontario, to its credit, did seek out public opinion in 2014 when it revised its policy about how doctors should relate to industry, but more can be done. All of the various bodies representing organized medicine in Canada need to publicize their monetary relationships with industry, their policies about physician-industry relationships and encourage public debate on how medicine and the industry should interact. With more information as a baseline, the public can start to be more involved in the discussion.

Beyond just making sure that the public is informed, there are other concrete steps that can be taken. Currently, there are no public representatives involved in the decision making about the promotion codes from the pharmaceutical industry association and the Pharmaceutical Advertising Advisory Board, although the board invited public input when it revised its code. There is also no public involvement in adjudicating whether there have been breaches of the codes. Both organizations should have to have public membership on their code committees that is independent of any relationship with industry. Medical societies and those organizations that accredit continuing medical education need to seek out public input into what topics are important to patients and how the public feels about continuing medical education being funded by drug companies. If industry money is publicly acceptable, then the public should have a say in how that money is used and what level of involvement industry should have in designing continuing medical education. More generally, these bodies along with medical schools and academic health science centres should be inviting members of the public to voice their opinions about interactions with industry in general. There are currently no members of the public on either the *CMAJ* Editorial Advisory Board[69] or the equivalent of the *Canadian Family Physician*.[70] Without any direct contact with the public how do these journals know that their relationships with industry are acceptable to the public? This situation could easily be corrected by having independent public membership on these boards.

Finally, the public cannot just sit back and passively wait to be invited to the table. It must actively demand to be there. A strong, coordinated public movement can drive changes in health policy, witness the advent of midwifery as a regulated profession in Ontario in the early 1990s, as part of a larger social movement that was critical of maternity care.[71] What happened with midwifery can also happen with drug policy. Individually, patients should be asking their doctors about how they relate to drug companies — how often they speak for the companies, whether they take meals or trips paid for by companies, do they take free samples from sales representatives — and whether or not doctors find these interactions acceptable. Consumer groups and organizations representing patients need to become much more active in this discussion through lobbying politicians to increase the amount of research funding, to fund independent drug information for doctors and to impose much stricter controls over promotion. These groups also need to make sure that organized medicine and industry hears what they think and not just once or twice but on an ongoing basis so that their message cannot be easily overlooked.

CONCLUSION

The medical profession has been given the responsibility and the privilege to prescribe medications in the best interests of individuals and society. By allying itself with the pharmaceutical industry it has forsaken its responsibilities to patients in favour of the private values of industry that are concerned with the need to earn a profit, not to protect public health. While the two can at times be synonymous, that happens mostly by coincidence rather than by design. When the medical profession adopts the values of private industry it is in essence saying that the needs of the private sector take precedence over the health of patients and society in general. The medical profession needs to reject these values and champion those of openness, safety and objectivity. In doing so, it will affirm the trust that society has placed in it.

Table 10.1: Recommendations for how to get doctors out of denial

Government (federal and/or provincial/territorial)

- Give control over promotion to an independent, government-funded agency made up of representatives of organizations that are independent of revenue from pharmaceutical promotion.
- Establish a Canadian version of the French Sales Charter to reinforce the position that the function of sales representatives is solely to encourage appropriate use of medications.
- Provide funding for a national sample of doctors to monitor the conduct of sales representatives.
- Require companies to declare all payments to doctors, make the names of the doctors public and investigate the impact of payments on prescribing behaviour.
- Provide funding for a widespread system of academic detailing.
- Provide funding for a national Canadian equivalent of the Australian NPS MedicineWise organization.
- Provide funding for medical schools to help underwrite the cost of continuing medical education.
- Rebate part of the cost of continuing medical education directly to doctors.
- Increase the support for independent research within academic health science centres and the overall budget of the Canadian Institutes of Health Research.
- Increase support for independent clinical trials.
- Set up a national pharmacare program that would cover the cost of medically necessary drugs.
- Set up a trial prescription program.

The medical profession

- Don't just declare conflict of interest but take the lead in establishing avoidance of conflict of interest as the standard.
- Establish strong and enforceable conflict-of-interest policies within academic health science centres, regulatory authorities, bodies that accredit continuing medical education and medical societies. Publicize these policies, monitor and enforce them with an effective pyramid of sanctions.
- Conflict-of-interest policies for academic health science centres should address all incentives, even relatively small items, including meals; payment for attendance at lectures and conferences, including online activities; continuing medical education for which physicians pay no fee; payment for time while attending meetings; payment for travel to meetings or scholarships to attend meetings; payment for participation in speakers' bureaus; the provision of ghostwriting services; provision of pharmaceutical samples; grants for research projects; and payment for consulting relationships.
- Doctors working in academic health science centres should not see sales reps.
- Faculty at academic health science centres should be prohibited from serving on company speakers' bureaus and should not be allowed to be authors on ghostwritten articles.
- Medical school conflict-of-interest policies should incorporate all of the items above and also include provisions about onsite educational activities, industry support for scholarships and research chairs and funds for students and the medical school curriculum.
- Industry should not be permitted to provide financial support for educational activities, including continuing medical education, either directly or through a subsidiary agency.

- The manual on promotion developed by Health Action International and the World Health Organization should be used for teaching students and residents about relationships with industry.
- All officials and employees with medical societies should be completely free of conflict of interest during their employment or tenure in office and for three years before.
- There should be a maximum percentage of medical societies' total revenue that comes from industry and from any individual company.
- Medical societies should release detailed financial statements that list all of their sources of income along with the amounts from each source and provide details about how industry money was used.
- Organizations that accredit continuing medical education such as the Royal College of Physicians and Surgeons of Canada, the Conseil québécois de développement professionnel continu des médecins, and the College of Family Physicians of Canada should develop policies about conflict of interest and produce income statements similar to those for medical societies.
- Medical journals should require editors, editorial teams, editorial boards and managers to be free of conflicts while working at journals and for three years before. Specifically these people should not have any direct financial ties (for example, stock ownership, speaker's fees, sitting on advisory boards) to any healthcare business advertising in the journal that they edit or work at.
- Journals should publish earlier versions of manuscripts along with reviewers' and editors' comments on the Internet so that readers can see the forces that went into revisions in the tone and content of published articles.

- Journals should publish the data from original research articles.
- Journals should publish detailed information about their sources of income, including the amount that they get from the sale of reprints, supplements and advertising and produce detailed financial analyses to show why it is necessary to continue to accept industry money.
- Medical journals should ban people who have signed on to ghostwritten articles as authors from publishing in the journal for a period of time long enough to make the penalty meaningful (say five years), retract the relevant article and make the penalty and the retraction public.
- Medical journals should change authorship criteria so that writers contributing to manuscript composition or revising the manuscript for intellectual content are required to be coauthors.
- Medical journals should make it clear to readers that whenever industry instigates and finances research and owns the data, the resulting publication is presented to readers as an industry project with academic contributions and not as an academic-led venture.
- The *CMAJ* and other Canadian journals should emulate the *BMJ* and refuse to publish certain types of articles from authors with conflicts of interest.
- Individuals should be invited to join clinical practice guideline panels through an open, transparent application process centred on rational, public selection criteria.
- Wherever possible, panelists should be free of any conflicts and chairs and co-chairs of committees should always be free of conflicts and a majority of the committee must always be free of conflicts.
- Panelists must disclose all industry-related professional activities, including research grants and speaker support, and for

the duration of guideline development divest themselves of direct financial interests (stock ownership, board positions, consultancy agreements) in commercial companies with an interest in any guideline recommendation.

- Panel decision makers should primarily be experts at reviewing scientific evidence and not content experts.

- Panelists should declare their *a priori* beliefs about a proposed intervention at the time they are nominated, and again at the conclusion of the panel's term.

- Only conflict-free panelists should be involved in determining the direction and strength of recommendations. Lack of consensus around evidence quality or recommendations should be resolved by explicit democratic processes involving conflict-free panelists.

- The Canadian Medical Association Infobase should only list clinical practice guidelines that follow the recommendations for conflict of interest listed above.

- The College of Family Physicians of Canada, the Royal College of Physicians and Surgeons of Canada and the Conseil québécois de développement professionnel continu des médecins should phase out accrediting industry-sponsored continuing medical education over a five-year period.

- In the meantime, an independent medical body should disperse any industry money for continuing medical education and industry should not be allowed to participate in the planning, development or delivery of continuing medical education, and both colleges and the Conseil should prohibit industry involvement in the planning, development and delivery of continuing medical education.

- Both colleges and the Conseil should explicitly state in their guidelines that industry is not permitted to suggest speakers or content to the planning committee.

- Medical organizations should develop educational objectives or a standard curriculum for continuing medical education.
- An Institute of Continuing Education should be created that would help eliminate conflicts of interest in continuing medical education.
- Researchers should use a standardized checklist to record conflicts of interest and this checklist should be used by research funders, journal editors and those supervising research at academic health science centres so that conflicts can be recognized, recorded and dealt with.
- Physicians in community practices should refuse to accept samples and gifts and refuse to see sales representatives.

The public

- All of the various bodies representing organized medicine in Canada need to publicize their monetary relationships with industry, their policies about physician-industry relationships and encourage public debate on how medicine and the industry should interact.
- As long as the pharmaceutical industry association and the Pharmaceutical Advertising Advisory Board are involved in regulating promotion they need to appoint independent members of the public to their code committees.
- As long as medical societies and those who accredit continuing medical education are willing to accept industry money, they need to seek out public input into what topics are important to patients and how the public feels about continuing medical education being funded by drug companies.
- The public should have an input into how medical societies use industry money for continuing medical education and what level of involvement industry should have in designing continuing medical education.

- Medical societies, organizations that accredit continuing medical education, medical schools and academic health science centres should invite members of the public to voice their opinions about interactions with industry in general.
- *CMAJ, Canadian Family Physician* and other journals should appoint independent members of the public to their editorial boards.
- Patients should ask their doctors about how they relate to drug companies.
- Consumer groups and organizations representing patients should lobby politicians to increase the amount of research funding, to fund independent drug information for doctors and to impose much stricter controls over promotion.
- Consumer groups and organizations representing patients need to make sure that organized medicine and industry hear what they think about physician-industry relationships on an ongoing basis.

ACKNOWLEDGEMENTS

In 2015, I was in Sydney, Australia, escaping from a particularly brutal winter in Toronto and finishing off work on my previous book, *Private Profits versus Public Policy: the Pharmaceutical Industry and the Canadian State*, and I realized that there was a second book, this one, that was waiting to be written. The first one purposely ignored the medical profession because it was about the industry and the government, but without talking about doctors and their organizations a large part of the story about pharmaceuticals is missing.

Two books in a little more than two years seemed excessive but one of my characteristics, for better or for worse, is being an obsessive compulsive and once seized with the idea of writing this book I couldn't let it go. However, I am enough of a realist to know that writing two books simultaneously is not a good idea and so this one got put on the back burner for a while. Once back in Toronto, I would make periodic visits to the Robarts and Gerstein Libraries at the University of Toronto to hunt down obscure references and add them to the material I planned to use. (I regard myself as particularly fortunate to have the resources of the University of Toronto's library system to call upon.)

In the summer of 2015, I was at the launch of a book published by James Lorimer and I approached him with the idea of this book. He gave me his card, encouraged me to write the book and said that I should contact him when my plans became more concrete. They did later that year and after a few emails and a meeting with Jim Turk I had a contract that eventually lead to what you are now reading.

Private Profits versus Public Policy was in many ways an

easier book for me to write than this one. Although the subject matter covered a much wider range of issues, this book is more personal because I am writing about a subject — the relationship between the medical profession and the pharmaceutical industry — that directly touches me as a doctor and that could affect my relationships with many of my colleagues. Also I have intimately participated in some of the events that I describe and I didn't want the story of these events to come off as if I have a vendetta that I am pursuing, nor did I want to appear self-righteous, which I have a tendency to do. I hope that I have been able to strike the right balance.

This book has been vastly improved by a number of people who took time from their busy lives to provide me with comments on some or all of the chapters. I owe a great debt of gratitude to: Elia Abi-Jaoude, Warren Bell, Pierre Biron, Alan Cassels, Justin Coleman, Jackie Duffin, Taylor Dysart, Marc-André Gagnon, John Hoey, Adam Hofmann, Anne Holbrook, Kelly Holloway, Peter Mansfield, Jill Masters, David Menkes, Barbara Mintzes, Nav Persaud, Colin Rose, Sheryl Spithoff, Geoff Spurling, Jim Turk and Robert Woollard. Debbie Ayotte, the Associate Director, Policy Research & Support at the Canadian Medical Association kindly searched through the association's archives to look for interactions between the association and the pharmaceutical industry in the decades before the mid-1950s. Laura Cook, James Lorimer and Jim Turk at Lorimer have all been a pleasure to work with and have helped immensely in seeing this book through to its final publication.

The ideas in this book did not just spring forth one day but are the subject of ongoing conversations, debates, discussions and arguments that I have had with a wide range of individuals over the course of over thirty-five years. In alphabetical order, so as not to offend anyone, they are: Elia Abi-Jaoude, John Abraham, Sharon Batt, Warren Bell, Lisa Bero, Alan Cassels, Janet Currie, Courtney Davis, Laura Esmail, Colleen Flood, Anne Rochon Ford, Colleen Fuller, Janice Graham, Paul Grootendorst, Roojin Habibi, Ken Harvey, David Healy, David Henry, the late Andrew Herxheimer, Hans Hogerzeil, Aidan Hollis, Richard Laing, Michael Law, Richard Lee, Trudo Lemmens, Mitchell Levine, Don Light, Ruth Lopert, Peter Lurie, Dee Mangin, Mike McBane, David Menkes, Steve Morgan, Bob Nakagawa, Nancy Olivieri, Nav Persaud, Harriet Rosenberg, Paula Rochon, Libby Roughead, Larry Sasich, Adrienne Shnier, Sergio Sismondo, Robyn Tamblyn, Leonore Tiefer, Brett Thombs, Sari Tudiver, Mary Wiktorowicz and Sid Wolfe. (My apologies to anyone I've forgotten.)

I've also had the opportunity to learn from reading some truly inspiring books written by John Abraham, John Abramson, Marcia Angell, Jerry Avorn, John Braitwaite, Howard Brody, Courtney Davis, Graham Dukes, Carl Elliott, Ben Goldacre, Peter Gotzsche, Jerome Kassirer, Charles Medawar and the late Milton Silverman. I can only hope that my book lives up to their standards.

For more than thirty years, Health Action International has been part of my life, drawing me out of my cozy Canadian environment and into the world of international pharmaceutical politics and letting me meet people I otherwise never would have known. I salute the dedication of my friends and colleagues, past and present, at Health Action International to the objective of ensuring that medications are used to promote social justice: Teresa Alves, Wilbert Bannenberg, Rose de Groot, Annelies den Boer,

Patrick Durisch, Marg Ewen, Kathy Glavanis-Grantham, Anita Hardon, the late Lisa Hayes, Elina Hemminki, the late Andrew Herxheimer, Catherine Hodgkin, Beryl Leach, Charles Medawar, Tessel Mellema, Kirsten Myhr, Orla O'Donovan, Katrina Perehudoff, Tim Reed, Ancel.la Santos, Phillipa Saunders, Jorg Schaaber, Staffan Svensson, Ellen 't Hoen, Bas van der Heide and Christian Wagner.

I cannot end without mentioning my two children, Esther Lexchin and David Oliver. Writing a book is not easy and neither is raising children, but you both, in your own ways, give me such pleasure. I could have done without writing this book but not without you two. Finally, there is my wife, Catherine Oliver, who stuck with me despite being forced to read the page proofs of my previous two books back in 1983 and 2016. I ambushed her at the late lamented Classics Bookstore on Saint Catherine Street in Montreal in the fall of 1982, and we have been together now for over tthirty-four years. I can't imagine my life without her.

Some of the material in this book was previously published in journals and other publications. I thank the publishers and editors for their permission to reprint excerpts here.

Material from the following articles is reprinted with permission of SAGE Publishing:

Lexchin J. The medical profession and the pharmaceutical industry: an unhealthy alliance. International Journal of Health Services. 1988;18:603–16.

Lexchin J. Pharmaceuticals, patents and politics: Canada and Bill C-22. International Journal of Health Services. 1993;23:147–60.

Material from the following book is reprinted with permission of New Star Books Ltd.:

Lexchin J. *The Real Pushers: A Critical Analysis of the*

Canadian Drug Industry. Vancouver: New Star Books, 1984.

Material from pages 90–97, 132 and 140–141 of the following book is reprinted with permission of University of Toronto Press:

Lexchin J. *Private Profits versus Public Policy: The Pharmaceutical Industry and the Canadian State*. Toronto: University of Toronto Press, 2016.

REFERENCES

INTRODUCTION

1. Jablonsky G. Physicians and the pharmaceutical industry. CMAJ. 1992;147:1415.
2. Solomon M. Long live the drug rep. Medical Post. 2008 October 24:10.
3. Ryan S. Re: "Long live the drug rep." Medical Post. 2008 December 19:11.
4. Steinman M, Shlipak M, McPhee S. Of principles and pens: attitudes and practices of medicine housestaff toward pharmaceutical industry promotions. American Journal of Medicine. 2001;110:551–557.
5. Foss K. Drug firms' freebies entice doctors: debate raging in medical community over pharmaceutical marketing practices. Globe and Mail. 2001 January 2:A1.
6. Hodges B. Interactions with the pharmaceutical industry: experiences and attitudes of psychiatry residents, interns and clerks. CMAJ. 1995;153:553–559.
7. Draaisma M. Doctors not bribed to pick drugs, says MDs' registrar. Edmonton Journal. 1988 November 21:B1.
8. Sah S, Fugh-Berman A. Physicians under the influence: social psychology and industry marketing strategies. Journal of Law, Medicine & Ethics. 2013;41:665–672.
9. Chimonas S, Brennan T, Rothman D. Physicians and drug representatives: exploring the dynamics of the relationship. Journal of General Internal Medicine. 2007;22:184–190 (direct quotes p184).
10. Sah S, Loewenstein G. Effect of reminders of personal sacrifice and suggested rationalizations on residents' self-reported willingness to accept gifts: a randomized trial. JAMA. 2010;204:1204–1211.
11. Walker M. Relationship with pharmaceutical companies. Canadian Family Physician. 2015;61:945.
12. Cialdini R. The power of persuasion. Stanford Social Innovation Review. 2003;1(2):18–27 (direct quotes p20).
13. Runnalls J. Donor dollars. Corporate Knights. Summer 2012. Available from: http://www.corporateknights.com/channels/education/donor-dollars-13478802/.
14. Canadian Association of University Teachers. Open for business on what terms? An analysis of 12 collaborations between Canadian universities and corporations, donors and governments. Ottawa; 2013.
15. Lexchin J. Reader upset at CFPC's involvement in prescribing survey. Canadian Family Physician. 1984;30:1454.
16. Rice D. The CFPC's executive director replies. Canadian Family Physician. 1984;30:1454–1455.
17. Industry. Canadian Dermatology Association; 2016. Available from:

http://www.dermatology.ca/industry/.

18. Searles G. An ethical debate: deciding the right Rx for physicians and the pharmaceutical industry 2013. Available from: http://www. dermatology.ca/wp-content/uploads/2013/09/Feb-2013-Ethical-Debate-Deciding-the-Right-Rx-for-Physicians-and-Pharma.pdf.

19. Oxorn H. The Society of Obstetricians and Gynaecologists of Canada: the first 50 years 1944–1994. New York: Parthenon Publishing Group Inc.; 1994.

20. Haque S. Pharmaceutical advertising. CMAJ. 2005;173:1066.

21. Senikas V. Pharmaceutical advertising. CMAJ. 2005;173:1066–1067.

22. Generic products as equivalents. CMAJ. 1963;88:94–95.

23. The positive role of pharmaceutical advertising. CMAJ. 1961;84:668.

24. Foulks J. The pharmaceutical industry. CMAJ. 1982;127:275–276.

25. Postlewaite G. The pharmaceutical industry. CMAJ. 1982;127:276.

26. Woods D. Roche: blending independent and commercial research. CMAJ. 1983;129:743–752 (direct quotes p752).

27. Woods D. Boehringer Ingelheim celebrates centenary. CMAJ. 1985;132:1417–1424.

28. Woods D. Sandoz: Swiss corporation moving towards global image. CMAJ. 1987;136:528–534.

29. Woods D. Upjohn celebrates a century of research and growth. CMAJ. 1986;135:694–697.

30. Institute of Medicine. Conflict of interest in medical research, education and practice. Washington, DC: National Academies Press; 2009.

31. Goozner M. The latest advisory committee stumbles at FDA: GoozNews.com; 2011. [updated December 5, 2011.] Available from: http://www.massdevice.com/latest-advisory-committee-stumbles-fda/.

32. Kassirer JP. Medicine's obsession with disclosure of financial conflicts: fixing the wrong problem. In: Snyder PJ, Mayes LC, Spencer DD, editors. Science and the media: Delgado's brave bulls and the ethics of scientific disclosure. Amsterdam, Boston, London: Academic Press; 2008, 79–89 (direct quotes p85).

33. Tobbell D. Pills, power, and policy: the struggle for drug reform in cold war America and its consequences. Berkeley: University of California Press; 2012.

34. Angell M. The truth about the drug companies: how they deceive us and what to do about it. New York: Random House; 2004.

35. Brody H. Hooked: ethics, the medical profession, and the pharmaceutical industry. Lanham: Roman & Littlefield Publishers, Inc.; 2007.

36. Avorn J. Powerful medicines: the benefits, risks, and costs of prescription drugs. New York: Alfred A Knopf; 2004.

37. Kassirer JP. On the take: how medicine's complicity with big business can endanger your health. New York: Oxford University Press; 2005.

CHAPTER 1

1. Canadian Association of University Teachers. Open for business on what terms? An analysis of 12 collaborations between Canadian universities and corporations, donors and governments. Ottawa; 2013.

2. Tobbell D. Pills, power, and policy: the struggle for drug reform in cold war America and its consequences. Berkeley: University of California Press; 2012.

3. Smith L. Panel discussion: the role of the Medical Section, C.Ph.M.A., in the Canadian pharmaceutical industry: Organization and aims of the medical section. CMAJ. 1958;79:924–925.

4. Routley T. Panel discussion: the role of the Medical Section, C.Ph.M.A., in the Canadian pharmaceutical industry: foreword. CMAJ. 1958;79:924.

5. Korcok M. Move to pharmaceutical industry right prescription for some Canadian doctors. CMAJ. 1988;138:749–751.

6. Many opportunities for MDs in the corporate drug world: pharmaceutical industry physicians don't have the stigma they did 20 years ago, perhaps because of a new emphasis on research. Medical Post. 1996 April 9:59.

7. Rasmussen N. The drug industry and clinical research in interwar America: three types of physician collaborator. Bulletin of the History of Medicine. 2005;79:50–80.

8. Director of Investigation and Research Combines Investigation Act. Material collected for submission to the Restrictive Trade Practices Commission in the course of an inquiry under Section 42 of the Combines Investigation Act. Ottawa; 1961 (direct quotes pp257–258).

9. Lang R. The politics of drugs: a comparative pressure-group study of the Canadian Pharmaceutical Manufacturers Association and the Association of the British Pharmaceutical Industry, 1930–1970. Westmead: Saxon House; 1974 (direct quotes pp108–109,112).

10. Minutes of proceedings and evidence no. 18: Hearing before the House of Commons Special Committee on Drug Costs and Prices. Ottawa: Queen's Printer; 1966 November 15 (direct quotes p1265).

11. Blishen B. Doctors & doctrines: the ideology of medical care in Canada. Toronto: University of Toronto Press; 1969 (direct quotes pp150,179,187).

12. Badgley R, Wolfe S. Doctors' strike: medical care and conflict in Saskatchewan. Toronto: Macmillan of Canada; 1967 (direct quotes pp31,59).

13. A submission of the Canadian Medical Association to the Royal Commission on Health Services. 1962 (direct quotes p7).

14. Canada. Royal Commission on Health Services. Ottawa: Queen's Printer; 1964.

15. Restrictive Trade Practices Commission. Report concerning the manufacture, distribution and sale of drugs. Ottawa: Queen's Printer; 1963.

16. House of Commons of Canada. Second (final) report of the Special Committee of the House of Commons on Drug Costs and Prices. Ottawa: Queen's Printer; 1967.

17. Lexchin J. The real pushers: a critical analysis of the Canadian drug industry. Vancouver: New Star Books; 1984.

18. Transactions of the ninety-fourth annual meeting of the Canadian Medical Association. CMAJ. 1961;85:517–545.

19. Department of Medical Economics Canadian Medical Association. News & Views on the Economics of Medicine. CMAJ. 1963;88:491–492 (direct quotes p491).

20. Waring G. Report from Ottawa. CMAJ. 1966;95:323.

21. Canadian Pharmaceutical Manufacturers Association. Submission to the Royal Commission on Health Services. 1962 (direct quotes p92).

22. Department of Medical Economics Canadian Medical Association. News & Views on the Economics of Medicine. CMAJ. 1964;91:1331–1332.

23. Gunton R. Report of the Committee on Pharmacy. CMAJ. 1965;93:459–465 (direct quotes p460).

24. The positive role of pharmaceutical advertising. CMAJ. 1961;84:668.

25. Generic products as equivalents. CMAJ. 1963;88:94–95 (direct quotes p94).

26. Patent protection in drug manufacture. CMAJ. 1964;90:1373–1374 (direct quotes p1373).

27. Parker J. Some implications of legalized substitution of prescribed pharmaceuticals. CMAJ. 1962;87:1318–1321.

28. Wigle W. Drug safety: the viewpoint of the pharmaceutical manufacturing industry. CMAJ. 1968;98:314–317.

29. Minutes of proceedings and evidence no. 30: Hearing before the House of Commons Special Committee on Drug Costs and Prices. Ottawa: Queen's Printer; 1967 January 26, 31.

30. Conder S. Medical research in Canada. Canadian Doctor. 1960;26(11):30–35.

31. Dixon B. The cost of drugs. Applied Therapeutics. 1961;3:362–365, 370.

32. Editorially speaking. Applied Therapeutics. 1961;3:595, 599 (direct quotes p595).

33. Nickerson M, Gemmell J. Doctors, drugs and drug promotion. CMAJ. 1959;80:520–524.

34. Palmer R. The case for prescribing by proper (non-proprietary) name. CMAJ. 1964;90:531–536.

35. Wightman K. Report of the Committee on Pharmacy. CMAJ. 1960;83:505–506.

36. Dunsworth F. Public relations and the medical profession. Nova Scotia Medical Bulletin. 1960;39:198–202.
37. The encircled physician. Nova Scotia Medical Bulletin. 1960;39:220–223.
38. The brand name — bane or benefit. Nova Scotia Medical Bulletin. 1960;39:299–302.

CHAPTER 2

1. Lang R. The politics of drugs: a comparative pressure-group study of the Canadian Pharmaceutical Manufacturers Association and the Association of the British Pharmaceutical Industry, 1930–1970. Westmead: Saxon House; 1974 (direct quotes p130).
2. Ruedy J. Report of the Committee on Pharmacy. CMAJ. 1967;97:700–701 (direct quotes p701).
3. The Canadian Medical Association brief to the Parliamentary Committee on Food and Drugs. CMAJ. 1966;95:324–330 (direct quotes p330).
4. House of Commons of Canada. Second (final) report of the Special Committee of the House of Commons on Drug Costs and Prices. Ottawa: Queen's Printer; 1967.
5. Waring G. Report from Ottawa. CMAJ. 1967;96:1119.
6. Bill C-190. CMAJ. 1968;98:262.
7. Department of Medical Economics Canadian Medical Association. Drug costs. CMAJ. 1968;99:972A–B (direct quotes p972A).
8. Hazlitt T. Fear of foreign drugs groundless, says Ottawa. Toronto Daily Star. 1967 December 4.
9. Genest J. Address of welcome. CMAJ. 1970;103:818–821 (direct quotes pp818–819).
10. Meeting highlight: government involvement in health care. Canadian Pharmaceutical Journal. 1971;104:212–213 (direct quotes p213).
11. Pharmaceutical industry studies current, future trends. Canadian Pharmaceutical Journal. 1977;110:171–173.
12. Goodman W. Drug substitution: remedy or rip off? CMAJ. 1983;128:198–201 (direct quotes p198).
13. Woods D. The pharmaceutical industry needs remedy for MacEachenism. CMAJ. 1982;126:337.
14. Gorecki P. Regulating the price of prescription drugs in Canada: compulsory licensing, product selection, and government reimbursement programmes. Technical Report No. 8. Ottawa: Economic Council of Canada; 1981.
15. Lexchin J. Pharmaceuticals, patents and politics: Canada and Bill C-22. International Journal of Health Services. 1993;23:147–160.
16. Woods D. The pharmaceutical industry: a prescription. CMAJ. 1983;129:675.

17. Canadian Medical Association. Brief to the Commission of Inquiry on the Pharmaceutical Industry. Ottawa; 1984 (direct quotes ppii,21–22,25).

18. Pharmaceutical Manufacturers Association of Canada. Submission to the Commission of Inquiry on the Pharmaceutical Industry. Ottawa; 1984 (direct quotes pp25,29).

19. Iacobacci M. Pressure groups and the federal government: the case of pharmaceutical lobbies regarding compulsory licensing. Ottawa; 1985 (direct quotes pp65–66).

20. Commission of inquiry on the pharmaceutical industry. Report. Ottawa: Supply and Services Canada; 1985.

21. Woods D. The Eastman prescription: a dispensable package. CMAJ. 1985;133:7.

22. Sawatsky J, Cashore H. Inside dope. This Magazine. 1986 September:4–12.

23. Toughill K. Drug firms to spend $93 million on research. Toronto Star. 1986 November 11:A2.

24. Minutes of Proceedings and Evidence of the Legislative Committee on Bill C-22: an Act to amend the Patent Act and to provide for certain matters in relation thereto: Hearing before the Legislative Committee of the House of Commons. Ottawa: Queen's Printer; 1987 January 20.

25. Gourdeau R. Drug research in Canada. Annals of the Royal College of Physicians and Surgeons of Canada. 1986;19:415–416 (direct quotes p415).

26. General Council votes to support Patent Act amendments affecting drugs. CMAJ. 1987;137:643.

27. Canadian Medical Association. Brief to the House of Commons Legislative Committee on Bill C-22: An Act to Amend the Patent Act. Ottawa; 1987 (direct quotes p5).

28. Coxe D. In Mussolini's boot step. Canadian Business. 1986 September:162.

29. Medical Research Council of Canada. The Medical Research Council of Canada and the pharmaceutical patent legislation. Ottawa; 1987 (direct quotes p8).

30. Minutes of Proceedings and Evidence of the Legislative Committee on Bill C-22: an Act to amend the Patent Act and to provide for certain matters in relation thereto: Hearing before the Legislative Committee of the House of Commons. Ottawa: Queen's Printer; 1987 February 11 (direct quotes p13:41).

31. Minutes of Proceedings and Evidence of the Legislative Committee on Bill C-22: an Act to amend the Patent Act and to provide for certain matters in relation thereto: Hearing before the Legislative Committee of the House of Commons. Ottawa: Queen's Printer; 1987 January 27 (direct quotes pp6:34,6:35).

32. Lexchin J. Postmarket safety in Canada: are significant therapeutic advances and biologics less safe than other drugs? A cohort study. BMJ Open. 2014;4:e004289.

33. Lexchin J. How safe are new drugs? Market withdrawal of drugs approved in Canada between 1990 and 2009. Open Medicine. 2013;8:e14–e19.

34. Minutes of Proceedings and Evidence of the Legislative Committee on Bill C-22: an Act to amend the Patent Act and to provide for certain matters in relation thereto: Hearing before the Legislative Committee of the House of Commons. Ottawa: Queen's Printer; 1987 February 4 (direct quotes p10:35).

35. Woods D. Drug legislation in the silly season. CMAJ. 1987;137:271.

36. Physician's Management Manuals. 1990;14(12):52–53.

37. Pharmaceutical Manufacturers Association of Canada. A presentation by the Pharmaceutical Manufacturers Association of Canada to the Senate Committee on Banking, Trade and Commerce studying Bill C-91. Ottawa; 1987.

38. Edward J. Science supports the case for brand-name drugs patent protection. Globe and Mail. 1992 December 29:A18.

39. Coalition backs patent protection plan for drugs. Medical Post. 1992 November 3:2.

40. Canadian Medical Association. Brief to the House of Commons Legislative Committee studying Bill C-91 "An Act to Amend the Patent Act." Ottawa; 1992.

41. Sullivan P. CMA to support increased patent protection for drugs but will attach strong qualifications. CMAJ. 1992;147:1699–1701.

42. Pharmaceutical Manufacturers Association of Canada. Presentation to the House of Commons Industry Committee on the review of Bill C-91. Ottawa; 1997 (direct quotes p16).

43. House of Commons of Canada, Industry Committee. Evidence. Ottawa; 1997. [updated March 19.] Available from: http://www.parl.gc.ca/content/hoc/archives/committee/352/indu/evidence/57_97-03-19/indu-57-cover-e.html.

44. Patented Medicine Prices Review Board. Annual report 2015. Ottawa; 2016.

45. Taylor K. The impact of the pharmaceutical industry's clinical research programs on medical education, practice and researchers in Canada: a discussion paper. Canadian pharmaceutical research and development: four short-term studies. Ottawa: Industry, Science & Technology Canada; 1991.

46. McFetridge D. Intellectual property rights and the location of innovative activity: the Canadian experience with compulsory licensing of patented pharmaceuticals. Ottawa: Carleton University; 1997.

47. Statistics Canada. Industrial research and development: intentions.

1999–2014. Document No.: 88-202-X.

48. Vitry A. Is Australia free from direct-to-consumer advertising? Australian Prescriber. 2004;27:4–6.

49. Mintzes B. Advertising of prescription-only medicines to the public: does evidence of benefit counterbalance harm? Annual Review of Public Health. 2012;33:259–277.

50. Merck Frosst. Direct-to-consumer advertising of prescription pharmaceuticals. A Merck Frosst position paper on how to use comprehensive patient information to deliver improved, cost-effective health outcomes. Submission to Health Canada consultation on direct-to-consumer advertising of prescription drugs. Ottawa; 1996 June 17 (direct quotes p1).

51. Pharmaceutical Manufacturers Association of Canada. Towards a better informed consumer of prescription medicines: a position statement by the Pharmaceutical Manufacturers Association of Canada to the Drugs Directorate's consultation workshop on direct to consumer advertising of prescription medicines. Ottawa; 1996 (direct quotes p17).

52. Canadian Medical Association. Position paper on direct to consumer prescription drug advertising. Ottawa; 1996 (direct quotes p1).

53. Canada's Research-Based Pharmaceutical Companies. Advertising prescription medicines in Canada: why it makes sense. Ottawa; 2003.

54. Haddad H. Brand-name ads. Ottawa Citizen. 2002 January 27:A13.

55. Herder M, Gibson E, Graham J, Lexchin J, Mintzes B. Regulating prescription drugs for patient safety: does Bill C-17 go far enough? CMAJ. 2014;186:E287–E292 (direct quotes pE288).

56. Robinson W. Standing Committee on Health, House of Commons. Evidence. 2014 June 12. Available from: http://www.parl.gc.ca/ HousePublications/Publication.aspx?Language=e&Mode=1&Parl=41 &Ses=2&DocId=6671393.

57. Rhines J. Proceedings of the Standing Senate Committee on Social Affairs, Science and Technology. Issue 20, Evidence. 2014 October 1. Available from: http://www.parl.gc.ca/Content/SEN/Committee/412/ soci/20ev-51604-e.htm?Language=E&Parl=41&Ses=2&comm_id=47.

58. House of Commons Canada Bill C-17: an act to amend the Food and Drugs Act, as passed by the House of Commons (June 16, 2014); 2014.

59. Canadian Medical Association. Bill C-17 an act to amend the Food and Drugs Act — protecting Canadians from unsafe drugs. Ottawa; 2014 (direct quotes p3).

60. Proceedings of the Standing Senate Committee on Social Affairs, Science and Technology: Hearing before the Standing Senate Committee on Social Affairs, Science and Technology (October 2, 2014); 2014.

61. Butler M. Why is the U.S. big pharma lobby sponsoring a conference on the future of health care in Canada? 2016. Available from: http://rabble.ca/print/blogs/bloggers/council-canadians/2016/09/why-us-big-pharma-lobby-sponsoring-conference-on-future-hea.

CHAPTER 3

1. MacDonald N, Downie J. Editorial policy: industry funding and editorial independence. CMAJ. 2006;174:1817.
2. Fassold R, Gowdey C. A survey of physicians' reactions to drug promotion. CMAJ. 1968;98:701–705.
3. Angus Reid Group. Credibility and the marketing mix. Toronto; 1991.
4. Cocking C. The abuse of prescription drugs. Weekend Magazine. 1977:16–19 (direct quotes p16).
5. Wittink D. Analysis of ROI for pharmaceutical promotion (ARPP). 2002. Available from: http://kurse.fh-regensburg.de/kurs_20/kursdateien/2010Analysis_of_ROI.pdf.
6. Davies G. Fueling growth efficiently, despite diminished access. Canadian Pharmaceutical Marketing. 2005:37–38.
7. Targeting doctors. Graph: top 50 drugs by promotion dollars. CBC-TV Disclosure. 2002.
8. Canadian pharmaceutical industry review 2015. Montreal: imshealth I brogan; 2016. Available from: http://imsbrogancapabilities.com/YIR_2015_FINAL.
9. Gettings J, O'Neill B, Chokshi D, Colbert J, Gill P, Lebovic G, et al. Differences in the volume of pharmaceutical advertisements between print general medical journals. PLoS One. 2014;9:e84790.
10. Chaisson G. Pharmaceutical marketing: an agency mecca. Marketing. 1992 December 14:35.
11. CAM Corp International. Total promotional expenses: 1996 to 2005. Englewood Cliffs, NJ; nd.
12. Canadian pharmaceutical industry review 2014. Montreal: imshealth I brogan; 2015. Available from: http://imsbrogancapabilities.com/YIR_2014_FINAL.
13. Canadian pharmaceutical industry review 2013. Montreal: ims I brogan; 2014. Available from: http://imsbrogancapabilities.com/YIR_2013_FINAL.
14. You and the ads. CMAJ. 1970;103:329.
15. Improved financial picture for 1970 forecast by finance committee. CMAJ. 1970;103:205.
16. Come out from under that bed. CMAJ. 1970;102:1306-1307 (direct quotes p1307).
17. Sanders M. The sparce index: medical excellence or drug dependence. CMAJ. 1970;102:531–532.

18. MacDermot H, Steinmetz N, Tetz W, Raine R, Stratford J, Jackson N, et al. Readers write about the journal. CMAJ. 1970;103:1019.

19. Mizgala H, Meldrum D. Readers write about the journal. CMAJ. 1970;102:1308.

20. Cosgrove G. Doctors bombarded by 'sexy' drug ads. Toronto Star. 1980 November 6.

21. Woods D. And now, a word for our sponsor . . . CMAJ. 1980;1980:1343.

22. Morgan P. Pharmaceutical advertising in medical journals. CMAJ. 1984;130:1412.

23. Squires B. Prescription drug advertising. In: Communicating risk, benefit, and cost of pharmaceuticals: proceedings of an invitational workshop. Vancouver: Canadian Public Health Association; 1992 February 2-4:50–52.

24. Advertiser wins CMAJ award. CMAJ. 1984;131:58.

25. Wilson C. Redefining the relationship: ethical prescribing in a pharmaceutical world. Canadian Family Physician. 2008;54:1341.

26. Lexchin J. CJEM and pharmaceutical advertisements: it's time for an end. CJEM. 2009;11:375–379.

27. Evans C. CJEM and pharmaceutical advertisements. CJEM. 2010;12:5.

28. The positive role of pharmaceutical advertising. CMAJ. 1961;84:668.

29. McCaffery M. The muzzle muddle. Canadian Family Physician. 1975;21(11):7.

30. Lexchin J. About those drug ads . . . Canadian Family Physician. 1976;22:109–110.

31. McCaffery M. About those drug ads . . . Canadian Family Physician. 1976;22:110.

32. Dixon T. Pharmaceutical advertising: information or influence? Canadian Family Physician. 1993;39:1298–1300.

33. Squires B. Truth in advertising. CMAJ. 1993;148:1663.

34. Whiteside C. Onsert with Canadian Family Physician questionable. Canadian Family Physician. 1997;43:613.

35. Reid T. Response. Canadian Family Physician. 1997;43:613.

36. Lewis S. Ketorolac in Europe. Lancet. 1994;343:784.

37. Ariano R, Zelenitsky S. Ketorolac (Toradol): a marketing phenomenon. CMAJ. 1993;148:1686–1688.

38. Spickler W. Ketorolac (Toradol): a new analgesic or an old NSAID? CMAJ. 1993;148:1693–1695.

39. Minutes of proceedings and evidence no. 5: Hearing before the House of Commons Special Committee on Drug Costs and Prices. Ottawa: Queen's Printer; 1966 June 23.

40. Katz M. Nude catches doctor's eye but drug ads reveal little. Montreal Star. 1973 July 24.

41. Problem child or child with a problem? Canadian Family Physician. 1973;19(10).
42. He is suffering from estrogen deficiency. Canadian Family Physician. 1973;19(4).
43. Raison A. The evolution of standards for pharmaceutical advertising in Canada. Pickering: Pharmaceutical Advertising Advisory Board; 1989 (direct quotes p27).
44. Pharmaceutical Advertising Advisory Board. Code of advertising acceptance. Pickering: PAAB; 2016. Available from: http://innovativemedicines.ca/wp-content/uploads/2015/06/IMC_Code_EN.pdf
45. Innovative Medicines Canada. Code of Ethical Practices. Ottawa: Canada's Research-Based Pharmaceutical Companies; 2016. Available from: http://innovativemedicines.ca/wp-content/uploads/2015/06/IMC_Code_EN.pdf.
46. Squires B. PAAB: a lesson in self-government. CMAJ. 1990;143:1151.
47. Lexchin J. PAAB: a lesson in self-government. CMAJ. 1991;144:844.
48. Squires B. PAAB: a lesson in self-government. CMAJ. 1991;144:844–845.
49. Kline S. Prescription drug advertising. In: Communicating risk, benefit, and cost of pharmaceuticals: proceedings of an invitational workshop. Vancouver: Canadian Public Health Association; 1992 February 2-4:52–56.
50. Mickleburgh R. More substance, less glitz urged in drug advertising. Images used to promote product often irritating, doctor urging guidelines says. Globe and Mail. 1993 January 14:A10.
51. Lexchin J. Enforcement of codes governing pharmaceutical promotion: what happens when companies breach advertising guidelines? CMAJ. 1997;156:351–357.
52. Lexchin J, Holbrook A. An assessment of the methodologic quality and relevance of references in pharmaceutical advertisements in a Canadian medical journal. CMAJ. 1994;151:47–54.
53. Pharmaceutical Adverising Advisory Board. PAAB code of advertising acceptance. Pickering: PAAB; 1986.
54. Pharmaceutical Adverising Advisory Board. PAAB code of advertising acceptance. Pickering: PAAB; 1997.
55. Lexchin J. How patient outcomes are reported in drug advertisements: review of Canadian medical journals. Canadian Family Physician. 1999;45:1213–1216.
56. Health Products and Food Branch (HPFB). Record of discussions — Canadian advertising preclearance agencies and Health Canada — April 5, 2012: Health Canada; 2012.
57. PAAB Views: Pharmaceutical Advertising Advisory Board; 2014. Available from: http://www.paab.ca/newsletters.htm.
58. Spurling G, Mansfield PR, Montgomery B, Lexchin J, Doust J, Othman N, et al. Information from pharmaceutical companies and

the quality, quantity, and cost of physicians' prescribing: a systematic review. PLoS Medicine. 2010;7:e1000352.

59. Huston P. Advertising in medical journals. CMAJ. 1994;151:7.

60. Rejection policy questioned. CMAJ. 1994;151:737.

61. Davidoff F, DeAngelis C, Drazen J, Nicholls M, Hoey J, Højgaard L, et al. Sponsorship, authorship and accountability. CMAJ. 2001;165:786–788 (direct quotes p787).

62. Haman A. Pure review: the big journals' new policy on the independence of researchers, while admirable, leaves enforcement too much up to individual editors' discretion, critics say. Medical Post. 2001 December 4:44.

63. The invisible hand of the marketing department. CMAJ. 2002;167:5.

64. Conflicts of interests and investments. CMAJ. 2004;171:1313.

65. Is medicine still a profession? CMAJ. 2006;174:743.

66. Austen I. Canadian medical group fires top editors of journal. New York Times. 2006 February 22;Sect. C:9.

67. Shuchman M, Redelmeier DA. Politics and independence — the collapse of the Canadian Medical Association Journal. New England Journal of Medicine. 2006;354:1337–1339.

68. Branswell H. CMA president says CMAJ editors fired over 'irreconcilable differences': Canadian Press; 2006 [updated April 13.] Available from: http://global.factiva.com.myaccess.library.utoronto.ca/ha/default.aspx.

69. Kassirer JP, Davidoff F, O'Hara K, Redelmeier DA. Editorial autonomy of CMAJ. CMAJ. 2006;174:945–950.

70. Steinbrook R, Kassirer J, Angell M. Justifying conflicts of interest in medical journals: a very bad idea. BMJ. 2015;350:h2942.

71. Rosenbaum L. Reconnecting the dots — reinterpreting industry-physician relations. New England Journal of Medicine. 2015;372:1860–1864.

72. Rosenbaum L. Understanding bias — the case for careful study. New England Journal of Medicine. 2015;372:1959–1963.

73. Rosenbaum L. Beyond moral outrage — weighing the trade-offs of COI regulation. New England Journal of Medicine. 2015;372:2064–2068.

74. Collier R. Competing interests are a complex problem. CMAJ. 2015;187:E373.

75. Collier R. The costs of vilifying pharma. CMAJ. 2015;187:E369–E370 (direct quotes pE369).

76. Collier R. Pharmaphobes, pharmascolds and conflict denialists. CMAJ. 2016;188:E3–E4 (direct quotes pE4).

77. Reid T. Welcome to Prescrire! Evidence-based reviews of drugs. Canadian Family Physician. 1999;45:1133–1134 (direct quotes p1133).

78. Announcement about Prescrire. Canadian Family Physician. 2001;47:967.

79. Pregent E. Singulair slam. Canadian Family Physician. 2000;46:1262–1263.
80. Grossman L. Drug information needs clarification. Canadian Family Physician. 2001;47:28–29.
81. Shulman R. Drug review "surprises" reader. Canadian Family Physician. 2000;46:2381–1283.
82. Van R. Outdated and misleading review of orlistat. Canadian Family Physician. 1999;45:2849–2852.
83. Duckmanton L. Drug information incorrect. Canadian Family Physician. 2000;46:780.
84. Pimlott N. Editor's response. Canadian Family Physician. 2011;57:1385.

CHAPTER 4

1. Canadian Institutes of Health Research. 2015-16: report on plans and priorities. Ottawa; 2015.
2. National Institutes of Health. Budget Bethesda: U.S. Department of Health and Human Services; 2016. Available from: https://www.nih.gov/about-nih/what-we-do/budget.
3. Patented Medicine Prices Review Board. Annual report 2015. Ottawa; 2016.
4. Re$earch Infosource Inc. Spotlight on university corporate research partnerships 2010–2014 medical/doctoral. 2015. Available from: http://www.researchinfosource.com/pdf/Spotlight2015CorporateMedicalDoctoral.pdf.
5. Rich P. Universities, drugs firms foster new partnership. Medical Post. 1992 February 25:25.
6. Dahlin K. Courting industry. University of Toronto Bulletin. 1994 May 30:9.
7. Lundh A, Lexchin J, Mintzes B, Schroll JB, Bero L. Industry sponsorship and research outcome. Cochrane Database of Systematic Reviews 2017, Issue 2. Art. No.: MR000033. Doi: 10.1002/14651858. MR000033.pub3.
8. Munro M. Doctor calls for guidelines for MDs, drug firms. Vancouver Sun. 1996 December 2:B3.
9. Buist S, Muhtadie L, Walters J. Big pharma showers Mac with cash. Hamilton Spectator. 2005 June 28:A1.
10. McIlroy A. Drug research walks thin line. Defining ethical boundaries critical when academic, corporate goals coincide. Globe and Mail. 2001 January 1:A1.
11. Buist S, Muhtadie L, Walters J. Connections and conflicts. Hamilton Spectator. 2005 June 28:A6.
12. Buist S, Muhtadie L, Walters J. Like a punch in the gut. Hamilton Spectator. 2005 June 27:A6.
13. Reznick R. The relationship between health professionals and the

pharmaceutical and device industries is under attack. Kingston, Ontario; 2010. [updated September 20.] Available from: http://meds. queensu.ca/blog/?p=332.

14. Reznick R. Building bridges to industry with Paul Lucas. Kingston, Ontario; 2015. [updated February 24.] Available from: https://meds. queensu.ca/blog/?p=2918.

15. Pharmacology conference: the medical profession and the pharmaceutical industry — ethical, clinical, scientific and financial issues at the interface. Montreal: McGill Department of Psychiatry; 2013. Available from: https://www.mcgill.ca/channels/event/ pharmacology-conference-medical-profession-and-pharmaceutical- industry-ethical-clinical-scientific-a-218715.

16. Frank D. Controversy and clarification regarding the symposium- debate on the pharmaceutical industry and medical profession. 2013. Available from: https://www.mcgill.ca/psychiatry/files/psychiatry/ channels/attach/controversy_and_clarification_regarding_the_ symposium.pdf.

17. Wazana A. Physicians and the pharmaceutical industry: is a gift ever just a gift? JAMA. 2000;283:373–380.

18. Thacker P. The ugly underbelly of medical research. The Project on Government Oversight; 2011. [updated January 13.] Available from: http://pogoblog.typepad.com/pogo/2011/01/the-ugly-underbelly-of- medical-research.html.

19. Psychopharmacology studies in affective disorders, anxiety disorders, and in the elderly. Harvard Department of Psychiatry; nd. Available from: http://www.hms.harvard.edu/psych/redbook/redbook- affectivedisorders-05.htm.

20. McIntyre RS, Harrison J, Loft H, Jacobson W, Olsen CK. The effects of vortioxetine on cognitive function in patients with major depressive disorder: a meta-analysis of three randomized controlled trials. International Journal of Neuropsychopharmacology. 2016;19(10):doi:10.1093/injp/pyw055.

21. Denis DeBlois. Montreal: The International Economic Forum of the Americas; 2016. Available from: http://forum-americas.org/profile/ denis-deblois.

22. Blackwell T. The selling of OxyContin. National Post. 2011 November 12.

23. Helwig D. Upjohn endows UWO. Ontario Medicine. 1989 January 9:5.

24. Morrissey D. Miles Canada to cover costs of cardiac lab. Hospital News — Toronto & SW Ontario. 1993 December:5.

25. Johnston C. Dr. Mak will head up new $100M cancer research institute at PMH. Ontario Medicine. 1993 March 8:15.

26. Moulton D. C-91 connection to drug-company grant poses problems for N.S. university. Medical Post. 1993 March 9:63.

27. Foss K, Luksic N. Lobbying for donor drug firm a mistake, U of T head admits Apotex chairman confirms top officials at hospitals wrote to Ottawa. Globe and Mail. 1999 September 16:A8.
28. Tripp R. Funding for obesity research centre questioned. Kingston Whig-Standard. 2007 January 27.
29. Stewart J. U of S adds research chair: pharmaceutical companies contribute to new position. Saskatoon StarPhoenix. 2009 June 16.
30. Merck Canada awards $4 M to Faculty of Medicine. Montreal: McGill University News and Events; 2013. [updated October 4.] Available from: https://www.mcgill.ca/channels/news/merck-canada-awards-4-m-faculty-medicine-230917.
31. Professorship in sustainable health care established at UBC. Vancouver: UBC News; 2015. [updated January 20.] Available from: http://news.ubc.ca/tag/initiative-for-sustainable-health-care/.
32. McGill University installs inaugural chair in pharmacoepidemiology. Montreal: McGill University News and Events; 2016. Available from: https://www.mcgill.ca/newsroom/channels/news/mcgill-installs-inaugural-chair-pharmacoepidemiology-261026.
33. McNaughton R, Huet G, Shakir S. An investigation into drug products withdrawn from the EU market between 2002 and 2011 for safety reasons and the evidence used to support the decision-making. BMJ Open. 2014;4:e004221.
34. Després J, Ross R, Boka G, Alméras N, Lemieux I, ADAGIO-Lipids Investigators. Effect of rimonabant on the high-triglyceride/low-HDL-cholesterol dyslipidemia, intraabdominal adiposity, and liver fat: the ADAGIO-Lipids trial. Arteriosclerosis, Thrombosis, and Vascular Biology. 2009;29:416–423.
35. MUHC endorses Pfizer's products. 2010. Available from: https://medicalmyths.wordpress.com/2010/04/09/muhc-endorses-pfizers-products/.
36. Jewesson P, Herar S. Activities of pharmaceutical industry representatives at a major teaching hospital. Canadian Journal of Hospital Pharmacy. 1996;49:256–260 (direct quotes p259).
37. Medical Advisory Committee University Health Network. Code of conduct for pharmaceutical representatives. 2004 May 13.
38. University Health Network. Policy & procedure manual. Administrative — code of conduct for pharmaceutical representatives. 2014 May.
39. Blackwell T. Western University launches rare probe after drug company allegedly exerted 'undue influence' on eye doctors. National Post. 2013 September 9.
40. Blackwell T. Drug company that offered to buy TVs for eye clinic did not exert 'excessive' influence, report finds. National Post. 2014 March 12.
41. Lacasse J, Leo J. Ghostwriting at elite academic medical centers in the United States. PLoS Medicine. 2010;7:e1000230.

42. Gøtzsche P, Hróbjartsson A, Johansen H, Maahr M, Altman D. Ghost authorship in industry-initiated randomised trials. PLoS Medicine. 2007;4:e19–e24.

43. Johnson E. Inside the business of medical ghostwriting. CBC News, Marketplace; 2003. [updated March 25.] Available from: https://web. archive.org/web/20100128111219/http://www.cbc.ca/marketplace/ pre-2007/files/health/ghostwriting/index.html.

44. Belluz J. The murky world of academic ghostwriting. Macleans. ca; 2011. [updated May 6.] Available from: https://web.archive. org/web/20110510024647/http://www2.macleans.ca/2011/05/06/ the-murky-world-of-academic-ghostwriting/comment-page-1/.

45. McHenry L. On the origin of great ideas: science in the age of big pharma. Hastings Center Report. 2005;35(6):17–19.

46. Bruser D, McLean J. Drug company accused of altering study by top SickKids pediatrician. Toronto Star. 2015 July 31.

47. Rochon P, Sekeres M, Hoey J, Lexchin J, Ferris L, Moher D, et al. Investigator experiences with financial conflicts of interest in clinical trials. Trials. 2011;12:9.

48. Schafer A. Biomedical conflicts of interest: a defence of the sequestration thesis — learning from the cases of Nancy Olivieri and David Healy. Journal of Medical Ethics. 2004;30:8–24 (direct quotes p17).

49. Downie J, Baird P, Thompson J. Industry and the academy: conflicts of interest in contemporary health research. Health Law Journal. 2002;10:103–122.

50. Lemmens T. Confronting the conflict of interest crisis in medical research. Monash Bioethics Review. 2004;23(4):19–40 (direct quotes p21).

51. Kendall J. Talking back to Prozac: David Healy was among the first psychiatrists to prescribe Prozac, now he's one of the fiercest critics of big pharma's "marketing" of depression. Did his outspoken views cost him his job? Boston Globe. 2004 February 1.

52. Healy D. Conflicting interests in Toronto: anatomy of a controversy at the interface of academia and industry. Perspectives in Biology and Medicine. 2002;45:250–263.

53. Healy D. Good science or good business? Hastings Center Report. 2000;30:19–22.

54. McIlroy A. Prozac critic sees U of T job revoked. Globe and Mail. 2001 April 14:A1.

55. Clark C. Top scientists allege U of T academic chill. Globe and Mail. 2001 September 6:A1.

56. Naylor C. Early Toronto experience with new standards for industry-sponsored clinical researach: a progress report. CMAJ. 2002;166:452–456 (direct quotes pp453,455).

57. Regulations amending the Food and Drug Regulations (1024 — clinical trials): regulatory impact analysis statement. Canada Gazette. 2000;134(4):227–260.
58. Harmonization of research policies. MedEMail. 2001 March 26.
59. Goldbloom D. Interactions with the pharmaceutical industry: task force report. Toronto; 2003.
60. University of Toronto Governing Council. Statement on conflict of interest and conflict of commitment. Toronto; 2007.
61. Rochon P, Sekeres M, Lexchin J, Moher D, Wu W, Kalkar S, et al. Institutional financial conflicts of interest policies at Canadian academic health science centres: a national survey. Open Medicine. 2010;4:E134–E138 (direct quotes pE135).
62. Lexchin J, Sekeres M, Gold J, Ferris L, Kalkar S, Wu W, et al. National evaluation of policies on individual financial conflicts of interest in Canadian academic health science centers. Journal of General Internal Medicine. 2008;23:1896–1903.
63. UBC Faculty of Medicine relationship with industry policy — summary. Vancouver: University of British Columbia; 2010. Available from: http://apt.med.ubc.ca/files/2013/12/Approved-Relationship-with-Industry-Policy-Feb-2010-Summary-Jul-13-20131.pdf.

CHAPTER 5

1. Gagnon M. The nature of capital in the knowledge-based economy: the case of the global pharmaceutical industry. Toronto: York University; 2009.
2. Millard W. Dispatch from the pharmasphere: an industry's fault lines on display. Annals of Emergency Medicine. 2008;51:175–180.
3. Lowy F, Gordon M, Moulton R, Spunt R, Thiessen J, Webster D, et al. Prescriptions for health: report of the pharmaceutical inquiry of Ontario. Toronto; 1990 (direct quotes p105).
4. Reid L, Herder M. The speakers' bureau system: a form of peer selling. Open Medicine. 2013;7(2):e31–e39 (direct quotes pe32).
5. Elliott C. The secret lives of big pharma's 'thought leaders'. The Chronicle of Higher Education; 2010. Available from: http://chronicle.com/article/The-Secret-Lives-of-Big/124335/.
6. Campbell E, Gruen R, Mountford J, Miller L, Cleary P, Blumenthal D. A national survey of physician-industry relationships. New England Journal of Medicine. 2007;356:1742–1750.
7. Advertisement. Physician's Management Manuals. 1990;14(12):52–53.
8. Dr. Labrie now will speak for the PMAC. Medical Post. 1991 October 8:16.
9. Dr. Cal Stiller: now a TV star. Ontario Medicine. 1992 February 3:25.

10. Regush N. Objectivity is an issue when reviewers have ties to drug firms. Montreal Gazette. 1992 June 6:B2.

11. McLean S. Arthritis drug lowers risk of stomach damage. Hospital News — Toronto & Region. 1993 May:6.

12. Goldman B. The night shift: real life in the heart of the E.R. Toronto: HarperCollins Publishers Ltd; 2010 (direct quotes pp85,86).

13. Blackwell T. The selling of OxyContin. National Post. 2011 November 12.

14. Blackwell T. Diclectin, popular morning sickness drug, less safe than key study said, new report warns. National Post. 2013 December 18.

15. Mendleson R, Bruser D, McLean J. Pregnancy drug maker Duchesnay financially linked to Motherrisk, obstetrician group. Toronto Star. 2015 April 24.

16. Ubelacker R. Med school pain course revised over concerns about possible pharma influence. Winnipeg Free Press, December 23, 2010. Available from: http://www.winnipegfreepress.com/breakingnews/ med-school-pain-course-revised-over-concerns-about-possible-pharma-influence--112369029.html.

17. Morrison S. Breathing becomes easier; new combination of two drugs in a single inhaler reduces risk of flare-up for asthmatics. Hamilton Spectator. 2002 February 13:A3.

18. Weeks C. Code of conduct sought to govern doctors and drug companies. Canada.com; 2007. [updated January 22.] Available from: http://sci.tech-archive.net/Archive/sci.med.nutrition/2007-01/ msg00566.html.

19. Bruser D, McLean J, Bailey A. Drug companies wine and dine family physicians. Toronto Star. 2016 February 16.

20. Crowe K. Ads disguised as news: a drug company's stealth marketing campaign exposed. CBC News; 2016. [updated October 5.] Available from: http://www.cbc.ca/news/health/vaginal-atrophy-analysis-1.3786547.

21. Blackwell T. The pill chill. National Post. 2005 April 27.

22. Dhalla I, Mamdani M, Sivilotti M, Kopp A, Qureshi O, Juurlink D. Prescribing of opioid analgesics and related mortality before and after the introduction of long-acting oxycodone. CMAJ 2009;181:891–896.

23. Weeks C. Ottawa urged to reconsider tamper-resistant oxycodone. Globe and Mail. 2016 April 29.

24. Sah S, Fugh-Berman A. Physicians under the influence: social psychology and industry marketing strategies. Journal of Law, Medicine & Ethics. 2013;41:665–672.

25. McKeen S. A prescription for profit: pitching pills: the success of new blockbuster prescription drugs seems as much a triumph of marketing as of medicine. Critics say it's time to change the rules of the game. Edmonton Journal. 2002 June 9:D6.

26. Seto A, Einarson T, Koren G. Pregnancy outcome following first trimester exposure to antihistamines: meta-analysis. American Journal of Perinatology. 1997;14:119–124.

27. Chin J, Gregor S, Persaud N. Re-analysis of safety data supporting doxylamine use for nausea and vomiting of pregnancy. American Journal of Perinatology. 2014;31:701–710.

28. SickKids: The Hospital for Sick Chldren. Motherisk program: summary of findings to date. 2015. [updated October 15.] Available from: http://www.motherisk.org/documents/SUMMARY-of-Findings_FINAL-Nov-30.pdf.

29. Kingston A. What you don't know about a leading morning-sickness drug. Maclean's; 2015. [updated October 23.] Available from: http://www.macleans.ca/society/health/what-you-dont-know-about-a-leading-morning-sickness-drug/.

30. Goldman B. I was part of big pharma's big influence. Globe and Mail. 2012 March 23.

31. Sylvain M. Rx&D redefines rules for training MDs as product speakers. Medical Post. 2007 January 16:61.

32. Rx&D. Code of conduct. Ottawa: Canada's Research-Based Pharmaceutical Companies; 2008.

33. Canadian Medical Association. Guidelines for physicians in interactions with industry. Ottawa: Canadian Medical Association; 2007. Available from: http://policybase.cma.ca/dbtw-wpd/Policypdf/PD08-01.pdf (direct quotes p3).

34. O'Malley A, Pham H, Reschovsky J. Predictors of the growing influence of clinical practice guidelines. Journal of General Internal Medicine. 2007;22:742–748.

35. Collier R. Clinical practice guidelines as marketing tools. CMAJ. 2011;183:E141–E142 (direct quotes pE141).

36. Lougheed M, Lemiere C, Ducharme F, Licskai C, Dell S, Rowe B, et al. Canadian Thoracic Society 2012 guideline update: diagnosis and management of asthma in preschoolers, children and adults. Canadian Respiratory Journal. 2012;19:127–164 (direct quotes p163).

37. Collier R. Clinical guideline writers often conflicted. CMAJ. 2011;183:E139–E140 (direct quotes pE139).

38. Canadian Diabetes Association. Clinical practice guidelines. 2014. Available from: http://guidelines.diabetes.ca/disclaimer.

39. Howlett M, Lillie D. The Canadian Diabetes Association guidelines: putting the evidence first. CMAJ. 2006;174:333–334.

40. Canadian Coordinating Office for Health Technology Assessment. CEDAC final recommendation on reconsideration and reasons for recommendation: insulin glargine (Lantus® - Aventis Pharma Inc.). 2005. Available from: https://www.cadth.ca/sites/default/files/cdr/complete/cdr_complete_Lantus_2005Sept28.pdf.

41. Clinical practice guidelines and conflict of interest. CMAJ. 2005;173:1297.
42. Neuman J, Korenstein D, Ross J, Keyhani S. Prevalence of financial conflicts of interest among panel members producing clinical practice guidelines in Canada and United States: cross sectional study. BMJ. 2011;343:d5621.
43. Choudhry N, Stelfox H, Detsky A. Relationships between authors of clinical practice guidelines and the pharmaceutical industry. JAMA. 2002;287:612–617 (direct quotes p615).
44. Skelly A. Statins in primary prevention: the debate flares up. Canadian HealthcareNetwork.ca; 2010. [updated September 10.] Available from: http://www.canadianhealthcarenetwork.ca/physicians/clinical/health-inde . . . diology/statins-in-primary-prevention-the-debate-flares-up-11122?print.
45. Ogilvie M, Boyle T. Big pharmacy's influence feared in Canada's patient care guideline authors, says study. healthzone.ca; 2011. [updated October 11.] Available from: https://www.thestar.com/life/health_wellness/2011/10/11/big_pharmacys_influence_feared_in_canadas_patient_care_guideline_authors_says_study.html.
46. De Lorgeril M, Salen P, Abramson J, Dodin S, Hamazaki T, Kostucki W, et al. Cholesterol lowering, cardiovascular diseases, and the rosuvastatin-JUPITER controversy. Archives of Internal Medicine. 2010;170:1032–1036 (direct quotes p1032).
47. Johnson K. Can you trust the latest Canadian contraceptive guidelines? "The Bayer facts" are revealing in their omission. 2011. [updated April 4.] Available from: https://katejohnsonmednews.wordpress.com/2011/04/04/can-you-trust-the-latest-canadian-contraceptive-guidelines-"the-bayer-facts"-are-revealing-in-their-omission/.
48. Lalonde A. SOGC clinical guideline development. CMAJ. 2011. [updated May 24.] Available from: http://www.CMAJ.ca/cgi/eletters/183/8/E443.full/reply#cmaj_el_649664.
49. Johnson K. Medical societies scramble to include disclosure on clinical guidelines. CMAJ. 2011;183:E443–E444.
50. Norris S, Holmer H, Ogden L, Burda B, Fu R. Conflicts of interest among authors of clinical practice guidelines for glycemic control in Type 2 diabetes mellitus. PLoS One. 2013;8:e75284.
51. Shnier A, Lexchin J, Romero M, Brown K. Reporting of financial conflicts of interest in clinical practice guidelines: a case study analysis of guidelines from the Canadian Medical Assocation Infobase. BMC Health Services Research. 2016;16:383.
52. Laupacis A. On bias and transparency in the development of influential recommendations. CMAJ. 2006;174:335–336.
53. Shuchman M. Drug firm threatens suit over MD's product review Globe and Mail. 1999 November 17:A1.

54. Talking points re: media reports — Dr. Holbrook and AstraZeneca. Ottawa: Rx&D; 2002. Available from: https://web.archive.org/web/20040110000851/http://www.canadapharma.org/Media_Centre/Backgrounders/Holbrook99_e.html.

55. Frame S. AstraZeneca responds. BMJ. 1999. [updated December 1.] Available from: http://www.bmj.com/rapid-response/2011/10/28/astrazeneca-responds.

56. Royal College of Physicians and Surgeons of Canada. National specialty societies. 2016. Available from: http://www.royalcollege.ca/rcsite/resources/national-specialty-societies-e.

57. Shnier A. Medical education and financial conflict of interest relationships with the pharmaceutical industry in Canada: an analysis of four areas of medical education. Toronto: York University; 2016.

58. Cassels A. Paying for what works: BC's experience with the reference drug program as a model for rational policy making. Vancouver: Canadian Centre for Policy Alternatives; 2002.

59. A position paper on drug-pricing strategies for prescription pharmaceuticals in Canada. Canadian Journal of Cardiology. 1997;13(1):33–45.

60. McLaughlin PR. Reference-based pricing of prescription drugs. Canadian Journal of Cardiology. 1997;13(1):31–32.

61. Industry. Canadian Dermatology Association; 2016. Available from: http://www.dermatology.ca/industry/.

62. Nevill T. Physicians and the pharmaceutical industry: an important relationship. The Microenvironment. 2011;2(1):1-2 (direct quotes p2).

63. Harrison J, Schiff J, Coursol C, Daley C, Dipchand A, Heywood N, et al. Generic immunosuppression in solid organ transplantation: a Canadian perspective. Transplantation. 2012;93:657–665 (direct quotes p657).

64. Rice D. The CFPC's executive director replies. Canadian Family Physician. 1984;30:1454–1455.

65. Smith M. Canadian society takes position on long-term hormone therapy. Journal of the National Cancer Institute. 2004;96:347–348.

66. Senikas V. Pharmaceutical advertising. CMAJ. 2005;173:1066–1067.

67. Eggertson L. New clinical guidelines say misconceptions have surrounded hormone therapy. CMAJ. 2009;180:504–505.

68. PMAC launches campaign against reference-based pricing. PMAC News. 1995:1–2.

69. Schneeweiss S, Walker A, Glynn R, Maclure M, Dormuth C, Soumerai S. Outcomes of reference pricing for angiotensin-converting-enzyme inhibitors. New England Journal of Medicine. 2002;346:822–829.

70. Schneeweiss S, Soumerai S, Maclure M, Dormuth C, Walker A, Glynn R. Clinical and economic consequences of reference pricing for

dihydropyridine calcium channel blockers. Clinical Pharmacology and Therapeutics. 2003;74:388–400.

71. Writing Group for the Women's Health Initiative Investigators. Risks and benefits of estrogen plus progestin in healthy postmenopausal women: principal results from the Women's Health Initiative randomized controlled trial. JAMA. 2002;288:321–333.

72. Frei R. Dermatologist pushes for drug price disclosure. Canadian HealthcareNetwork.ca; 2014. [updated July 11.] Available from: http://www.canadianhealthcarenetwork.ca/physicians/news/drugs/dermatologist-pushes-for-drug-pricedisclosure-35077.

73. Hugenholtz H, Cass D, Dvorak M, Fewer D, Fox R, Izukawa D, et al. High-dose methylprednisolone for acute closed spinal cord injury — only a treatment option. Canadian Journal of Neurological Sciences. 2002;29:227–235.

CHAPTER 6

1. Gass D. Ethical issues in sponsorship of CME. CMAJ. 1982;127:681.

2. Hollobon J, Lipovenko D. Drugs are the safeguards safe? Relying on firms for data on drugs called haphazard. Globe and Mail. 1982 October 22:5.

3. Guidelines for drug-company-supported CME. CMAJ. 1986;135:384A.

4. Ad Hoc Committee on Physician-Pharmaceutical Industry Guidelines. Guidelines for an ethical association with the pharmaceutical industry: a discussion document. Ottawa; 1990.

5. Mickleburgh R. Canadian MDs agree to stringent code on gifts. Guidelines ban free trips and other non-medical presents from pharmaceutical companies. Globe and Mail. 1991 August 14:A1.

6. Nixon A. Stress and the ethical physician. CMAJ. 1991;145.

7. Physicians and the pharmaceutical industry. CMAJ. 1992;146:388A–C (direct quotes p388C).

8. Woollard R. Addressing the pharmaceutical industry's influence on professional behaviour CMAJ. 1993;149:403–404 (direct quotes p404).

9. Toughill K. Rules for doctors at drug-firm seminars stir up controversy. Toronto Star. 1992 April 11:C5.

10. Evenson B. Medicine & the hard sell. Ottawa Citizen. 1993 April 1:B3.

11. Rauchman S. Doctors, drug companies still blur guidelines: CMA's code of ethical conduct faces revision after only two years. Medical Post. 1993 March 16:28.

12. Physicians and the pharmaceutical industry (update 1994). CMAJ. 1994;150:256A–C (direct quotes p256B).

13. Physicians and the pharmaceutical industry (update 2001). CMAJ. 2001;164:1339–1344.

14. Guidelines for physicians in interactions with industry. Ottawa: Canadian Medical Association; 2007. Available from: http://policybase. cma.ca/dbtw-wpd/Policypdf/PD08-01.pdf.

15. Kermode-Scott B. Pharma-physician codes of conduct evolving. Medical Post. 2005 Nov. 15:50.

16. Driver D. CME rethink. Medical Post. 2010 October 5:30-31 (direct quotes p31).

17. Borsellino M. Doctors and drug industry suffer ongoing discomfort. Medical Post. 2005 September 13:38.

18. Hanson D. Message from the president: physicians and the pharmaceutical industry. Insert to CMAJ. 2003;168(6).

19. Elston M, MacKean P, McDonald J, Hanson D. Rx&D code of marketing practices [announcement]. CMAJ. 2003;168:714.

20. Rx&D. Code of marketing practices. Ottawa; 2002.

21. Yeo M. Marketing Rx&D: one step forward, two steps back. CMAJ. 2003;168:1273–1274.

22. Hanson D. Marketing Rx&D: the CMA president responds. CMAJ. 2003;168:1274.

23. Yeo M. Marketing Rx&D: rebuttal. CMAJ. 2003;168:1275.

24. Ogle K. Marketing Rx&D. CMAJ. 2003;168:1238–1239 (direct quotes p1239).

25. The Canadian Medical Association and Pfizer Canada collaborate on first-of-its kind education program for physicians. CNW; 2009. [updated December 1.] Available from: http://www.newswire.ca/news-releases/ the-canadian-medical-association-and-pfizer-canada-collaborate-onfirst-of-its-kind-education-program-for-physicians-539048111.html.

26. Weeks C. Medical association takes heat for Pfizer funding. Globe and Mail. 2009 December 2.

27. Gage R. Rules on gifts from firms set for MDs in Manitoba. Globe and Mail. 1989 August 21:A8.

28. Walker R. Drug company perks could cost doctors right to practise. Calgary Herald. 1989 April 11:A2.

29. McQuaig L. MDs using Squibb drug in study receive computers for office use. Globe and Mail. 1988 December 15:A1-A2.

30. Lowy F, Gordon M, Moulton R, Spunt R, Thiessen J, Webster D, et al. Prescriptions for health: report of the pharmaceutical inquiry of Ontario. Toronto; 1990 (direct quotes p11).

31. Task Force on the Relationship Between the Pharmaceutical Industry and Physicians. Draft guidelines for physicians in their relationship with pharmaceutical companies. Toronto; 1991.

32. Loranger R. A summary of responses to the draft guidelines. Toronto: College of Physicians and Surgeons of Ontario; 1991.

33. Physicians and the pharmaceutical industry. College Notices. 1992 August.

34. Taylor P. Drug company's gifts test doctor's ethics. The lingering question is this: What free things can doctors accept without compromising their professional reputations and the care of their patients? Globe and Mail. 1997 August 1:A7.

35. Berger P. Letter to Dr. Chandar Rao and Dr. John Bonn. Toronto; 2000 July 20.

36. Bonn J. Fifth International Congress on drug therapy in HIV infection. Letter to Dr. Anne Phillips. Toronto; 2000 September 1.

37. Elston M. Letter to Dr. Philip Berger. Ottawa; 2000 October 5.

38. Shnier A. Medical education and financial conflict of interest relationships with the pharmaceutical industry in Canada: an analysis of four areas of medical education. Toronto: York University; 2016 (direct quotes pp88–92).

39. Physicians' relationships with industry — update: new policy approved. Toronto: College of Physicians and Surgeons of Ontario; 2014. Available from: http://policyconsult.cpso.on.ca/?page_id=2938.

40. Agrawal S, Saluja I, Kaczorowski J. A prospective before-and-after trial of an education intervention about pharmaceutical marketing. Academic Medicine. 2004;79:1046–1050.

41. College of Physicians and Surgeons of Ontario. Physicians' relationships with industry: practice, education and research (draft). Toronto; 2014. [updated March 11.] Available from: http://policyconsult.cpso.on.ca/wp-content/uploads/2014/03/Physicians-Relationships-with-Industry-Draft.pdf.

42. Canada's Research-Based Pharmaceutical Companies. Re: draft policy physicians' relationship with industry: practice, education and research. Submission to College of Physicians and Surgeons of Ontario. Ottawa: Rx&D; 2014 May 9.

43. Ontario College of Family Physicians. Feedback on physicians' relationships with industry: practice, education and research. Submission to College of Physicians and Surgeons of Ontario. Toronto; 2014 May 14.

44. College of Physicians and Surgeons of Ontario. Policy statement #2-14: physicians' relationships with industry: practice, education and research. Toronto; 2014 (direct quotes p2).

45. McLeod C. Gifts for enrolling patients in drug trials acceptable. Medical Post. 2003 June 24:7.

46. Reid L, Herder M. The speakers' bureau system: a form of peer selling. Open Medicine. 2013;7(2):e31–e39.

47. Sinclair D. Funding for continuing medical education. CMAJ. 2008;178:1575.

48. Marlow B. Rebuttal: is CME a drug-promotion tool? No. Canadian Family Physician. 2007;53:1877.

49. Angus Reid Group. Credibility and the marketing mix. Toronto; 1991.

50. Ferley S. Medical publications highly valued as an information source by Canadian physicians. Canadian Pharmaceutical Marketing. 2011 September:45–46.
51. Woods D. PMAC to spend almost $1 million annually to reach "stakeholders." CMAJ. 1986;134:1387–1388.
52. Williams A, Cockerill R, Lowy F. The physician as prescriber: relations between knowledge about prescription drugs, encounters with patients and the pharmaceutical industry, and prescription volume. Health and Canadian Society. 1995;3:135–166.
53. Physicians' evaluation of different media channels. Keith Communications Inc.; 2012. Available from: http://www.keithhealthcare.com/?p=78.
54. Ferley S. What's really happening with physicians' media usage: insight from the 2013 PMB Medical Media Study. Canadian Pharmaceutical Marketing. 2013 September/October:36–38.
55. Leslie C. Relationship between MDs and pharma changing. Medical Post. 2015 September 15:45.
56. Biomedical Ethics Committee RCPSC. Ethical responsibilities of physicians in their dealings with pharmaceutical companies. Annals of the Royal College of Physicians and Surgeons of Canada. 1990;23:45–48.
57. Hébert P. The need for an Institute of Continuing Health Education. CMAJ. 2008;178:805–806 (direct quotes p806).
58. Campbell C. Funding for continuing medical education. CMAJ. 2008;178:1577–1578.
59. Royal College of Physicians and Surgeons of Canada. CPD accreditation: group learning activities. Co-developing an activity — a physician organization and a non-physician organization. Ottawa: Royal College of Physicians and Surgeons of Canada; 2014. Available from: http://www.royalcollege.ca/rcsite/cpd/accreditation/guidelines/cpd-guidelines-process-for-co-development-with-non-accredited-physician-organization-e.
60. Conseil Québécois de développement professionnel continu des médecins. Relations between medical organizations and business corporations: code of ethics for parties involved in continuing medical education. 2003.
61. Bates D. Reader objects to drug co. sponsorship of CME courses. Canadian Family Physician. 1976;22:815.
62. Bourbonniere C. Ethical issues in sponsorship of CME. CMAJ. 1982;127:681.
63. Dean M. Guidelines for CME need revamping. Canadian Family Physician. 1996;42:1295–1296.
64. Gutkin C, Handfield-Jones R. Guidelines for CME need revamping — response. Canadian Family Physician. 1996;42:1296–1297.

65. Huo S, Scialli A, McGarvey S, Hill E, Tügertimur B, Hogenmiller A, et al. Treatment of men for "low testosterone": a systematic review. PLoS One. 2016. DOI: org/10.1371/journal.pone.0162480.
66. Watkins W. Letter to Dr. Joel Lexchin. Ottawa: Canadian Medical Association; 2004 March 16.
67. Marlow B. Letter to Dr. Joel Lexchin. Mississauga: College of Family Physicians of Canada; 2004a January 28.
68. Marlow B. Letter to Dr. Joel Lexchin. Mississauga: College of Family Physicians of Canada; 2004b February 26.
69. Lexchin J. A hypertensive snow bird. CMAJ. 2005;173:1357.
70. Marlow B. A hypertensive snow bird. CMAJ. 2005;173:1357–1358.
71. Rosengarten M. A hypertensive snow bird. CMAJ. 2005;173:1358.
72. Dawes M. A hypertensive snow bird. CMAJ. 2005;173:1358.
73. Cook G. A hypertensive snow bird. CMAJ. 2005;173:1358.
74. What's wrong with CME? CMAJ. 2004;170:917.
75. Marlow B. The future sponsorship of CME in Canada: industry, government, physicians or a blend? CMAJ. 2004;171:150–151.
76. Marlow B. Is continuing medical education a drug-promotion tool? No. Canadian Family Physician. 2007;53:1650–1651 (direct quotes p1651).
77. Marlow B. Funding for continuing medical education. CMAJ. 2008;178:1576–1577.
78. Wilson B. Continuing medical education programs being placed under closer scrutiny. CMAJ. 2010;182:E683–E684 (direct quotes pE684).
79. Department of Continuing Professional Development: College of Family Physicians of Canada. Commercial involvement and program development. CPF in Focus. 2012;4(5):2.
80. Collier R. CME accreditation: separating education from promotion. CMAJ. 2014;186:E670.
81. Bruser D, McLean J, Bailey A. Drug companies wine and dine family physicians. Toronto Star. 2016 February 16.
82. Lemire F. The CFPC's relationship with the health care and pharmaceutical industry. Canadian Family Physician. 2014;60:396.
83. Spithoff S, Lexchin J, Kitai C. It's time to examine pharma funding of doctors' education. Healthy Debate; 2015. Available from: http://healthydebate.ca/?s=spithoff.
84. College of Family Physicians of Canada. The CFPC's relationship with the health care/pharmaceutical industry. Mississauga; 2013.
85. Silverman E. Steps to reduce pharma influence over Canadian docs criticized. Pharmalot; 2016. [updated January 26.] Available from: https://www.statnews.com/pharmalot/2016/01/26/drug-firms-doctors-conflict-of-interest/.
86. Hall J, Lemire F. Professional development and industry funding: a

response from the CFPC. Healthy Debate; 2015. [updated December 18.] Available from: http://healthydebate.ca/opinions/college-of-family-physicians-of-canada-pharmaceutical-industry-funding.

87. Lemire F. Complete dissociation from the health care and pharmaceutical industry: response. Canadian Family Physician. 2015;61:669.

88. Royal College of Physicians and Surgeons of Canada. National standard for support of accredited CPD activities. Ottawa: Royal College of Physicians and Surgeons of Canada; 2016. Available from: http://www.royalcollege.ca/rcsite/cpd/providers/tools-resources-accredited-cpd-providers/national-standard-accredited-cpd-activities-e.

89. Royal College of Physicians and Surgeons of Canada, The College of Family Physicians of Canada, Collège des Médecins du Québec. National standard for support of accredited CPD activities. 2016. Available from: http://www.royalcollege.ca/rcsite/cpd/providers/tools-resources-accredited-cpd-providers/national-standard-accredited-cpd-activities-e.

CHAPTER 7

1. Give me the child until he is seven and I'll give you the man. Confused at a higher level: the view from Carleton College's physics department; 2010 January 2. Available from: https://arjendu.wordpress.com/2010/01/02/give-me-the-child-until-he-is-seven-and-ill-give-you-the-man/.

2. Shapiro M. Getting doctored. Kitchener: Between The Lines; 1978.

3. Square D. Does that free sleeve of golf balls demean the profession? CMAJ. 2003;168:884.

4. Persaud N. High cost, dubious benefit. CMAJ. 2010;182:175–176.

5. Ubelacker R. Med school pain course revised over concerns about possible pharma influence. Winnipeg Free Press. 2010 December 23. Available from: http://www.winnipegfreepress.com/breakingnews/med-school-pain-course-revised-over-concerns-about-possible-pharma-influence--112369029.html.

6. Glauser W. Pharma influence widespread at medical schools: study. CMAJ. 2013;185:1121–1122 (direct quotes p1122).

7. Ferris LE. Report on the informal inquiry into concerns raised about the University of Toronto's interfaculty pain curriculum (IPC). 2010. Available from: http://www.medicine.utoronto.ca/sites/default/files/Final%20Report%20from%20the%20IPC%20Informal%20Inquiry%20Dec%206th%202010.pdf (direct quotes p14).

8. Holloway K. Uneasy subjects: medical students' conflicts over the pharmaceutical industry. Social Science & Medicine. 2014;114:113–120 (direct quotes pp118,119).

9. Barfett J, Lanting B, Lee J, Lee M, Ng V, Simkhovitch P. Pharmaceutical marketing to medical students: the student perspective. McGill Journal of Medicine. 2014;8:21–27 (direct quotes p21).

10. Industry Funding Working Group. Defining the relationship: an evidence based review and recommendations on the role of industry funding in medical schools. Canadian Federation of Medical Students; 2011. Available from: http://www.cfms.org/files/position-papers/cfms_industry_funding_working_group_paper.pdf.

11. Belluz J. Students demand boundaries between drug firms and medical schools. Maclean's. 2013 September 23.

12. Mintzes B. Educational initiatives for medical and pharmacy students about drug promotion: an international cross-sectional survey. World Health Organization, Health Action International, European Union; 2005. Document No.: WHO/PSM/PAR/2005.2.

13. Kondro W. Cost recovery trumps concerns about conflicted interest. CMAJ. 2008;179:225–226 (direct quotes p225).

14. Hébert P, MacDonald N, Flegel K, Stanbrook M. Competing interests and undergradaute medical education: time for transparency. CMAJ. 2010;182:1279.

15. Association of American Medical Colleges. Industry funding of medical education: report of an AAMC task force. Washington, DC; 2008.

16. Association of Faculties of Medicine of Canada. Industry funding of medical education: anticipated questions and associated answers. Ottawa; 2008 December.

17. Gold I. The first national AFMC dialogue on conflict of interest. Gravitas. 2010;43(3):9–10 (direct quotes p9).

18. Institute of Medicine. Conflict of interest in medical research, education and practice. Washington, DC; 2009 (direct quotes p46).

19. Williams R. Principled partnerships — a uniquely Canadian approach to innovation. Gravitas. 2010;43(3):6.

20. Driver D. CME rethink. Medical Post. 2010 October 5: 30-31 (direct quotes p31).

21. Canadian Press. Medical schools urge limits to drug makers' influence on students. CBC News; 2008. Available from: http://www.cbc.ca/news/technology/medical-schools-urge-limits-to-drug-makers-influence-on-students-1.740789.

22. Mathieu G, Smith E, Potvin M-J, Williams-Jones B. Conflict of interest policies at Canadian universities and medical schools: some lessons from the AMSA pharmfree scorecard. BioéthiqueOnline. 2012;1(13).

23. Beyaert M, Takhar J, Dixon D, Steele M, Isserlin L, Garcia C, et al. A review of Canadian medical school conflict of interest policies. Creative Education. 2013;4:217–222.

24. Shnier A, Lexchin J, Mintzes B, Jutel A, Holloway K. Too few, too weak: conflict of interest policies at Canadian medical schools. PLoS One. 2013;8:e68633.

25. Saunders M-E. Bursary program launched for med students. Telegraph-Journal. 2009 April 3:C3.

26. Hofmann A. Reject pharmaceutical's medical funding. Telegraph-Journals. 2009 April 7:A6.

27. Williams R. Pharmaceutical partnerships improve care. Telegraph-Journal. 2009 April 9:A8.

28. Forrest D, Ruedy J. Proposed guidelines for housestaff interaction with pharmaceutical companies. Annals of the Royal College of Physicians and Surgeons of Canada. 1993;26:291–293.

29. Hodges B. Interactions with the pharmaceutical industry: experiences and attitudes of psychiatry residents, interns and clerks. CMAJ. 1995;153:553–559 (direct quotes p553).

30. Chakrabarti A, Fleisher W, Staley D, Calhoun L. Interactions of staff and residents with pharmaceutical industry: a survey of psychiatric training program policies. Annals of the Royal College of Physicians and Surgeons of Canada. 2002;35(Supplement):541–546 (direct quotes p541).

31. Stark T. Interactions between physicians and the pharmaceutical industry. A study into the perceptions of the early career psychiatrist. Calgary: University of Calgary; 2014.

32. Wazana A, Granich A, Primeau F, Bhanji N, Jalbert M. Using the literature in developing McGill's guidelines for interactions between residents and the pharmaceutical industry. Academic Medicine. 2004;79:1033–1040.

33. Razack S, Arbour L, Hutcheon R. Proposed model for interaction between residents and residency training programs, and pharmaceutical industry. Annals of the Royal College of Physicians and Surgeons of Canada. 1999;32:93–96.

34. Fogel M. Survey of pharmaceutical promotion in a family medicine training program. Canadian Family Physician. 1989;35:1603–1605.

35. Sergeant M, Hodgetts G, Godwin M, Walker D, McHenry P. Interactions with the pharmaceutical industry: a survey of family medicine residents in Ontario. CMAJ. 1996;155:1243–1248.

36. Mahood S, Zagozeski C, Bradel T, Lawrence K. Pharmaceutical policies in Canadian family medicine training: survey of residency programs. Canadian Family Physician. 1997;43:1947–1951.

37. Lussier M-T, Vanier M-C, Authier M, Diallo F, Gagnon J. Drug sample management in University of Montreal family medicine teaching units. Canadian Family Physician. 2015;61:e417–e424.

38. Agrawal S, Saluja I, Kaczorowski J. A prospective before-and-after trial of an education intervention about pharmaceutical marketing. Academic Medicine. 2004;79:1046–1050.

39. Kelcher S, Brownoff R, Meadows L. Structured approach to pharmaceutical representatives: family medicine residency program. Canadian Family Physician. 1998;44:1053–1060.
40. Education Council, Residency Training Programme in Internal Medicine, Department of Medicine, McMaster University, Hamilton, Ont. Development of residency program guidelines for interaction with the pharmaceutical industry. CMAJ. 1993;149:405–408.
41. Guyatt G. Academic medicine and the pharmaceutical industry: a cautionary tale. CMAJ. 1994;150:951–953 (direct quotes p952).
42. Erola J. We need dialogue and discussion, not a new Berlin Wall. CMAJ. 1994;150:955–956 (direct quotes p955).
43. Stearns E. Relations with the pharmaceutical industry. CMAJ. 1994;151:414–415.
44. Danby F. Interacting with the pharmaceutical industry. CMAJ. 1994;151:732.
45. Colby W. Guidelines for interaction with the pharmaceutical industry. CMAJ. 1995;152:1040-1041.

CHAPTER 8

1. Lowy F, Gordon M, Moulton R, Spunt R, Thiessen J, Webster D, et al. Prescriptions for health: report of the pharmaceutical inquiry of Ontario. Toronto; 1990 (direct quotes p100).
2. Jewesson P, Herar S. Activities of pharmaceutical industry representatives at a major teaching hospital. Canadian Journal of Hospital Pharmacy. 1996;49:256–260.
3. Schulte C. An inviting task: how often does the average physician have interactions with pharmaceutical companies? An Alberta doctor counted and the answer may surprise you. Medical Post. 2001 May 22:28.
4. Canadian pharmaceutical industry review 2015. Montreal: imshealth | brogan; 2016. Available from: http://imsbrogancapabilities.com/ YIR_2015_FINAL.
5. Leslie C. Relationship between MDs and pharma changing. Medical Post. 2015 September 15:45.
6. Pharmaceutical industry is 'reorienting' its promotional activities. Canadian Family Physician. 1977;23:262.
7. Chamberlain A. Communicating health: doctor, drug firm ties coming into question. Guidelines abound in tricky relationship. Toronto Star. 1994 May 10:C1.
8. Deutsch N. Better drug information with less hype? Physician's Management Manuals. 1994;18(6):33–34.
9. Elston M, MacKean P, McDonald J, Hanson D. Rx&D code of marketing practices [announcement]. CMAJ. 2003;168:714.

10. Sylvain M. Rx&D reins in free lunches. Medical Post. 2005 January 25:9.
11. Abraham C. MDs' pitch-and-swing days over; New guidelines restrict golf, travel freebies that drug companies doled out to doctors. Globe and Mail. 2005 February 26:A6.
12. Kermode-Scott B. Pharma-physician codes of conduct evolving. Medical Post. 2005 Nov. 15:50.
13. Williams R. Principled partnerships — a uniquely Canadian approach to innovation. Gravitas. 2010;43(3):6.
14. Foss K. Drug firms' freebies entice doctors: debate raging in medical community over pharmaceutical marketing practices. Globe and Mail. 2001 January 2:A1.
15. Blackwell T. Drug firm's violations of ethics 'unprecedented': Industry code: Company paid for doctors' trips to conference on French Riviera. National Post. 2005 March 19:A2.
16. Innovative Medicines Canada. Code of ethical practices. Ottawa; 2016. Available from: http://innovativemedicines.ca/wp-content/uploads/2015/06/IMC_Code_EN.pdf (direct quotes pp8,36).
17. Waring G. Report from Ottawa. CMAJ. 1966;95:323.
18. Gowdey C, Fassold R. Survey of doctors' reactions to the promotion of new drugs. Canadian Pharmaceutical Journal. 1968;101:344–350.
19. Fassold R, Gowdey C. A survey of physicians' reactions to drug promotion. CMAJ. 1968;98:701–705.
20. Hall K, Parker W. Physician's views of the pharmacist's professional role. Canadian Pharmaceutical Journal. 1976;109:311–314.
21. Parboosingh J, Lockyer J, McDougall G, Chugh U. How physicians make changes in their clinical practice: a study of physicians' perception of factors that facilitate this process. Annals of the Royal College of Physicians and Surgeons of Canada. 1984;17:429–435.
22. Woods D. PMAC to spend almost $1 million annually to reach "stakeholders." CMAJ. 1986;134:1387–1388.
23. Palmer W, Ross D. Introducing a new drug into your practice. Canadian Family Physician. 1987;33:2529–2533.
24. Williams A, Cockerill R, Lowy F. The physician as prescriber: relations between knowledge about prescription drugs, encounters with patients and the pharmaceutical industry, and prescription volume. Health and Canadian Society. 1995;3:135–166.
25. Angus Reid Group. Credibility and the marketing mix. Toronto; 1991.
26. Strang D, Gagnon M, Molloy W, Bédard M, Darzins P, Etchells E, et al. National survey on the attitudes of Canadian physicians towards drug-detailing by pharmaceutical representatives. Annals of the Royal College of Physicians and Surgeons of Canada. 1996;29:474–478.
27. Ferley S. Medical publications highly valued as an information source by Canadian physicians. Canadian Pharmaceutical Marketing. 2011(September):45–46.

28. Ferley S. What's really happening with physicians' media usage: insight from the 2013 PMB Medical Media Study. Canadian Pharmaceutical Marketing. 2013(September/October):36–38.

29. Swanson R, Hall W, Jennett P. Pharmaceutical representatives — educators or product marketers? Academic Medicine. 1994;69:128–129.

30. IMS Health Canada. IMS Health Canada's 2002 detailing survey. 2002.

31. Davies G. Fueling growth efficiently, despite diminished access. Canadian Pharmaceutical Marketing. 2005(September):37–38.

32. Chalkley P. Targeting accessible physicians. Canadian Pharmaceutical Marketing. 2009(April):29–30.

33. Regush N. MDs not always expert on drugs they prescribe. Montreal Gazette. 1982 October 26;A1,A8 (direct quotes pA8).

34. Roslin A. B.C. Health Minister won't prevent gifts going to doctors. Georgia Straight; 2008. [updated September 10.] Available from: http://www.straight.com/article-161048/abbott-wont-prevent-gifts-going-doctors.

35. Zoutman D, Ford B, Bassili A. A call for the regulation of prescription data mining. CMAJ. 2000;163:1146–1148.

36. Targeting doctors: the health data trade. CBC-TV Disclosure; 2002 March 5.

37. Government acts to prohibit sale of prescription information [press release]. Victoria; 1997 April 11.

38. Targeting doctors. Graph: top 50 drugs by promotion dollars. CBC-TV Disclosure; 2002 March 5.

39. Coutts J. Pharmaceutical group's head defends sale of medical data. Erola acknowledges that drug firms should inform doctors. Globe and Mail. 1996 March 28:A6.

40. Minutes of proceedings and evidence no. 4: Hearing before the House of Commons Special Committee on Drug Costs and Prices. Ottawa: Queen's Printer; 1966 June 16 (direct quotes p95).

41. Innovative Medicines Canada. Code of ethical practices. Ottawa: Innovative Medicines Canada; 2016. Available from: http://innovativemedicines.ca/wp-content/uploads/2015/06/IMC_Code_EN.pdf.

42. Kenneth O. Wylie, M.D., President Canadian Medical Association (advertisement). CMAJ. 1978;119:1336.

43. Summary publication. Drug symposium: drug information for the health care team. Montreal; 1975 May 30–31.

44. Hollobon J, Lipovenko D. Drugs are the safeguards safe? Relying on firms for data on drugs called haphazard. Globe and Mail. 1982 October 22:5.

45. Foster C. Sales pitch still crucial to pharmaceutical firms. Globe and Mail. 1982 September 10:R2.

46. Chamberlain A. Training key to increase its sales, drug firm says. Toronto Star. 1993 November 11:B1.

47. Kirkey S. MD raises alarm over drug promotion: industry critic urges better system to monitor marketing techniques. Ottawa Citizen. 1997 February 1:A4.

48. Rx&D. Where we stand: detailing. Ottawa: Canada's Research-Based Pharmaceutical Companies; 2010, 2.

49. Ross V. Between bliss and bedlam. Maclean's. 1980 December 8:38–40, 42 (direct quotes p40).

50. Wipond R. Meet your doctor's generous friend. Focus online. 2013 July/August.

51. Mintzes B, Lexchin J, Sutherland J, Beaulieu M-D, Wilkes M, Durrieu G, et al. Pharmaceutical sales representatives and patient safety: a comparative prospective study of information quality in Canada, France and the United States. Journal of General Internal Medicine. 2013;28:1368–1375.

52. Nissen S, Wolski K. Effect of rosiglitazone on the risk of myocardial infarction and death from cardiovascular causes. New England Journal of Medicine. 2007;356:2457–2471.

53. Restrictive Trade Practices Commission. Report concerning the manufacture, distribution and sale of drugs. Ottawa: Queen's Printer; 1963 (direct quotes pp226,270).

54. Tardif L, Bailey B, Bussières J-F, Lebel D, Soucy G. Perceived advantages and disadvantages of using drug samples in a university hospital center: a case study. Annals of Pharmacotherapy. 2009;43:57–63.

55. Lussier M-T, Vanier M-C, Authier M, Diallo F, Gagnon J. Drug sample management in University of Montreal family medicine teaching units. Canadian Family Physician. 2015;61:e417–e424.

56. Sylvain M. Ethics: pharma marketing sways Canadian doctors. Medical Post. 2008 September 26.

57. Fassold R, Heath E, Gowdey C. An appraisal of drug sampling. University of Western Ontario Medical Journal. 1967;38(2):42–46.

58. Katz M. Drug companies bear gifts and unproven claims. Montreal Star. 1973 July 23:D1.

59. Rx&D. Code of marketing practices. Ottawa; 2002 (direct quotes p10).

60. Berger P. The masters of the giveaway. Globe and Mail. 1983 December 3:6.

61. McQuaig L. MDs using Squibb drug in study receive computers for office use. Globe and Mail. 1988 December 15:A1,A2.

62. McQuaig L. MDs' watchdog will allow computer deal. Globe and Mail. 1989 February 21:A4.

63. Walker R. Free trips worry doctor. Calgary Herald. 1989 April 12:B1.

64. The hills are alive. CFPC-Update. 1989;6(2):1–2 (direct quotes p1).

65. Berger P. The industry is acting improperly in promoting HIV drugs. Globe and Mail. 1997 March 20:A19.

66. CTV's W5 examines big pharma largesse heaped on docs. CTV W5. 2002 May 19.
67. Blackwell T. The pill chill. National Post. 2005 April 27:A1.
68. Pharma launches voluntary guidelines for payment disclosures. CBC Radio — The Current; 2016. [updated April 8.] Available from: http://www.cbc.ca/radio/thecurrent/the-current-for-april-4-2016-1.3519317/apr-8-2016-episode-transcript-1.3520603#segment1.
69. Law M, Cheng L, Dhalla I, Heard D, Morgan S. The effect of cost sharing on adherence to prescription medications in Canada. CMAJ. 2012;184:297–302.
70. Lexchin J, Kawachi I. Voluntary codes of pharmaceutical marketing: controlling promotion or licensing deception. In: Davis P, editor. Contested ground: public purpose and private interest in the regulation of prescription drugs. New York: Oxford University Press; 1996, 221–235.

CHAPTER 9

1. Commission of inquiry on the pharmaceutical industry. Report. Ottawa: Supply and Services Canada; 1985.
2. OECD. Health at a glance 2015: OECD indicators. Paris; 2015.
3. Patented Medicine Prices Review Board. Annual report 2015. Ottawa; 2016.
4. Lexchin J, Mintzes B. A compromise too far: a review of Canadian cases of direct-to consumer advertising regulation. International Journal of Risk & Safety in Medicine. 2014;26:213–225.
5. Klass A. There's gold in them thar pills. Middlesex, England: Penguin Books Ltd.; 1975 (direct quotes p159).
6. Hamilton R, Shields D. The dictionary of Canadian quotations and phrases: revised and enlarged edition. Toronto: McClelland and Stewart Limited; 1979.
7. Squires B. Prescription drug advertising. In: Communicating risk, benefit, and cost of pharmaceuticals: proceedings of an invitational workshop. Vancouver: Canadian Public Health Association; 1992 February 2-4:50–52 (direct quotes p50).
8. Moses H, Dorsey E, Matheson D, Their S. Financial anatomy of biomedical research. JAMA. 2005;294:1333–1342.
9. Canadian Institutes of Health Research. Annual report 2007–2008. Available from: http://www.cihr-irsc.gc.ca/e/36882.html.
10. Canadian Institutes of Health Research. Canadian Institutes of Health Research 2015–2016 report on plans and priorities. Ottawa; 2015.
11. Lundh A, Lexchin J, Mintzes B, Schroll JB, Bero L. Industry sponsorship and research outcome. Cochrane Database of Systematic Reviews 2017, Issue 2. Art. No.: MR000033. Doi: 10.1002/14651858. MROOOO33.pub3 (direct quotes p21).
12. Kjaergard L, Als-Nielsen B. Association between competing interests and authors' conclusions: epidemiological study

of randomised clinical trials published in the BMJ. BMJ. 2002;325:249–252.

13. Friedman LS, Richter ED. Relationship between conflicts of interest and research results. Journal of General Internal Medicine. 2004;19:51–56.

14. Stelfox H, Chua G, O'Rourke K, Detsky A. Conflict of interest in the debate over calcium-channel antagonists. New England Journal of Medicine. 1998;338:101–106.

15. Tatsioni A, Siontis G, Ioannidis J. Partisan perspectives in the medical literature: a study of high frequency editorialists favoring hormone replacement therapy. Journal of General Internal Medicine. 2010;25:914–919.

16. Fugh-Berman A, McDonald C, Bell A, Bethards E, Scialli A. Promotional tone in reviews of menopausal hormone therapy after the Women's Health Inititative: an analysis of published articles. PLoS Medicine. 2011;8:e1000425.

17. Wang A, McCoy C, Murad M, Montori V. Association between industry affiliation and position on cardiovascular risk with rosiglitazone: cross sectional systematic review. BMJ. 2010;340:c1344.

18. Moynihan R. Key opinion leaders: independent experts or drug representatives in disguise? BMJ. 2008;336:1402–1403.

19. Opinion leader development. KOL; 2014. Available from: http://www.kolonline.com/services-development.asp.

20. Elliott C. The secret lives of big pharma's 'thought leaders'. The Chronicle of Higher Education; 2010. Available from: http://chronicle.com/article/The-Secret-Lives-of-Big/124335/.

21. Millard W. Dispatch from the pharmasphere: an industry's fault lines on display. Annals of Emergency Medicine. 2008;51:175–180.

22. Pharma brands earmark $38 million for thought leaders. PR Newswire; 2006. Available from: http://www.prnewswire.com/news-releases/pharma-brands-earmark-38-million-for-thought-leaders-53883072.html.

23. Hensley S, Martinez B. New treatment: to sell their drugs, companies increasingly rely on doctors — for $750 and up, physicians tell peers about products; talks called educational — Dr. Pitt's busy speaking tour. Wall Street Journal. 2005 July 15:A1.

24. Guyatt G, Akl E, Hirsh J, KeAron C, Crowther M, Guttuerman D, et al. The vexing problem of guidelines and conflict of interest: a potential solution. Annals of Internal Medicine. 2010;152:738–741.

25. Cosgrove L, Bursztajn H, Erlich D, Wheeler EE, Shaughnessy A. Conflict of interest and the quality of recommendations in clinical guidelines. Journal of Evaluation in Clinical Practice. 2013;19:674–681.

26. Shnier A, Lexchin J, Romero M, Brown K. Reporting of financial conflicts of interest in clinical practice guidelines: a case study analysis of guidelines from the Canadian Medical Assocation Infobase. BMC Health Services Research. 2016;16:383.

27. Bowman M. The impact of drug company funding on the content of continuing medical education. Möbius. 1986;6:66–69.

28. Bowman M, Pearle D. Changes in drug prescribing patterns related to commercial company funding of continuing medical education. The Journal of Continuing Education in the Health Professions. 1988;8:13–20.

29. Katz H, Goldfinger S, Fletcher S. Academia-industry collaboration in continuing medical education: dresscription of two approaches. The Journal of Continuing Education in the Health Professions. 2002;22:43–54.

30. Cervero R, Gaines J. Is there a relationship between commercial support and bias in continuing medical education activities? An updated literature review. Chicago: Accreditation Council for Continuing Medical Education; 2014.

31. Fugh-Berman A, Hogenmiller A. CME stands for commercial medical education: and ACCME still won't address the issue. Journal of Medical Ethics. 2016;42:172–173.

32. Rutledge P, Crookes D, McKinstry B, Maxwell S. Do doctors rely on pharmaceutical industry funding to attend conferences and do they perceive that this creates a bias in their drug selection? Results from a quesionnaire survey. Pharmacoepidemiology and Drug Safety. 2003;12:663–667.

33. Kesselheim A, Mello M, Studdert D. Strategies and practices in off-label marketing of pharmaceuticals: a retrospective analysis of whistleblower complaints. PLoS Medicine. 2011;8:e1000431.

34. Steinman M, Bero L, Chren M-M, Landefeld S. Narrative review: the promotion of gabapentin: an analysis of internal industry documents. Annals of Internal Medicine. 2006;145:284–293.

35. Boyd E, Cho M, Bero L. Financial conflict-of-interest policies in clinical research: issues for clinical investigators. Academic Medicine. 2003;78:769–774.

36. King M, Essick C, Bearman P, Cole J, Ross J. Medical school gift restriction policies and physician prescribing of newly marketed psychotropic medications: difference-in-differences analysis. BMJ. 2013;346:f264.

37. Epstein A, Busch S, Busch A, Asch D, Barry C. Does exposure to conflict of interest policies in psychiatry residency affect antidepressant prescribing? Medical Care. 2013;51:199–203.

38. McCormick B, Tomlinson G, Brill-Edwards P, Detsky A. Effect of restricting contact between pharmaceutical company representatives

and internal medicine residents on posttraining attitudes and behavior. JAMA. 2011;286:1994–1999.

39. Holbrook A, Lexchin J, Pullenayegum E, Campbell C, Marlow B, Troyan S, et al. What do Canadians think about physician-pharmaceutical industry interactions? Health Policy. 2013;112:255–263.

40. Redelmeier D. On the psychology of pharmaceutical industry gifts to physicians. Journal of General Internal Medicine. 2009;25:7–8.

41. Grande D, Frosch D, Perkins A, Kahn B. Effect of exposure to small pharmaceutical promotional items on treatment preferences. Archives of Internal Medcine. 2009;169:887–893.

42. Lexchin J. New drugs and safety: what happened to new active substances approved in Canada between 1995 and 2010? Archives of Internal Medicine. 2012;172:1680–1681.

43. Lexchin J. How safe are new drugs? Market withdrawal of drugs approved in Canada between 1990 and 2009. Open Medicine. 2013;8:e14–e19.

44. Lexchin J. Postmarket safety warnings for drugs approved in Canada under the Notice of Compliance with conditions policy. British Journal of Clinical Pharmacology. 2015;179:847-859.

45. Chew L, O'Young T, Hazlet T, Bradley K, Maynard C, Lessler D. A physician survey of the effect of drug sample availability on physicians' behavior. Journal of General Internal Medicine. 2000;15:478–483.

46. Boltri J, Gordon E, Vogel R. Effect of antihypertensive samples on physician prescribing patterns. Family Medicine. 2002;34:729–731.

47. Symm B, Averitt M, Forjuoh S, Preece C. Effects of using free sample medications on the prescribing practices of family physicians. Journal of the American Board of Family Medicine. 2006;19:443–449.

48. Miller D, Mansfield R, Woods J, Wofford J, Moran W. The impact of drug samples on prescribing to the uninsured. Southern Medical Journal. 2008;101:888–893.

49. Patented Medicine Prices Review Board. Generic drugs in Canada: international price comparisons and potential cost savings. Ottawa; 2011. Available from: http://www.pmprb-cepmb.gc.ca/CMFiles/Publications/Analytical%20Studies/NPDUIS-GenericDrugs-IPCs-e-sept30.pdf.

50. Canadian Generic Pharmaceutical Association. Market trends. 2016. Available from: http://canadiangenerics.ca/sustainable-healthcare/market-trends/.

51. Tardif L, Bailey B, Bussières J-F, Lebel D, Soucy G. Perceived advantages and disadvantages of using drug samples in a university hospital center: a case study. Annals of Pharmacotherapy. 2009;43:57–63.

52. Allan G, Lexchin J, Wiebe N. Physician awareness of drug cost: a systematic review. PLoS Medicine. 2007;4:e283.

53. Spurling G, Mansfield PR, Montgomery B, Lexchin J, Doust J,

Othman N, et al. Information from pharmaceutical companies and the quality, quantity, and cost of physicians' prescribing: a systematic review. PLoS Medicine. 2010;7:e1000352.

54. Daemmrich AA. Pharmacopolitics: drug regulation in the United States and Germany. Chapel Hill: University of North Carolina Press; 2004 (direct quotes p4).

55. Ford A, Saibil D, editors. The push to prescribe: women and Canadian drug policy. Toronto: Women's Press; 2009.

CHAPTER 10

1. Evans P, Sewell WH Jr. Neoliberalism: policy regimes, international regimes and social effects. In: Hall P, Lamont M, editors. Social resilience in the neoliberal era. Cambridge: Cambridge University Press; 2013, 35–68.

2. Mayes C, Kerridge I, Habibi R, Lipworth W. Conflicts of interest in neoliberal times: perspectives of Australian medical students. Health Sociology Review. 2016. 25:256-271 (direct quotes p265).

3. Private MRI service launches at 2 Saskatchewan clinics. CBC News; 2016. [updated March 1.] Available from: http://www.cbc.ca/news/canada/saskatchewan/private-mri-service-now-offered-saskatchewan-1.3471351.

4. Plasma for profit: why is Health Canada allowing paid plasma collection? Canadian Union of Public Employees; 2016. [updated March 9.] Available from: http://cupe.ca/plasma-profit-why-health-canada-allowing-paid-plasma-collection.

5. De Bettignier J-E, Ross T. The economics of public-private partnerships. Canadian Public Policy. 2004;30:135–154.

6. McKee M, Edwards N, Atun R. Public-private partnerships for hospitals. Bulletin of the World Health Organization. 2006;84:890–896.

7. Gilbert E. Failing grade for public-private partnership hospitals. CMAJ. 2009;180:380.

8. Mehra N. Flawed failed abandoned. Toronto: Ontario Health Coalition; 2005. Available from: http://www.ontariohealthcoalition.ca/wp-content/uploads/FULL-REPORT-April-7-2005.pdf.

9. Hancock G. Not bishops but businessmen. New Internationalist. 1977;50:11–13 (direct quotes p13).

10. Consumers International. Branding the cure: a consumer perspective on corporate social responsibility, drug promotion and the pharmaceutical industry in Europe. London; 2006 (direct quotes pp9,26).

11. Best Medicines Coalition, Health Charities Coalition of Canada, Canadian Medical Association, Canadian Nurses Association, Canadian Pharmacists Association, Innovative Medicines Canada.

Canadian consensus framework for ethical collaboration. nd. Available from: http://innovativemedicines.ca/wp-content/uploads/2016/06/IMC_CONCENSUS_2016_HR_nobleed.pdf.

12. Innovative Medicines Canada. Patients, healthcare professionals and the research-based pharmaceutical industry align on ethical collaboration. Ottawa; 2016. [updated June 10.] Available from: http://innovativemedicines.ca/patients-healthcare-professionals-and-the-research-based-pharmaceutical-industry-align-on-ethical-collaboration/.

13. Roslin A. B.C. Health Minister won't prevent gifts going to doctors. Georgia Straight; 2008. [updated September 10.] Available from: http://www.straight.com/article-161048/abbott-wont-prevent-gifts-going-doctors.

14. Garai P. Advertising and promotion of drugs. In: Talalay P, editor. Drugs in our society. Baltimore: Johns Hopkins Press; 1964, 189–202 (direct quotes p195).

15. Habibi R, Guénette L, Lexchin J, Reynolds E, Wiktorowicz M, Mintzes B. Regulating information or allowing deception? Pharmaceutical sales visits in Canada, France and the United States. Journal of Law, Medicine & Ethics. 2016;44:602-613.

16. Mintzes B, Lexchin J, Sutherland J, Beaulieu M-D, Wilkes M, Durrieu G, et al. Pharmaceutical sales representatives and patient safety: a comparative prospective study of information quality in Canada, France and the United States. Journal of General Internal Medicine. 2013;28:1368–1375.

17. Prescrire Editorial Staff. 15 years of monitoring and one simple conclusion: don't expect sales representatives to help improve healthcare quality. Prescrire International. 2006;15:154–159.

18. Rosenthal M, Mello M. Sunlight as disinfectant — new rules on disclosure of industry payments to physicians. New England Journal of Medicine. 2013;368:2052–2054.

19. Yeh J, Franklin J, Avorn J, Landon J, Kesselheim A. Association of industry payments to physicians with the prescribing of brand-name statins in Massachusetts. JAMA Internal Medicine. 2016;176:763–768.

20. DeJong C, Aguilar T, Tseng C-W, Lin G, Boscardin C, Dudley R. Pharmaceutical industry-sponsored meals and physician prescribing patterns for Medicare beneficiaries. JAMA Internal Medicine. 2016;176:1114–1122.

21. Blackwell T. Canadian drug companies agree to divulge how much they pay doctors, health groups. National Post. 2016 March 28.

22. Pharma launches voluntary guidelines for payment disclosures. CBC Radio — The Current; 2016. [updated April 8.] Available from: http://www.cbc.ca/radio/thecurrent/the-current-for-april-4-2016-1.3519317/apr-8-2016-episode-transcript-1.3520603#segment1.

23. Chhina H, Bhole V, Goldsmith C, Hall W, Kaczorowski J, Lacaille D. Effectiveness of academic detailing to optimize medication prescribing behaviour of family physicians. Journal of Pharmacy & Pharmaceutical Sciences. 2013;16:511-529.

24. Jin M, Naumann T, Regier L, Bugden S, Allen M, Salach L, et al. A brief overview of academic detailing in Canada: another role for pharmacists. CPJ. 2012;145:142–146.e2.

25. Therapeutics Initiative. Independent healthcare evidence. Vancouver; 2016. Available from: http://www.ti.ubc.ca/.

26. NPS MedicineWise. Annual report 2015: foundations for a Medicinewise tomorrow. Surry Hills, NSW; 2016.

27. Gadzhanova S, Roughead E, Bartlett M. Improving cardiovascular disease management in Australia: NPS MedicineWise. Medical Journal of Australia. 2013;199:192–195.

28. Spithoff S. Industry involvement in continuing medical education: time to say no. Canadian Family Physician. 2014;60:694–696 (direct quotes p695).

29. Tax industry to fund CME? Yes, in France. Global CME Newsletter; 2011 October/November. Available from: http://www.wentzmiller. org/cmenewsletters2011.html.

30. Migdal A. U of T labs get $98-million upgrade from Ottawa, Queen's Park. Globe and Mail. 2016 July 28.

31. National Institutes of Health. Budget. Bethesda: U.S. Department of Health and Human Services; 2016. Available from: https://www.nih. gov/about-nih/what-we-do/budget.

32. Canadian Institutes of Health Research. 2015–16: report on plans and priorities. Ottawa; 2015.

33. Canadian Institutes of Health Research. Strategy for patient-oriented research: a discussion paper for a 10-year plan to change health care using the levers of research. Government of Canada; 2010. Available from: http://www.cihr-irsc.gc.ca/e/41232.html.

34. Patented Medicine Prices Review Board. Annual report 2015. Ottawa; 2016.

35. Morgan S, Gagon M-A, Mintzes B, Lexchin J. A better prescription: advice for a national strategy on pharmaceutical policy in Canada. Healthcare Policy. 2016;12:18–36.

36. Ho K, MacKeigan L. A model to estimate drug plan cost savings from a trial prescription program. Journal of Managed Care Pharmacy. 2001;7:391–401 (direct quotes p396).

37. Bliss M. William Osler: a life in medicine. Toronto: University of Toronto Press; 1999 (direct quotes p361).

38. Stossel T. Regulating academic-industrial research relationships solving problems or stifling progress? New England Journal of Medicine. 2005;353:1060–1065.

39. Brennan T, Rothman D, Blank L, Blumenthal D, Chimonas S, Cohen J, et al. Health industry practices that create conflicts of interest: a policy proposal for academic medical centers. JAMA. 2006;295:429–433 (direct quotes pp430,431).
40. Cain D, Loewenstein G, Moore D. The dirt on coming clean: perverse effects of disclosing conflicts of interest. Journal of Legal Studies. 2005;34:1–25.
41. Ayres I, Braithwaite J. Responsive regulation. Transcending the deregulation debate. New York: Oxford University Press; 1992.
42. Pearl R. Medical conflicts of interest are dangerous; for some patients, what their doctors don't tell them could be hazardous to their health. Wall Street Journal Online. 2013 April 24.
43. Shnier A, Lexchin J, Mintzes B, Jutel A, Holloway K. Too few, too weak: conflict of interest policies at Canadian medical schools. PLoS One. 2013;8:e68633.
44. Mansfield P, Lexchin J, Wen L, Grandori L, McCoy C, Hoffman J, et al. Educating health professionals about drug and device promotion: advocates' recommendations. PLoS Medicine. 2006;3:e451.
45. Mintzes B, Mangin D, Hayes L, editors. Understanding and responding to pharmaceutical promotion: a practical guide. Health Action International and World Health Organization; 2010.
46. Lexchin J, Light D. Commercial influence and the content of medical journals. BMJ. 2006;332:1444–1447.
47. Rose D. Medical journal bans drug company ads. Sydney Morning Herald. 2011 February 3.
48. Matheson A. Ghostwriting: the importance of definition and its place in contemporary drug marketing. BMJ. 2016;354:i4578.
49. Chew M, Brizzell C, Abbasi K, Godlee F. Medical journals and industry ties. BMJ. 2014;349:g7197.
50. Scott I, Guyatt G. Clinical practice guidelines: the need for greater transparency in formulating recommendations. MJA. 2011;195:29–33 (direct quotes p29).
51. Institute of Medicine. Clinical practice guidelines we can trust. Washington, DC; 2011.
52. Lenzer J, Hoffman J, Furberg C, Ioannidis J. Ensuring the integrity of clinical practice guidelines: a tool for protecting patients. BMJ. 2013;347:f5535.
53. Canadian Medical Association. Submit a guideline. 2016. Available from: https://www.cma.ca/En/Pages/submit-guideline.aspx.
54. Collier R. Clinical practice guidelines as marketing tools. CMAJ. 2011;183:E141–E142.
55. Fletcher S. Continuing education in the health professions: improving healthcare through lifelong learning. Chariman's summary of the conference. Josiah Macy Jr Foundation; 2008 (direct quotes p221).

56. Hébert P. The need for an Institute of Continuing Health Education. CMAJ. 2008;178:805–806 (direct quotes p805).

57. Christie T. Reformers resist aggressive drug marketing tactics. The Register-Guard. 2008 March 2.

58. Sylvain M. Yukon doctors ban pharma sponsorship from annual meeting. Medical Post. 2007 February 2:37.

59. Ontario College of Family Physicians. Feedback on physicians' relationships with industry: practice, education and research. Toronto: College of Physicians and Surgeons of Ontario; 2014. Available from: http://policyconsult.cpso.on.ca/wp-content/uploads/2014/05/Ontario-College-of-Family-Physicians.pdf.

60. Driver D. CME rethink. Medical Post. 2010 October 5:30-31.

61. Lexchin J. Continuing education. In: Rowe B, Lang E, Brown M, Houry D, Newman D, Wyer P, editors. Evidence-based emergency medicine. Chichester: Wiley-Blackwell; 2009, 34–42.

62. Rochon P, Hoey J, Chan A-W, Ferris L, Lexchin J, Kalkar S, et al. Financial conflicts of interest checklist 2010 for clinical research studies. Open Medicine. 2010;4:E69–E91.

63. Boyle T. Toronto doctors say no to free samples from drug firms. Toronto Star. 2013 October 26.

64. Leslie C. Relationship between MDs and pharma changing. Medical Post. 2015 September 15:45.

65. Spurling G, Mansfield P. General practitioners and pharmaceutical sales representatives: quality improvement research. Quality and Safety in Health Care. 2007;16:266–270.

66. Ura A. Trying to limit outside influence in prescribing drugs. New York Times. 2014 June 15:27A.

67. Wisconsin Medical Society. Policy compendium 2015–2016: the relationship of the profession to the health products industry. 2015. Available from: https://www.wisconsinmedicalsociety.org/_WMS/about_us/governance/policy_compendium/2015/2015-2016_policy_compendium_june15_addendum.pdf (direct quotes p105).

68. Canadian Institute for Health Information. Prescribed drug spending in Canada, 2016: a focus on public drug programs. Ottawa: 2016.

69. CMAJ editorial advisory board 2017 [cited 2017 March 1]. Available from: http://www.cmaj.ca/site/misc/edboard.xhtml.

70. CFP editorial advisory board 2017 [cited 2017 March 1]. Available from: http://www.cfp.ca/site/misc/EAB/about_eab.xhtml.

71. Kaufman K. A history of Ontario midwifery. Journal of the Society of Obstetricians and Gynaecologists of Canada. 1998;20:976-81.

INDEX

The letter *f* following a page number denotes a figure, the letter *t* denotes a table and the letter *b* denotes a box.